ERNIE BANKS

MR. CUB
AND THE
SUMMER OF '69

Phil Rogers

TRIUMPH
BOOKS

Library of Congress Cataloging-in-Publication Data

This book is available in quantity at special discounts for your group or organization. For further information, contact:

Triumph Books
542 South Dearborn Street
Suite 750
Chicago, Illinois 60605
(312) 939-3330
Fax (312) 663-3557
www.triumphbooks.com

Printed in U.S.A.
ISBN: 978-1-60078-519-1
Design by Sue Knopf
All photos courtesy of AP Images unless otherwise noted.

To Phyllis Merhige,
Katy Feeney,
Ernie Banks,
and pioneers everywhere

Contents

FOREWORD

By Thomas Boswell

When we are sifting for childhood heroes, we look for what we lack. Even though I grew up in Washington, D.C., I looked all the way to Chicago to find Ernie Banks. Then I didn't let him go.

The late '50s were full of major sports heroes. I could have found something that appealed deeply to me in Johnny Unitas, Arnold Palmer, or Willie Mays. I certainly read enough profiles of all of them, and other stars, in every sports magazine. There were local D.C. heroes, like home run champion Roy Sievers, who I fell for hard as a kid. But with all the rest of sports to choose from, I picked Banks and followed his last 15 seasons avidly.

By '69, after I graduated from college, Ernie was the last childhood hero that I still rooted for every day. In September, as his Cubs battled America's darling, the Miracle Mets, I clung to Banks, then 38, as he staggered toward his only chance to play in a World Series. When the Cubs failed, I took a lesson from their fall—supplied by Banks—that has never left me.

If you want a defining trait, one that survives defeat, attracts affection from others, and mysteriously restores itself, then it's hard to beat enthusiasm.

"It's a great day for a ballgame. Let's play two," isn't just a quotation that'll probably end up in Bartlett's [Familiar Quotations]. It's philosophy.

Believe me, as someone who's covered baseball for 35 years at the Washington Post, nobody wants to play 324 games, not even Ernie. "Let's play two," is a world view and a deep one, not a quip.

The outward joy that Banks professed, even if it was partly innate to his temperament, was also a daily act of will: a lifelong private commitment to enthusiasm as a guiding principle.

For countless people, including me, it's hard to find anybody among family or friends who's a living example of that combination of attitude and energy. When you find a Banks who sticks to those guns all his life, that's the definition of a role model.

"He who would be calm must first put on the appearance of calm," Shakespeare wrote. In other words, our emotions do not simply come from inside us and express themselves outwardly. The process can work in reverse. By putting on the outward appearance of calm—or confidence or enthusiasm or whatever quality we value—we can increase our tendency to feel that way.

Every day for 19 seasons, Banks put on that appearance of joy and convinced himself and probably some teammates that they were "playing" ball not so much competing as publicly scrutinized pros.

So how did that sensibility stand up to The Collapse—the epitome of the sport as pain, not play?

When the Cubs crashed in September, losing 11-of-12 to go from five games ahead to 4½ behind, it all happened so fast that it seemed more grotesque than dramatic and, by the end, darkly comic. Banks slumped, too. But after seven straight losses, he made a personal stand. Against the Phils, he drove in a run in the first inning, then homered in the eighth to give the Cubs a 2–1 lead; they blew it, of course. The next day, in the only Cubs win of the whole smashup, Banks drove in four of their five runs. That was the old man's statement—not nearly enough, but something.

On the final day of the season, when manager Leo Durocher, the grouch who said, "Nice guys finish last," was disengaged from his team and stuck with the disgrace of his defeat, Banks was still showing up—just to play baseball. On the season's last day, Banks, the oldest man in the lineup, played his 155th game of the year and had a triple, a homer, and he drove in three runs to finish the season with 106 RBIs, a total he hadn't topped since his twenties.

You need all kinds of role models as you grow up. That '69 Cubs choke sealed it for me—Banks would remain one of mine. No team could fail worse.

Mostly, Banks stunk, too. But I didn't respect him any less. And nobody else seemed to, either.

By '77, Ernie had been voted into the Hall of Fame. Durocher got in by the back door of the Old Timers Committee in '94—three years after he died. Banks has been going to Cooperstown every August for a third of a century, enjoying the chatter with his fellow immortals. Leo never got to sit on the veranda of the Otesaga Hotel overlooking Lake Glimmerglass and preen. Let's play two, or nice guys finish last? Excuse me, but I call it a parable.

In a baseball sense, Banks is an immortal because he averaged 41 homers and 115 RBIs per year as a shortstop from 1955–60, making himself the equal of Mays, Mickey Mantle, or anybody else in the game for those half-dozen years.

There'd never before been a middle infielder with such power. And to this day, there still hasn't. Banks won a Gold Glove, too. Switching to first base and remaining a solid hitter until he'd amassed 512 homers assured him a place in the Hall.

But it is the Other Banks, the man who exemplified an entire stance toward how we approach life, who will be remembered long after most of baseball's 500–home-run men are forgotten.

Perhaps fans of the '50s, when Banks emerged, were particularly susceptible to what he embodied. From 1929 through the early '50s, the whole country, and especially the Greatest Generation, endured a unique sequence of traumas from the Depression to World War II to McCarthyism.

The virtues that were required to survive those times were admirable but perhaps tended toward a narrow spectrum. My friends and I seemed to come from families who'd all walked 20 miles to school—uphill both ways. My grandfather, a small-town farmer who almost went broke in the '30s, worked dawn to dusk. I saw him grab a snake out of a ditch, crack it like a whip, and throw it back dead. My father, an Army sergeant, was in the Normandy invasion, but he never talked about it. Another relative, who started a union, was accused of being un-American and blackballed.

These days, it almost seems quaint to make a list of taken-for-granted American traits back then: determination, the need for rigorous education, delayed gratification, and even stoicism. But Banks added something different and exciting for many of us.

Arriving in the big leagues just seven years after Jackie Robinson broke the color line, no sensible fan thought that Banks had come up easy. He'd even played in the Negro Leagues.

Everyone assumed that even if Banks' temperament tended toward cheerfulness, there was something else at work. Ernie *made himself* want to "play two," even on days when he undoubtedly didn't. And yet that habit of enthusiasm, that determination to focus on the love of the game for its own sake, seemed to become a reinforcing principle for him. The more he repeated it, lived it, the more it became true.

In short, maybe you could *make yourself* be happy.

All Banks fans will have their own affectionate version of Ernie. I imagine Banks on a hot August afternoon at Wrigley Field when the ivy vines are drooping and the Cubs flag in center field is near the bottom of the pole. He says, for the millionth time, "It's a beautiful day for a ballgame. Let's play two."

A few eyes roll. But the hint has been dropped, the seed planted once more, that the focus of the day actually is baseball, the game they love. "Ernie must be nuts," the Cubs think. "But, hell, I guess I would like to play one."

So, they do.

ACKNOWLEDGMENTS

I t's only every now and then that an opportunity comes along that is truly too good to turn down. This book was one of those for me.

Shortly before being approached about this project, I had heard Ernie Banks interviewed on Chicago talk radio. The station replayed the familiar sound bite of Jack Brickhouse calling Banks' 500th home run and then asked Ernie what he thought when he heard it. The answer was surprising. He said he thought it was all anybody knew about him. This didn't seem right because Ernie Banks, Mr. Cub, is definitely one of Chicago's brand names.

He also happened to be one of the best players in the National League at the start of the NL's golden age, a period of unparalleled success driven by the aggressive pursuit of African American talent. Ernie was one of the best shortstops who ever played, and there's no argument about that claim. For good measure, Banks was born and educated in Dallas, like me, although the circumstances of our childhoods could not have been more different, due mostly to the color of our skin and my peaking as a baseball player in Little League, a level of play not available to Ernie.

You would think the market would be flooded with books about Ernie Banks. But for whatever reason, that hasn't been the case. In fact, the only Banks book was an autobiography he co-wrote in 1971. That is stunning given how beloved of a figure he deservedly is for so many people.

I'll admit I did not know that much about Banks when I started this project. I can't swear I ever saw him play live (although I have a vague recollection of the Cubs being in the visiting dugout when my grandfather and parents took me to a game in the Astrodome's initial year). But I've known about him all my life, and I took the assignment understanding the importance of telling his story the right way. I hope I have succeeded in that.

Because this is an unauthorized biography, I wasn't assured of any cooperation from Ernie Banks. But we did spend time together, and I will be forever grateful to him for making that happen.

Next to Ernie Banks, the people most responsible for me being able to pull this off were my wife, Anne McElaney, and son, Dylan Rogers. Their good humor and patience throughout a Banks-filled summer was very much appreciated, and I loved having them there to listen to Ernie tell stories about his remarkable life and career. I'll never forget those times. Thanks also to my daughter, Shelby Rogers, for being Shelbyrific.

I also owe a major debt of gratitude to the other people who helped me understand Banks and the strange life he led, transitioning from a young Negro Leaguer listening to his heroes tell stories on the Kansas City Monarchs' bus to an icon beloved by Chicagoans, many of whom wanted him in their team's uniform but maybe not in the house across the street.

I'd especially like to thank the regal Monte Irvin for being generous with his time and recollections (and for opening his home up to Dylan, as well). Ditto Nolan Ryan, Lou Brock, Phil Niekro, and Tom Seaver. I'd like to thank Ken Burns, Bud Selig, Ron Santo, Kermit Eby, and Tom Boswell for their direct contributions to the book, and Jane Leavy and Joe Posnanski (whose biographies of Sandy Koufax and Buck O'Neil, respectively, are among the best books I've read) for inspiration.

I'd like to thank all the writers who covered Banks diligently and honestly throughout the years, especially the late Jim Enright and Rick Talley, whose coverage would stand up in any generation. I owe major thanks and several cheeseburgers to the staff of the National Baseball Hall of Fame and Museum, in particular the keepers of an amazing set of archives—Tim Wiles, Bill Francis, and Freddy Berowski. Also thanks to Hall president Jeff Idelson and PR man extraordinaire Brad Horn.

I would also like to thank the staff at the Highland Park Library and Naperville's Nichols Library for their invaluable assistance. For a variety of reasons, thanks to Barry Horn, Gene Wojciechowski, Dave Rogers, Ed English,

Dan McGrath, Richard Justice, Tracy Ringolsby, Larry Stone, Bob Elliott, Dave Eanet, Dave Van Dyck, Paul Sullivan, and Melissa Isaacson.

I'd like to thank my co-workers at the *Chicago Tribune* and the staff at Triumph Books, especially Mitch Rogatz and Tom Bast for thinking of me, Don Gulbrandsen for pulling it together, and Karen O'Brien for her careful editing.

INTRODUCTION

J ust one more hit. One more lousy hit.

Is that too much to ask?

That's what Ernie Banks was thinking when he stood in the on-deck circle at Shea Stadium, swinging a weighted bat and watching Ron Santo dig in to hit against Jerry Koosman. The Cubs had men on first and second and no outs in the eighth inning, tied 2–2 with the New York Mets in the biggest game of Banks' long career.

He was in his 17th season, and 1969 had been unlike any of those before it. The Cubs were baseball's lovable losers, in first place for only 37 of 2,586 days in the previous 16 seasons, just 12 of which came after the end of April and none later than July 4.

This was September, and the Cubs led the Mets by 2½ games. The New Yorkers had been gaining ground for weeks, causing the Bleacher Bums to squirm on their barstools back at Ray's Bleachers behind the center-field wall of Wrigley Field in Chicago. This was the Cubs' chance to show the Mets that the race was going to go to the team that had led all season, the one that had chased success the longest.

No player was ever more optimistic than Banks. He expected Santo to come through, even if his elbow was killing him after being drilled by Koosman earlier in the game. But the Cubs' captain hit a ground ball to Mets shortstop Bud Harrelson, who started an easy double play.

Two outs. Glenn Beckert standing on third base with the go-ahead run.

This wasn't going to be easy, but Banks had a chance.

As the 38-year-old first baseman walked to home plate, the scoreboard showed he was batting .253, his career average in decline. His chances against Koosman, a hard-throwing lefthander, probably weren't that good. Banks had homered off him here back in July, but that was one of only four hits in the seven games he had faced him.

Banks wasn't thinking about any of this, at least he was trying not to think about any of this. He was doing everything he could to clear his head, to make the task in front of him as simple as possible.

He had once told his friend Lou Brock that hitting was about three things—the baseball, the pitcher, and the hitter. And once the pitcher threw the ball, he was out of the equation. It was just the hitter and the ball, simple as that. "So whaddya mean, you can't hit Koufax?" he asked Brock.

This was no different. It was a baseball, a pitcher, and a hitter. And Banks knew he had an advantage. He had good hands, quick hands, hands he had used to pick cotton as a boy, hands that would pull the cotton from the bulbs and stuff it into a sack as fast as they could. The journey that had brought him to a packed stadium in Queens, New York, was the essential American Dream.

He had been blessed with ability and had maximized it by finding strong role models and learning from them, by showing up for work day after day with a baby-faced smile and a determination to treat others as he hoped to be treated. He never felt he was owed anything, including a hanging curveball with two outs and the go-ahead run on third base.

But if Koosman happened to hang a curve…

1

KILLING WITH KINDNESS

When Ernie Banks walked into Wrigley Field on a hot summer night in 2010, it had been almost 39 years since Philadelphia Phillies third baseman Deron Johnson couldn't handle the ground ball that went down as the last of his 2,583 hits for the Chicago Cubs.

The Cubs enjoyed an off night on a trip to Washington and Cincinnati and were sitting in fifth place under new management. Mike Quade, a native of Chicago's northwest suburbs who had fallen in love with baseball watching Banks, Billy Williams, Ron Santo, and Fergie Jenkins, had just replaced Lou Piniella as manager—the team's 24th managerial change since Banks retired.

Maybe Quade would be the one. Maybe 2011 would be the season.

In baseball, as in life, you never know. Even with a team that couldn't win when it had the equivalents of Alex Rodriguez at shortstop, Evan Longoria at third base, Josh Hamilton in left field, and Roy Halladay at the front of the starting rotation.

If you love the game, you love your favorite players. You love them forever if they are named Ernie Banks, if they smiled at you, if they said something silly while they signed an autograph. To be at Wrigley Field on this night is to understand how there can still be an innocence in hero worship, at least for the players lucky enough to have competed before sports talk radio, steroids, and fantasy baseball.

Fantasy baseball?

For Banks and the players of his generation, the fantasy was just to play baseball, to make an honest living playing a game with a stick and a ball.

It always starts out so simple, and before long it turns into something else altogether. For the lucky few, like Ernie Banks, the game never got ugly, even if much about life out of uniform was more difficult than people knew.

Banks has been at Wrigley Field often since his last game there in 1971, continuing a treasured relationship with the only team he ever played for and the tortured fans who continue sports' longest, saddest vigil, waiting for the championship season that never happens.

Banks knows the disappointment as well as anyone, but you wouldn't say he has suffered.

He had his moments, for sure.

In June 1964, Banks was upset when the Cubs traded his roommate, Lou Brock, to the St. Louis Cardinals. But it wasn't his style to show it, so he simply made a quiet vow to the young outfielder.

"Don't worry, Lou," Banks said. "You'll still be able to get into the Series. I'll send a ticket down to you in St. Louis."[1]

Brock got the last laugh. After helping take the Cardinals to the 1964 World Series, where they beat the Yankees in seven games, Brock sent Banks a package that contained the box his Series ring had been in—without, of course, the ring.

Banks could laugh about that, as he can laugh about almost anything. He laughed often on this night, speaking to a room packed with Cubs fans from the ages of 55 to 85, some of whom brought along children or grandchildren in the hope the younger generation would get to know the player they idolized as adolescents or young adults.

Banks kept a cap on his head, concealing the retreat of what had once been a nice head of hair. He had put on some weight during the four decades since his retirement, but he still had a physique that almost any man his age would envy. He was a little rounder around the middle, perhaps, but hardly overweight. He wore a yellow polo shirt bearing the logo of Cog Hill's No. 2 course, Dubsdread, which had long been on the rotation of great golf courses he loved to play while in Chicago.

Many of the fans came bearing relics for Banks to sign—old programs, baseballs he allegedly hit over Wrigley Field's ivy-covered walls, or photographs. They chose to celebrate the times when they were younger rather than stay home and dissect the 2010 Cubs guided by the little known Quade, who inherited the job when Lou Piniella gave up and went home to Florida, hoping like so many before him to wash off the stain of Cub-specific failure before going elsewhere to resume a less aggravating life.

There is no elsewhere for Ernie Banks, and that's all right with him.

His franchise had gone 63 years without a championship when he retired in 1971, and the team would be no more successful without him than it had been when he was one of the best players in the game—a wiry, country-strong shortstop whose power hitting placed him on the same level as Henry Aaron and Willie Mays in the late 1950s. The four-year tease that was the Piniella era extended the Cubs run without a championship to 102 years.

But like the T-shirts say, anybody can have a bad century. Why let the final score spoil the fun? Banks never did, although he burned to know the joy that Brock must have experienced while standing with his teammates at the top of the baseball world. He dreamed about what a World Series parade down Michigan Avenue would be like. It is his nature to dream, and few Americans have ever had dreams as outlandish and far-flung.

On this night at Wrigley, a gentleman in the crowd rose to tell Banks that he remembered reading how he often visited zoos when the Cubs were on the road and wondered if he still has an affinity for studying animals.

Banks answered the question thoughtfully but did not stop there. Thinking about zoos makes him think about circuses, and thinking about circuses makes him think about one of a thousand career paths he considered.

"I loved clowns," Banks said. "I read about clowns. I wanted to be a clown. I was going to Sarasota [Florida] to clown school, to train to become a clown. I liked clowns because they wore big shoes, red nose, sad face. Clowns looked sad but they made people laugh. That was always interesting to me."

In any conversation with Banks, it seems, there are always unexpected twists and turns. When he's asked to talk about baseball, he finds a way to turn the subject to business. Asked about his businesses, he turns it into a conversation about interpersonal relationships.

Banks says his "whole life was about education," and that he has always had a desire to learn something every day, which was still true as he approached his 80th birthday. He reels off a list of colleges he has attended, all strictly for the knowledge and not for a particular course of study—Northwestern University, the University of Chicago, Arizona State, Truman College, and Columbia College.

"I went back to school after I retired," Banks said. "I felt like my brain needed a massage. I didn't know anything when I finished playing. What can I do? What have I learned? It's all of that. It's like, 'Wow, I have to start out all over and catch up to guys who went to Harvard and Yale and Princeton and all that.'"

With the help of the late Phil Wrigley, who owned the Cubs during Banks' 19 seasons, Banks got into the car business and a variety of other enterprises. He would win some and lose some financially, just as he would love and lose in marriage.

On this night, he was married to 54-year-old Liz, his fourth wife in a line of commitments that began when he proposed to his high school sweetheart while in Germany with the Army. Marriage was perhaps the one area of his life where he had genuine regrets, although you'd never hear him talk about them.

Over and over again, he is asked to explain his trademark expression—"Let's play two." The stories he provides as its origin have changed wildly through the years, but as he's aged Banks has come up with an answer that provides a ring of truth.

He said he wanted to play doubleheaders because he was happiest at the ballpark.

"I was married, and that was the only place I could make my own decisions, when I came to ballpark—when to swing, when not to swing, when to run," Banks said at Wrigley's stadium club. "I couldn't do that at home. That's why I said let's play two. I didn't want to go home because I couldn't make those decisions."

Banks never gave up on love or life. That isn't in his nature.

He believes he was fortunate to have played before the lights were installed at Wrigley Field. "In my time, we had baseball in the afternoon and love at night," he said.

Banks has never understood how anyone could choose to live by themselves, without a husband or a wife. He loves to play matchmaker, making it a goal to be invited to more weddings every year than he had been the year before. At last count, his high was climbing toward 40 different couples who had asked him to help celebrate their nuptials in a calendar year.

Mark Grace was single throughout his tenure as the Cubs' first baseman. Banks spent most of those 13 years trying to find Mrs. Grace.[2]

In public appearances, like conversations, Banks often breaks out in song to make his point. That's a skill that would suit him at home, as well, especially at bedtime.

Ernie and Liz adopted a newborn in 2008, Banks' fourth child. He was 77 when Alyna Olivia came home from the hospital and ready to sing lullabies to her just as he once had to his twin sons, Jerry and Joel, and his daughter, Jan.

That's all well and good—"Happy for you, Ernie," "Way to go, Ernie"—but when Chicagoans of a certain age congregate at an event Banks is attending, the thing they want to do is talk about baseball, particularly the Chicago Cubs.

They want to tell Banks what he means to them. They want to tell him how they saw him hit a home run at Wrigley Field when their father took them to their first game; how they were there on Opening Day 1969, and how they saw him hit grand slams, especially those fans old enough to know about 1955 when he set the record with five. They want to thank him for being so considerate, so giving of his time, and then ask him to give just a little bit more, enough to sign this picture they've had squirreled away in their home office since the Nixon administration.

Banks is happy to do it, although he admits that at one point in time his motivation was driven by the fear this was all going away as fast as it had arrived.

"I tried to sign every kid's autograph," Banks told the crowd at Wrigley. "Because in my mind I thought that one day I might have to ask this kid for a job."

>> «

Jarvis fires away... That's a fly ball, deep to left, back, back... HEY-HEY! He did it! Ernie Banks got number 500! The ball tossed to the bullpen... everybody on your feet... this... is IT! WHEEEEEEE!

Jack Brickhouse's time-capsule call of Banks' 500th home run preceded Banks' appearance on a Chicago talk radio station in the spring of 2010. After playing the often-replayed clip, the host asked Banks what he thought about when he heard it.

His answer was, frankly, sad. "I think that's about all anyone knows about me," Banks said. "People know I hit 500 home runs. Some people know the number was 512. But after all the time I was with the Cubs, that's about all that people really know."

No player chatted with more players, stadium workers, and baseball fans than Banks during his stay with the Cubs from September 1953 through '71. No player was ever more accessible for interviews, whether with Chicago reporters or those based in New York and elsewhere.

Yet in a *Sport* magazine piece that ran at the end of the '71 season, writer Paul Hemphill described Banks as having kept the public at arm's length, his substance obscured by his style, the person beneath his pleasant, often-cherubic exterior still a mystery after all these years.

Hemphill's story was "The Last Days of Ernie Banks" and contained the contents of a one-on-one interview conducted in a private area at Wrigley Field while also describing the non-stop flow of chatter between Banks and everyone whose path he crossed. The purpose of the piece, Hemphill wrote, was to "make some sense of this man who has managed to show not a sliver of his inner self in nearly two decades of being in the spotlight."

Writers have never stopped trying to explain the questions that come with the Chicago icon known as Mr. Cub. How can a genuine baseball great—one of the best players ever at shortstop, arguably the game's most important position—devote his career to a losing organization and emerge as a more cheerful retiree than players whose dresser drawers are stuffed with World Series rings?

The *New York Times'* Malcolm Moran, a reporter too young to have known Banks in the era when he was a favorite of writers like Dick Young and Jim Murray, was beyond puzzled by a Banks sighting, in uniform, at Wrigley Field before Game 1 of the 1984 National League Championship Series.

Briefly kicked to the curb by Dallas Green after the Tribune Company's purchase of the team from the Wrigley estate, Banks had been given back his post-playing career job as a low-responsibility ambassador for the franchise. It figured he would be somewhere at the ballpark for the start of the Series against San Diego, the Cubs' first playoff action since the 1945 World Series. But what was with holding court in the dugout, wearing a No. 14 uniform with a patch that read, "NL EASTERN DIVISION CHAMPIONS"?

Banks was there to throw out the ceremonial first pitch—a memorable effort, as he would fling it from the pitching rubber to the plate behind his back, a move he said he borrowed from Satchel Paige, one pulled off with the gracefulness that was lacking when Leon Durham allowed Tim Flannery's ground ball to go through his legs in Game 5—but he looked awkward in uniform, almost as if he might try to sneak onto the field in the top of the first.

"There was something a little sad about [this]," Moran wrote. "Hall of Famers appear in suits and ties, and wave before they throw out the first ball, and then take their box seat. Banks dressed in the clubhouse with players who were not yet born when he first put on the Cub uniform.... And yet somehow Banks' appearance performed the same function as the ivy on the outfield walls, the reminder of a time when scorecards did not cost $3, as they did here today, and pencils were nowhere near 20 cents."

Banks told Moran and other reporters that it was wrong to consider the Cubs losers. "They're what you call good sports," he said. "To be a good sport, you have to prove that you're a good loser. But to prove that you're a good loser, you have to lose. This is what I'm saying: The only way to prove that you're a good sport is to lose."[3]

≫ ≪

In a 2005 *Chicago Tribune* feature, David Haugh wrote that Banks sometimes tells friends he hasn't suffered enough. "They say, 'What do you mean you didn't suffer enough?'" he said. "I see people in other parts of the world, they have no shoes, sleep on the floor, no food. That's real suffering. When I see some people struggling, I have empathy for them, but they really don't know what the bottom is."

Banks said his goal is to win a Nobel Peace Prize. "I've looked at people who have won it, [Desmond] Tutu, Lech Walesa, people who gave of themselves, helped others, and made this a better world," Banks said. "I can imagine myself in Stockholm. I visualize that, dream at night about that, being on that stage. That's the legacy I'm searching for."

Haugh closed the piece with writings of Oriah Mountain Dreamer in *The Invitation*, which Banks said summarized his outlook on life.

It doesn't interest me what you do for a living. I want to know what you ache for, and if you dare to dream of meeting your heart's longing.

It doesn't interest me how old you are. I want to know if you will risk looking like a fool for love, for your dreams, for the adventure of being alive.

It doesn't interest me what planets are squaring for your moon. I want to know if you have touched the center of your own sorrow, if you have been open to life's betrayals or have become shriveled and closed from fear of further pain. I want to know if you can be with joy, mine or your own, if you can dance with the wildness and let ecstasy fill you to the tips of your fingers and toes without causing us to be careful, be realistic, or to remember the limitations of being human.

It doesn't interest me if the story you're telling me is true. I want to know if you can disappoint another to be true to yourself, if you can bear the accusation of betrayal and not betray your soul. I want to know if you can be faithful, and therefore trustworthy. I want to know if you can see beauty even when it's not a pretty day, and if you can source your life from God's presence. I want to know if you can live with failure, yours and mine, and still stand on the edge of a lake and shout to the silver of the full moon, "Yes!"

It doesn't interest me to know where you live or how much money you have. I want to know if you can get up after a night of despair, worn and bruised to the bone, and do what needs to be done for the children.

It doesn't interest me who you are or how you came here. I want to know if you will stand in the center of the fire with me and not shrink back.

It doesn't matter to me where or what or with whom you have studied. I want to know what sustains you from the inside when all else falls away. I want to know if you can be alone with yourself. And if you truly like the company you keep in empty moments.[4]

Not exactly the kind of talk you hear around the batting cage, is it? No wonder Banks feels few really know him. Beneath the smile, at the end of the day, he opts to position himself as someone who would have more in common with Deepak Chopra than Sammy Sosa.

Or does he just want us to think that?

John Roseboro, whose career with the Dodgers paralleled Banks' with the Cubs, is one of the few who went on the record to say that he felt Banks was full of it. "Maybe it's sacrilege, but I believe Banks was a con artist," Roseboro notoriously said. "No one smiles all the time naturally unless they're putting it on and putting you on. Every day of our lives isn't a good one."[5]

Banks' nature could easily seem contrived. As he approached his 80th birthday, he often wore a cap that carried the slogan "Busy is Good," a carryover of his lifelong love of motivational gimmicks. One day during the 1969 season, he walked around the clubhouse with a piece of paper attached to his chest that said, "Want to wake up each day with a smile? Sleep with a hanger in your mouth."[6]

While Banks constantly engages friends and strangers alike in conversations, he rarely gets beyond the most superficial level, asking about mothers-in-law and Little League baseball, music, and mutual friends.

"He's got this shtick he goes through, and that's the way it is," one of Banks' fellow Hall of Famers said. "He just jabbers."

Sometimes Banks doesn't listen to the reply. "One time he asked me how my mother was doing," the Hall of Famer said. "I said, 'Ernie, she passed a few years ago.' He said, 'That's good, that's good.' I just shook my head."

Banks' out-of-the blue phone calls are sources of amusement for his friends. You never know when they are coming, one friend said, and you never know where Banks is going.

Sports Illustrated's Mark Kram described Banks' love of the telephone in a piece that ran in the most fateful month of Banks' career, September 1969. Kram wrote that Banks had called up Frank Robinson in Baltimore and warned that he would be seeing him in October. He had called up his old friend Lou Brock in St. Louis to say that, as great and gallant as the Cardinals were, Brock should forget about "a run for our pennant."

Banks awoke Willie Mays to have a conversation typical of his sneak attacks:

"Hello. Willie? That you?" Banks asked.

"Who is this?" Mays replied, sounding sleepy.

"Who is this? It's Ernie Banks. Listen, Willie. First of all, I want to congratulate you on an outstanding performance last night. You're a wonderful player and fine person. You know that, don't you? We won again this afternoon. Did you know that?"

"I know that," Mays said. "Don't you think I know what's going on?"

"Wonderful. Then you know the Cubs are going all the way," Banks said. "Nothing's going to stop this team."

"Are you calling me to tell me that?"

"I'm calling you to tell you to go out there tonight and give it your all against the Cardinals. You're a superstar! I want to see you play like a superstar."

"Who's pitching for them?" Mays asked.

"Bob Gibson! You hit him. You always hit him. When you come up to the plate against Gibson, it's murder. I feel sorry for him tonight."

By now Mays was laughing. "All right," he said. "I got to get dressed to go to the ball park."

"Good. That's positive thinking. And when you get there, remember, you're Willie Mays. No. 24! An immortal!"[7]

Mays didn't question why his friend was calling to give him a pep talk. Like the aging Banks, Mays was on the downside of his career in '69, and it was natural for Banks both to pay respect to Mays while trying to stoke his fire to play against one of the Cubs' rivals.

Henry Aaron got his share of those calls when he was playing, too. They continued in retirement, slowing at times but never stopping.

"There [has never] been another ballplayer with Ernie's disposition," Aaron said. "It might seem odd that we became good friends because in addition to being rivals, we were opposite personalities. He was as outgoing as I wasn't. Ernie was so upbeat and happy all the time that a lot of people thought he was phony. Well, if Ernie's a phony, he must be a hell of an actor because he's been fooling me for [most of my life]."[8]

Filmmaker Ken Burns first met Banks when he was taping his seminal documentary on baseball in the early 1990s. The two have bumped into each other from time to time since then, and Burns has received his share of telephone calls from Banks, interested in discussing a variety of subjects.

Burns said that at first he didn't know what to make of Banks' sunny outlook and chatter. But over time he took into account the people who helped shape Banks, especially Negro League legend Buck O'Neil, who provided Burns a window to look into baseball from the African American perspective.

"Think about who his mentor is," Burns said. "It took me a while. I was sort of like, 'Duh.' His mentor is Buck O'Neil, and what is Buck O'Neil's message? [It] was and is this kind of joyous tolerance, this affirmation in the face of adversity, this kind of transcendent grace that through the whole sordid history of the human race that does not for a second suggest that humans are actually made in God's image, Buck resurrects that possibility. I think Ernie is the kind of inheritor of that kind of optimism.

"Because he's in this modern era, it's shaded in some ways, but I realize I was hearing the echoes of Buck. Not to take anything away from Ernie, but that exuberance, that 'let's play two' cliché, wasn't a cliché. It was real. Clichés are just truths that were overused, but they still are truths. To me the real subject of the [documentary *Baseball*] is resilience. It is the best game that's ever been invented, and it always reveals its profound resilience, this human resilience. It is a game that mirrors life. None of us are getting out of it alive, and loss is the greatest teacher."

Banks endured more than probably anyone else who ever played for the Cubs, with the possible exception of fellow African Americans like Gene Baker and George Altman. Sammy Sosa went through a lot to get to the United States as a baseball player, but once he got to the big leagues, the world was his oyster.

In the 1950s and '60s, as a black from segregated Texas starring for a team with a fan base that was 99 percent white at a time when baseball was ahead of America in its attempt at creating a society where equality was the standard, Banks navigated the most swirling of waters. Yet he somehow came out as one of the handful of truly great players from the Cubs franchise, with a smile on his face and the daily slights seemingly forgotten.

In its essence that is a miracle, and Banks speaks of his career in exactly those terms. To truly understand it you have to put baseball's breaking of the color barrier in context and take a hard look at what an ugly place America could be in the era when Banks played.

"I have often described [integrating baseball in the 1940s] as our proudest and most important moment," said Bud Selig, who, as a Milwaukee fan, befriended Hank Aaron almost four decades before becoming baseball's commissioner. "Think about it. Branch Rickey signs Jackie [Robinson] in 1945, [Robinson] goes to Montreal in '46, where he has some trauma, comes up to the big leagues the next year. It's four years before Harry Truman integrated the military, it's seven and a half years before *Brown vs. Board of Education*, it's 18 years before the Civil Rights movement.

"This is baseball's proudest and most dramatic moment. I have a lot of reasons to have a lot of respect for Branch Rickey, who I think was the greatest baseball executive of all time. But I think that alone makes him the greatest baseball executive of all time. I remember he had a great quote in '50 or '51. Someone was concerned the Dodgers would have an all-black team. He said, 'I'm paid to win here.' That was right. That was the way it was supposed to be. It took a lot. Some clubs were very slow [to integrate], some not at all. I don't think people understand the great significance, which is why Jackie Robinson was no question one of the most influential Americans of the 20th century. Not a scintilla of question."

Pioneering players dealt with isolation and racial abuse. Selig developed his compassion through the experience of his friend, Aaron, and appreciates what Banks would have faced at Wrigley Field.

"It's so interesting because in many ways [Banks was] the hero when people went to Wrigley Field, and that was it," Selig said. "Life away from the field was completely different. It was very frustrating for players. Henry and I have spent many hours talking about it. No question. Very true."

Banks dealt with so much, including a feeling from blacks involved in the civil rights movement that he and others like him should use their stature to push for change, if not downright demand it. What Banks did was show up for work almost every day with a smile on his face, making friends as easily as he piled up hits.

Because it is a difficult subject to discuss, it often seems necessary to tap dance around our racial differences and experiences. It seems better to make assumptions and accept certain truths on their face without opening ourselves up to a genuine consideration of our lives. But just because we try to ignore something doesn't mean it no longer exists.

Banks was arguably *the* poster child for a racially mixed Chicago, even when few places in Chicago really were racially mixed. It was comforting to see Banks hitting home runs and then doing polite interviews with Jack Brickhouse, even if there were large areas of the city in which he could not park his Cadillac without fear of having its tires cut, as happened once outside a reporter's home.

"Race is always there," Burns said. "It's always there, no matter what people want to say.... We play a lie to this thing, this belief that we've escaped the specific gravity of race in this country. We haven't escaped it. Chicago certainly didn't escape it in the 1960s. We take advantage of Buck O'Neil, we take advantage of Ernie Banks because we like our progressivism to come with a good nature.

"If it's Curt Flood and you're going to upset the apple cart, if it's Barry Bonds with his complicated baggage, well, that's not the kind of African American we want to have around. We're very quick to do this. We gave Franklin Roosevelt eight and a half years to clean up the Depression, which he didn't do, with a stimulus program a lot larger than [the one overseen by Barack Obama in 2009–10], and then the biggest stimulus program in the history of the world came along, called World War II. But now? Black guy can't do it in a year? Throw the bum out."

Banks never seemed visibly angry. He played in 2,528 games with the Cubs, and never once was he ejected. He maintained excellent relationships with his teammates and every manager he ever played for, including Leo Durocher, who resented Banks' popularity and constantly worked to replace him in the lineup, deeming him over the hill when he was still among baseball's most reliable run producers.

The Banks-Durocher relationship demonstrated how far Banks was willing to go to get along with someone. His response to Durocher was both calculated and true to his essence.

"When somebody resented me, didn't like me—and that was the case with Leo—I kind of killed them with kindness," Banks said. "On the bench, I'd always sit beside him, on the plane sit beside him, in the dugout sit beside him. He's always looking around and seeing me.... When you light a fire under my heels, it just made me better. I focused more, concentrated more, reached inside of me and got more out of myself.... Overall, he made me a better player toward the end of my career."9

Banks took a similar attitude toward any teammates or rivals who treated him badly. He would earn respect with his performance on the field—every day, all season, every season.

"What we tried to do was take it out on the ball, go out and play good baseball and change their minds," said Monte Irvin, a fellow Hall of Famer who began his career in the Negro Leagues. "Win 'em over. Most of your teammates were for you. There were very few guys you didn't get along with."

Banks didn't challenge authority while drawing a high salary in a white-run enterprise, so many African Americans considered Banks a sellout. That hurt him. But like the other disappointments he experienced, he rarely if ever gave voice to his side of the story, at least not in any depth.

"He told 'em, 'I don't have time to march but I contribute,'" Irvin said. "'I try to play good baseball to make up for it that way. Give the kids somebody to look up to, so the fans come to the ballpark pleased.' That's what he thought. I think that's a pretty good attitude."

In his later years, the Rev. Jesse Jackson would work to have a statue of Banks built outside Wrigley Field. But when he was working alongside Martin Luther King Jr. for better schools and housing in segregated Chicago in the 1960s, Jackson was frustrated by Banks' silence.

While Banks was truly a bridge guy, making white Chicago feel comfortable when placed shoulder to shoulder with black Chicago, it was difficult for those facing daily hardships without his advantages to see him as part of the struggle. Imagine the toll that must have taken on Banks, who would think about it a lot more than he shared when he was in public.

Where was Banks in the civil rights struggle?

"You know who I'd ask [about that]?" Burns said. "Michael Jordan. Where's his activism? Where's his sense of being a spokesman or a role model for African Americans? Where's his outspokenness about hip-hop culture and the negative influences of that gangster stuff? Where is he when the questions of the day are happening? He's on the golf course because somewhere he understood where his meal came from. It was not in any way [from] rocking the boat.

"It's so interesting that you make your bargain with the man, somehow—which makes Jackie all the more remarkable. He made his bargain, and then he lived his life. He was arguing just days before he died, getting honored at the 25-year mark, saying, 'I'm very honored, but I'll be even more honored when I look over and see a third-base coach who is black.'"

The first hotel Banks stayed in as a professional baseball player was so shabby it literally had holes in the roof, allowing moonlight and rain to enter his room.[10] Not so many years later he'd be staying in some of America's finest hotels, but he would never feel as comfortable as he did in the hotels he shared with his teammates from the Negro League's Kansas City Monarchs. It would be enlightening to hear him accurately detail the human side of his life's journey, but this is a story he's never really chosen to tell.

"Some things happen to my life I just want to keep to myself, enjoy," Banks said. "My grandkids don't even know I played baseball. [I hold onto the memories] just to share with them some of the experiences I had."

Burns believes there are two reasons why Banks was never open about all aspects of his life, including matters of race. The first is a question of whether he was truly capable of verbalizing all he endured in his journey, especially the feeling of being treated like a second-class citizen while knowing he had been blessed with gifts. The second is a question of knowing how his bread is buttered.

"Ernie has a different kind of thing. He's going to come up in a world that's been segregated for his whole life. He knows. He gets it. Right?" Burns said. "All of a sudden he's now in this world that's delivering him fame and immortality and let's just say a living, right? It's hard to question that. It's like the soldiers in our World War II films. If you've seen your best friend get his head shot off, it's not like it looks like in the movies, even the most realistic movies. It's worse. You don't come home and talk about that. You lock that away. I think there's a disconnect.

"Somewhere along the line, whatever introspection we want—even Buck didn't do it; he just carried on in that utterly Christian way—what is there to do? [From Banks' perspective], how is it possible I've spent 19 years of my life without any interaction with white people because even in the north they have segregated you into the neighborhoods that you, quote, belong and then you're the sort of spice in this gumbo called the Chicago Cubs, beloved by everybody, embraced by everybody. What do you do with that? I don't know. In some ways you could just short circuit.

"Maybe that's where there's no place to actually talk about it. I'm sure he does think about it. I also know he has to be so careful. He doesn't want to not be Mr. Cub, right? This was Jackie Robinson's thing. As soon as he didn't have to turn the other cheek, after three years he was described as uppity by the very same sportswriters who treated him like he was this magnificent new thing. The backlash is really intense. Look at Barry Bonds. He was the repository of all our negative feelings because he was such an SOB. Yeah, but so was Joe DiMaggio. Ted Williams was difficult. But it all comes with that subtle thing of race. Nobody says there's an angry white guy."

2

February

The sky was falling.

It often felt that way in Chicago at the end of the 1960s.

The United States was at war in Vietnam. Jimi Hendrix's screeching transfixing guitar and Jim Morrison's haunting voice, delivering lyrics both poetic and unsettling, provided a serenade along streets from Haight-Ashbury to Greenwich Village, including hundreds of middle-class, white-bread towns in between. With the debate fueled by a diverse cast of characters that included Martin Luther King, George Wallace, Joan Baez, and Richard Nixon, America was finally wrestling with the myth it had perpetuated since Thomas Jefferson sidestepped the hypocrisy of being both a founding father and a slave owner—the myth about freedom for all and all men being created equal.

Baseball, which the fictional Terence Mann called "the one constant through all the years" in the movie *Field of Dreams*, marked the time as it had since before Cap Anson learned to hit. And there was nowhere that baseball could be sweeter than at Wrigley Field, on the corner of Clark and Addison, a ballpark that Ernie Banks said is "like the Taj Mahal."

One day in July 1967, a sea of change was experienced by the team playing there, and their fans, whose happiness had long been based on the lowest of expectations.

Fergie Jenkins had thrown a three-hitter to beat Pete Rose and the Cincinnati Reds, which was nice, but the real fun didn't start until a few minutes later. That's when the ground around Jenkins literally began to shake.

"Wrigley Field was packed, and after the game was over, the fans all stayed there to see what would happen on the east coast, whether the Cardinals would lose, to see if our pennant would fly on top of that pole," Jenkins said. "See, we had pennant flags to show the standings of the teams, and I can recall that when they announced we went into first place—the Mets had beaten St. Louis—there was a cheer for, man, 10 minutes.

"A lot of us were in the dressing room, and when this cheer came up, we knew with all the excitement that something was happening. We said to each other, 'Hey, the fans are still in the ballpark.' And we were happy to hear we were in first place for the first time."

Jenkins and his teammates went back out on the field and looked toward the big green scoreboard atop the center-field bleachers. There they watched the attendants raise the Cubs' pennant to the top of nine others representing National League teams.[1]

The Cubs, the so-called Lovable Losers who had known only one winning season in 20 years, were in first place this late in a season for the first time since 1945 when Charlie Grimm made the mistake of starting an overworked Hank Borowy on two days rest in Game 7 of the World Series.

In '67, the euphoria was short-lived. The Cardinals would steam to the NL pennant, with the Cubs winding up in third place. They would finish third again in '68, with St. Louis winning its third pennant in five years and losing to Detroit in the World Series.

The Cards were led by Bob Gibson and Lou Brock, the latter of which was Banks' former roommate who had been stupidly traded after starting his Hall of Fame career with the Cubs. They won 97 games, 13 more than the Cubs, but in the second half of the season it was the Cubs who were the NL's best team.

Leo Durocher, long judged as morally unacceptable by Phil Wrigley, the second-generation Cubs owner whose biggest vice was overhauling car engines that could have hummed along after only an oil change, had arrived as the Cubs' manager before the 1966 season. Durocher once would have laughed at the prospect of managing such a laughingstock but had been out of favor for a decade since successful runs managing the Dodgers and Giants.

The Cubs' early returns under Durocher had made the National League like the country itself—unsettled. They had made such progress that it was no longer crazy to speak of them as serious contenders, and they weren't alone in sparking the imagination.

The expansion New York Mets had established a new low-water mark with their 40–120 record in 1962 and through '68 had lost 343 more games than they had won, an average finish of 49 games below .500. But the Mets' luck turned when they landed the rights to USC's Tom Seaver in a lottery.

With Whitey Herzog cutting his management teeth as an assistant to GM Johnny "Grandma" Murphy, the Mets had surrounded Seaver with a stable of promising pitchers, including Gary Gentry, Nolan Ryan, and Jerry Koosman. They, too, had brought in a manager with a lofty reputation, former Brooklyn Dodgers slugger Gil Hodges, who was pried away from his contract to manage the Washington Senators only because that team was hurting financially.

"Hodges changed the losing mindset," Mets third baseman Ed Charles said. "He was an upfront type of manager, very knowledgeable about the game, very firm in what he expected from players."[2]

Few outside of New York and Chicago saw the Mets and Cubs as being ready to stop the powerful Cardinals from repeating as champions, but they were clearly on the rise with teams like the Pirates, Giants, and Reds descending.

With baseball's second wave of expansion adding teams in San Diego, Montreal, Kansas City, and Seattle, commissioner Spike Eckert and the owners had decided it was time to add a divisional format. They aligned the 24 teams in four divisions of six teams apiece, with the Cubs placed in the NL East while Cincinnati and Atlanta (relocated from Milwaukee) were assigned to the West, and they added a league championship series before the World Series.

Numerical odds of a team advancing to postseason play had grown from 10 to 17 percent, and many baseball men fretted that life would be too easy for frontrunners. Among those was the Cubs' manager.

"It's going to be much harder in this divisional play for a club to catch up," Durocher said. "You only have to worry about five clubs. The others don't bother me. My only worry about the Western teams is when I play them, and we only play each other 12 times."[3]

Among sportswriters and fans, the question mark about the NL was who would win the West—Henry Aaron's Braves or the Giants, now led by Willie

McCovey, with Willie Mays as a supporting actor. There was near consensus in picking the East.

"The East is the personal property of the St. Louis Cardinals, perhaps the best and deepest ballclub to be seen [this spring]," the *New York Times'* Arthur Daley wrote. "Under the driving lash of Leo Durocher, the Chicago Cubs have become a genuine threat. They finished third a year ago and conceivably could be a winner this season if geographers had placed them in the Western Division. Unfortunately for them, however, they are in the East."[4]

Daley failed to mention one team that had caught the Cubs' eyes.

"I know it's going to be tough, especially with the Cardinals and Mets," said Don Kessinger, the Cubs' 26-year-old shortstop. "The Mets are going to surprise a lot of people."[5]

>> <<

But even before players could get on the field, fans were confronted with a true surprise. Players, organized under former United Steelworkers' negotiator Marvin Miller, were threatening baseball's first strike.

To say that management was appalled would be an understatement. Gussie Busch and the other barons who controlled baseball were in a state of apoplexy at this development. Men who got paid to play a boy's game actually had the nerve to feel they should have some control over how the revenues they produced were distributed.

"Let 'em strike," Braves general manager Paul Richards said. "Maybe if they do, it will get the guys who don't want to play out of the game and let the fellows who appreciate the major leagues play."

Not that Richards thought it would come to this, of course. "I don't think the players have enough guts to strike," he added.[6]

At issue was ownership's contribution to the players' pension fund—and the difference between the sides was laughably small. The players were seeking to increase the owners' contributions from $4.1 million to $5.9 million annually, and the owners' opening offer was $5.1 million. That left a gap of only $800,000, but neither side was in a mood to compromise.[7]

In its infancy, the players' union was looking to build cohesiveness among the players and gain leverage for future negotiations over much bigger issues, like salaries and an end to the reserve clause, which effectively could bind a player to his team indefinitely.

Miller had negotiated one work agreement for the players, getting the minimum salary raised to $10,000 and the maximum pay cut reduced to 20 percent in 1968. But his earliest victory had been to get players to refuse to sign their baseball card contracts, organizing them against the Topps Company, which was forced to increase players' annual payments from $125 to $250 and to pay the union 8 percent of sales up to $4 million and 10 percent on sales more than that.

Miller's approach was to ask players to not sign their contracts for 1969 until there was an agreement on the pension issue. That would mean a collective holdout as teams did not allow unsigned players to work out with their teammates.

Miller held a press conference at the site of the winter meetings—the Palace Hotel in San Francisco—to announce his plans. More than 450 players had signed off on his plan, and he read their names, beginning with stars like Banks, Mays, Aaron, Roberto Clemente, Pete Rose, Frank Robinson, Harmon Killebrew, and Don Drysdale.

There was no movement in the talks in December and January, and a cloud hung over the normal date for teams to open their camps in Arizona and Florida.

Minor leaguers and rookies who weren't union members weren't included among the potential holdouts, so camps would definitely open. The questions were how many familiar faces would be there and if the exhibition schedule would be impacted. Bowie Kuhn, who had just replaced Eckert as commissioner, sat in his New York office, growing more worried with each passing day.

Not wanting to take a chance, the White Sox canceled a series of games that John Allyn and his co-owner brother, Arthur Allyn Jr., had scheduled in Mexico City. But there were some good signs for the owners.

Young Orioles pitcher Jim Palmer, injured the previous year, ignored the boycott.[8] Banks, fresh off partnering with Dick Butkus in a celebrity golf tournament, reported on time to the Cubs' camp in Scottsdale, Arizona. He declared himself management, not labor, as Wrigley and Durocher had named him a player-coach in 1967. Veteran backup catcher Gene Oliver was also in a group of 18 players on the field for the first workout.[9]

Banks worked alongside few people he knew but carried himself as if this was business as usual when the workouts began.

"Yessir, yessir, yessir, World Series '69, the Chicago Cubs versus the Detroit Tigers," Banks declared in his familiar sing-song style, before conducting a phantom interview. "What kind of pitch did you hit for your home run, Mr. Banks?" "Oh, a mediocre fastball, Mr. Newspaperman."

Bill Libby, in Scottsdale to write a profile of Banks for *Sport* magazine, took it all in. "The kids and free agents looked at [Banks] like he was crazy," Libby wrote. "He didn't notice. He never does."[10]

Meanwhile Ron Santo, designated as the Cubs' captain by Durocher, was like most players. He was anxious to get back to work and nervous about damaging the good thing he had going.

The Cubs' perennial All-Star third baseman traveled to Arizona but stayed out of camp, telling writers he would start working out on March 1 without regard to the negotiations. "Mr. Wrigley has been good to me," Santo said. "I'm going to be good to him."[11]

Santo didn't stop there, either. He talked about how the paternal Wrigley had been an asset in getting his Chicago pizza business off the ground.

"He's helped me with money and given me counsel," Santo said. "I wouldn't be in the pizza business right now without his help. I just refuse to fight him. I know all players aren't fortunate enough to play for an owner like Mr. Wrigley, but that's no reason for me to oppose him."

Santo said he was getting calls from teammates about whether or not to report.

"I know they have been treated as fairly as I have, so what am I going to tell them?" he said. "Just the truth as I know it."[12]

Glenn Beckert, Don Kessinger's double-play partner since 1965, was in the group of Cubs players lined up to follow Santo into camp without union approval.

"The whole mess comes from a lack of communication with the players," Beckert said, criticizing Miller and the union leadership. "An average guy like me doesn't know what's going on. Most of what I know about it I read in the papers."[13]

The *Chicago Tribune's* George Langford saw the Cubs' "breakaway," as he called it, as a sign the union could not stand up to management. He cited the players' reluctance to stay out of camp as "a tribute to Philip K. Wrigley, the team owner, and to the high-level men within the organization who have maintained an unusual rapport with the players over the years."

Veteran players elsewhere were similarly struggling with the notion of biting the hand that fed them.

Carl Yastrzemski had won the Triple Crown for Boston in 1967, a feat for which he had been rewarded with a two-year contract. These types of contracts would go to utility infielders and long relievers 20 years later, but Yastrzemski and Banks were the only players known to have them as the '69 season approached, as players were only starting to gain a collective voice.

Like Santo, Yastrzemski was finding it tough to challenge his boss. He wouldn't hold out long, if he did hold out. In the end, however, no one would need to hold out long.[14]

The hyper-sensitive Kuhn wilted at the first hint of unhappiness by the public and the press. He ordered negotiator John Gaherin to make a deal, backing down from a fight just as a lot of baseball executives were seeing waves of players on the verge of joining Palmer, Banks, and others in camps.

The dispute ended a week later with owners raising the pension contribution to $5.45 million. Spring training began with the '69 season safe from the kind of work stoppages that would haunt baseball over the next three decades.[15]

Wrigley declared the settlement a tie, comparing it to a game stopped by darkness. "I think it ended with both sides saving face," the Cubs' owner said. "But I thought it was a foregone conclusion from the start of all the fussing that there would be no delay in our spring plans."[16]

John Holland, the Cubs' general manager, said the contentious bargaining "left no scars" on his team, and that indeed was the case.

"I was never worried about it," Durocher said. "And one thing that particularly did not worry me was Mr. Miller, in case you want to know."[17]

Miller's big victories would come later. Banks, Santo, and company could only hope that Durocher had a few ahead of him, too.

3

Two Different Americas

Picking cotton is back-breaking work.

On plantations throughout the south, both before and after Eli Whitney invented the cotton gin in 1794, the cotton industry was among the primary reasons for America's slave trade. The economies of states like Georgia, Alabama, Mississippi, and Louisiana were based around the inexpensive labor of field hands who either were given or earned just enough to survive.

There weren't a lot of plantations in Texas, at least not once you got as far west as Dallas. There were, however, farms and cotton fields that stretched as far as the eye could see across the prairies.

One phenomenon that economists have discovered about America's slave trade is that the costs for growers actually went down after the Civil War. You could hire labor more cheaply when you did not need to take care of the needs of the workers, as had been the case on plantations. The black men and women who were declared free by Abraham Lincoln, along with generation after generation of their ancestors, paid a high price for their freedom.

So it was for Eddie and Essie Banks.

Eddie was born in East Texas, not far from the Louisiana border. Essie was from Shreveport, just across the state line. They moved to Dallas to raise their family, which would ultimately include 12 children born to the enduring Essie over a period of 31 years. Eddie thought the move would give him a chance to earn more money, working in a bigger city. And it also allowed him to continue his childhood passion—baseball.

In 1931, Essie gave birth to their second child. It was their first son, and they named him Ernest without bothering to add a middle name.

They lived in an all-black neighborhood near downtown Dallas, close enough to see the bright lights of the city but in a world that few of the people who shopped in Neiman Marcus and Sanger Harris could comprehend. There were few luxuries for children in Banks' neighborhood, with even Christmas generally more of a reminder of what they didn't have than a season of gift giving. Thanksgiving meant bringing home live chickens to be killed and prepared, and one year Ernie and his oldest sister, Edna, had to wrestle a neighbor who had stolen their bird.[1]

One of Ernie's rare presents was a BB gun from his father. There were times he used it to shoot rats, chasing them away from the house, which Essie maintained in a clean, orderly fashion. For the most part, this seemed a safe, even at times idyllic community, in which to begin life.[2]

"All the families were poor and hard-working," Banks said. "On summer evenings most of our parents relaxed on the front porches, but as soon as darkness fell, they called us to come inside. When it got dark, you went home and stayed there for the rest of the night."

There was no mixing of races in the Dallas of Banks' youth. A black man might work for a white family but they would not socialize, and anyone who challenged the social order was asking for trouble. The Ku Klux Klan was on the rise in the 1920s, with most of its growth occurred in urbanizing cities that were experiencing their own growth spurts, such as Dallas, Houston, Detroit, and Atlanta. Eddie and Essie, like other black parents, feared for their children who might not understand the distinctions of race and class.

Eddie was among 8.5 million Americans working for the Works Progress Administration after the Depression. He worked building highways and streets and repairing public buildings. In his free time, he took on any odds jobs he could find and passed down his work ethic to his oldest son.

It fell to Ernie to take care of many responsibilities around the house that the family rented for $20 a month, such as keeping kerosene in the lamps, and bringing in wood for the two stoves and water to heat upon it. From the time he was old enough to do the most menial of tasks, he was expected to bring home whatever money he could, always turning it over to Essie.

"Despite the hardships, my parents always stressed togetherness within the family," Banks said. "They taught us love and the importance of right thinking. We had to share everything, from clothes to money and food, and we were glad to give whatever we earned to our mother, who determined where it was needed most. This kind of sharing was my first lesson in teamwork."[3]

Banks shined shoes, mowed lawns, and worked in a hotel kitchen for a while. The job he remembers the most fondly was picking cotton.

Eddie would get him up at 5:00 AM, long before the sun peeked across the flat horizon, and they would walk to a blacks-only café in the neighborhood for a quick breakfast. Then a truck would arrive for them and the other pickers, who would climb in the back and ride 30 miles northeast toward the town of Greenville almost always standing up and jammed next to each other. When they reached the fields, they would work until dark.

"Each picker carried a huge sack over his shoulder, tossing the cotton into it as he worked," Banks said. "The older men could pick with both hands and toss the cotton into the sack in one smooth motion. I used a different method, crawling along the rows on both knees, picking as I moved.... At the end of each day, the grower paid off at the rate of $2 per hundredweight. Five or six dollars was pretty good for a day's work. I never made that much, but a lot of the pickers did."[4]

What kid would remember this experience with relish?

One who loved his father and sought his approval. And one who was hungry. The morning breakfast, paid for with nickels and dimes, was every bit as big of a treat for a young Ernie as steak would be for the businessmen who flocked to the Old Warsaw restaurant on Maple Avenue.

Ernie would get a glass of milk and either coffee cake or a sweet roll, sitting on a stool next to his young father. He would listen to the chatter of neighbors and savor a time he considered special, and very much worth the long, hard workday he would face in the cotton fields.

» «

Banks' old home at 1723 Fairmount Street was razed along with all the others on his street in the 1980s, when a Dallas city abuzz over Tom Landry and watching J.R. Ewing set out to create an arts district. Where Banks' home once stood is now a parking lot that services the Morton H. Meyerson Symphony Center, designed by architect I.M. Pei and built at a cost of more than $80 million.

Everything a young Banks had needed had been in the neighborhood that now is parking lots and other elements of urban renewal. His school was three blocks away, the grocery store was closer, and the Moorland branch of the YMCA was only eight blocks away. Banks couldn't afford to participate in Y programs, but he got to know the staffers, who would look the other way when he shot baskets and used the facilities, and eventually he wound up working in the Y while in high school.

"It was a small universe," Banks said. "I was never exposed to anything outside of my neighborhood."

Essie Banks described Ernie as an almost model son who never "prowled" at night and was a regular at Sunday school and church. "He liked to stretch out on top of his bed and read for hours," she said in a *Saturday Evening Post* story. "He was an average student in school."

Eddie Banks was a good athlete who favored baseball. He spent eight years as a catcher for a semi-pro team called the Dallas Green Monarchs after World War I.

"I was a pretty good hitter, but I couldn't carry Ernie's bat," Eddie, who died in 1978, told the *Chicago American's* Jim Enright in 1960. "We didn't have so many great hitters in my day, and the competition wasn't nearly as keen. Everything is different these days. The hitters are better, the pitching is better, baseball is better, and so is the world. It's a much faster pace now."[5]

Ernie started life more as a dreamer than a doer. He had no interest in playing baseball and no idea where a sport could carry a kid with talent.

"This is the miracle I'm talking about," Banks said. "I didn't want to play baseball.... I wanted to be an international lawyer. Throughout all my life growing up, I've always said to myself, 'Gosh, human beings are [the] only ones [who] can make life complicated and unpleasant.' Every time I found people, they always started talking about what they had, where they'd been, what they'd done, and their children. I felt like slapping 'em and saying, 'Snap out of it, talk about something [that]can make this a better world.' Do something, say something [that] can make this a better world. Throughout my life that's what I've always been searching for—my footsteps to make this a better world, and

Barack [Obama] did this, to win a Nobel Peace Prize. That was my thought when I was quite young."

Eddie Banks' goals weren't quite as ambitious. He just wanted his oldest son to follow in his footsteps as a baseball player. "He wanted me to be a baseball player," Banks said of his father. "But I had no idea I wanted to be a baseball player."

When Eddie came home from work, he would pay Ernie to play catch. What kid could turn down that offer?

"I started Ernie out early," Eddie said. "He was only eight, and a very little fellow at that, when I purchased his first ball and glove. We used to play catch every afternoon after I came home from work. The bat came later, and that almost wrecked everything. Drives off Ernie's bat broke so many windows in the neighborhood that we were always in trouble. In fact, his mother used to yell at me, 'Why don't you quit that silly baseball and help Ernie get a job? He'd be better off delivering newspapers or cutting grass.'"[6]

Eddie omitted how he convinced Ernie to join him in the daily games of catch. Ernie said he wasn't exactly thrilled the day Eddie showed up with a baseball glove and bat. "I wouldn't have anything to do with them," Banks said. "So Dad gave me 10 cents to play catch with him. From then on, whenever he wanted to play catch, he'd bribe me with nickels and dimes."[7]

Eddie arranged for Ernie and his brother, Benjamin, to serve as bat boys for the Green Monarchs.

"He was still so small his mother had to cut the uniform they bought for him to about half its original size," Eddie once said. "He was the most bat-less batboy you ever saw. He'd be playing catch with some of the players when he should have been doing his regular chores. Ernie was such a happy-go-lucky kid nobody minded too much that he was spending more time playing than working."[8]

Eddie had started a new job as a clerk at a grocery store. Most of his co-workers were white, and many of them weren't thrilled to be working alongside a black. Ernie hoped that his father could get him a job there, too, but every time he asked he was told the work was too hard, that he wasn't old enough or strong enough.

Having proven himself in the cotton fields, Banks was confused.

"Later I learned his talk was a cover-up," Banks said. "There were frequent fights between the blacks and whites on the job and a lot of name-calling. My dad didn't want me exposed to it."[9]

>> <<

Banks and his friends would spend as much time as they could at the YMCA. It seemed he was a natural in every sport he tried.

At segregated Booker T. Washington High School, Banks played end on the football team; averaged 20 points a game in basketball, including one 38-point game; and starred on the track team both as a runner and high jumper who once cleared 5'11" when he was 16 years old.

His career in competitive sports had started almost by default, however.

Banks has recounted how he was watching Washington's football team practice. He was a sophomore, on the tall side but only about 150 pounds. All the players were much bigger.

Bill Blair, a man from the neighborhood known for his baseball skills and a friendly way with kids, asked Banks why he didn't try out for the team. "Bill, I'm too small for this game," he said. "Look at all those big guys out there."

Blair didn't consider that a good answer. "You can catch the ball, and you can run," he said before yelling to the coach, Raymond Hollie.

"Ray!" he shouted. "This boy can make your team!"

Hollie invited Banks to go in the gym and put on a uniform. Once he had the shoulder pads on, he didn't feel undersized anymore. "I felt like I weighed 200 pounds," Banks remembered. "I caught some passes, and this was my real start in athletics."

Baseball was the one sport Banks didn't play in high school. The school didn't have a team but did field one for fast-pitch softball, on which he starred. There had been no organized baseball in his neighborhood—no pee-wee or Little League—so he had never really had a chance to play the game he watched his father and other men play on the weekends.

But his ability in softball was obvious to everyone. He had a gracefulness in the field and the kind of bat speed that scouts spend a lifetime searching to find. He could run, he could throw, and everyone spoke well of him, even the neighbors whose windows he had broken. He landed a spot on the top summer team in the community so he could keep playing after the high school season ended.[10]

One day in 1946 that team played one from another part of Dallas. It featured a ringer named Hank Thompson, a left-handed hitter who had just been released from the army after serving as a machine gunner with the 1695th Combat Engineers at the Battle of the Bulge in the densely forested Ardennes Mountains region of Belgium.[11] Originally a support unit in the segregated army, the all-black unit served alongside whites in combat but only after the high number of white troops killed and wounded by the Germans had made this necessary.

Thompson had played for the Kansas City Monarchs before being drafted into the army, and he returned to the Monarchs a short time after facing Banks' team outside Dallas. He played for the St. Louis Browns three months after Jackie Robinson had broken baseball's color line in 1947 and only a couple weeks after Larry Doby had become the first black to play in the American League.

Banks had heard about Thompson before the game but was spellbound watching him.

"I watched every move he made with a bat," Banks said. "With just one smooth swing, Hank hit a ball onto the roof of a house behind the outfield fence. It was the longest home run I had ever seen in softball. Other home-run balls had hit that house, but none had hit it with the velocity of Thompson's. When I saw Hank's even and quick swing, I decided his style was for me. He had great wrist timing, and for the rest of that summer I copied his style and stance. I wasn't able to hit the ball as far as Thompson did, but I was spraying a lot of line drives."[12]

Blair would surface again. An on-and-off member of the Negro Leagues' Indianapolis Clowns, the Washington grad was watching his alma mater play softball during a trip home in 1947, Ernie's sophomore year. He came out to scout the pitcher, "a fellow named Brannon," whom he thought might have the stuff to play professionally. He would leave talking about the 16-year-old shortstop he had recently introduced to football.

"Brannon was the fastest pitcher I had ever seen," said Blair, who would become the publisher of the *Elite News*, which served Dallas' black community. "I never saw anyone who could throw like him. I never saw anyone get the solid licks off him. And here was this willowy kid walloping ball after ball off him. Ernest, I could tell right away, was going to be something special."[13]

Blair returned to watch Banks play a few more games. Eventually, he sought out Eddie to tell him his oldest son had a future in baseball, if he could play it as well as he played softball.

Ernie wasn't sure this was a good idea. "I've never played baseball," he told Blair.

"If you can play softball, you can play baseball," Blair said.

Blair asked Eddie if he could take Ernie to a tryout. Ernie couldn't believe he was really going to get a chance.

"How could he place a skinny 16-year-old shortstop in baseball?" Ernie said. "We all wondered."

Robinson had joined the Brooklyn Dodgers a couple months earlier. But Blair didn't have the imagination to envision Banks one day playing against him.

"The major leagues for Ernest?" Blair said, repeating a question. "That was the furthest thing from my mind. It wasn't the way you thought back then."[14]

Blair was looking for players who could fill out the low-level black touring teams that were feeders for the Monarchs and the other teams in the two top Negro Leagues. He returned to the Banks home with Johnny Carter, the owner-manager of the deceptively named Detroit Colts, who were based 411 miles from Dallas in the West Texas town of Amarillo.

Carter arrived driving a 1946 Dodge, which Banks described as the nicest car he'd ever seen, and Banks said he was "so well dressed that you would have thought he was a model who had just stepped out of a Neiman Marcus window display."

Banks had never been inside that Dallas institution but had window shopped while downtown, not far from the house on Fairmount Street, imagining himself wearing such fine clothes. Carter asked for permission to take Ernie to Amarillo for a tryout. Eddie was totally in favor, and Essie signed off on the idea when Carter promised that Banks would be back to Dallas in time for his junior year at Washington.[15]

Ernie couldn't have said no even if he wanted to. The quest for the Nobel Peace Prize and a career in international law would have to wait.

>> <<

Dressed in grimy overalls and working on one of his beloved luxury cars outside the garage of a mansion on Lakeview Avenue, opposite Lincoln Park, a man was hailed down by a family experiencing trouble on their drive.

The family was black, the man white, but there was nothing awkward about their dialogue.

"You fix flats, mister?" asked the man driving a Ford.

The mechanic nodded his head.

"Will you fix this one?"

The mechanic nodded again.

He took out his jack, raised the car, took the wheel off, and rolled it into his well-appointed garage. There he hammered off the shoe, filled a tin drum with water, inflated the tube with air and dropped it in the water. Spinning it around, he quickly found the leak. He lifted the tube up to his work bench, applied a patch, and got to work getting the tire back on the Ford.

When he was done, he grabbed a rag and dried off his hands.

"How much?" the grateful driver asked.

"A buck."

The driver reached into his pocket, pulled out his wallet, and handed over a $1 bill. Phil Wrigley, at that time president of the Wrigley Company and owner of the Cubs, took it.

"Thank you," said the driver, not bothering to ask the mechanic for his name.[16]

No matter. The unexpected chance to fix a stranger's tire made this a good day for Philip Knight Wrigley, one of the most decent men to ever own an American sports team.

» «

Born to the manor, Wrigley never quite took to it. As a second-generation magnate whose primary focus was to oversee the family's chewing gum business, Wrigley never thought of himself as particularly special.

He spent a lifetime walking in other people's shoes, even though his own were the finest one could buy at Marshall Fields or Brooks Brothers. He learned responsibility at a young age, watching his flamboyant father, William Wrigley Jr., run the business he had founded in 1891 and the baseball team he had purchased in 1925.

William Wrigley Jr. had also been privileged but hardly spoiled. His father owned a soap factory outside Philadelphia, where the family lived. But he told his son how he had worked for $1.50 a week as a boy, stirring the bubbling soap mix with a paddle. He talked his father into letting him become a salesman when he was barely in his teens, traveling through Pennsylvania, New York, and New England selling scouring soap from a four-horse team with bells on the harness.

William Wrigley Jr. set out on his own at the age of 30, heading west. He landed in Chicago with his savings of $32 and started what would become the biggest gum company in the world, eventually giving him a fortune of more than $40 million.[17]

Wrigley had a good product. He had come to appreciate Americans' love of chicle (what we now call chewing gum) when he used it as an incentive to get more people to buy his father's packages of baking soda. He spread the word about his product by becoming a pioneer in advertising. He twice invested $100,000 in national advertising campaigns that didn't return any significant sales. But instead of backing down, he upped the ante, as was his style. Wrigley invested $250,000 in a third campaign, and suddenly Americans were all ears.

The Wrigley advertising budget grew to $4 million annually in the 1920s, when double-page, color ads practically underwrote the cost of printing *The Saturday Evening Post*.[18] Wrigley's budget tripled in that decade, creating jobs in Chicago and affording the company's founder a chance to fully invest in a hobby.

While the older Wrigley was himself a transplant, he epitomized the brashness of Chicago. He hated the city's image as a weak sister to New York. He had found himself drawn to baseball and purchased a small interest in the Cubs in 1915 when Charles Weeghman, owner of the Chicago Whales of the Federal League, acquired majority control from Cincinnati newspaperman Charles Taft. Wrigley purchased control in 1921, the season that Hall of Famer Johnny Evers was fired as manager midway through a seventh-place finish in the eight-team National League.

"I bought the Cubs not only because I love baseball, but because I was once joshed about a large city like Chicago having such poor ball clubs," Wrigley said. "When I was on the road selling soap years before, other salesmen used to kid me about Chicago's weak clubs."

The Cubs had been to the World Series twice since beating the Detroit Tigers in 1908 but hadn't finished higher than third under Weeghman. This would allow Chicago sportswriter Phil Hersh to write, "Thus, the perfect epitaph for the Wrigley years: Bought a laughingstock, sold a laughingstock."

>> <<

Phil Wrigley, known as P.K. in the public, was as retiring in his personal style as his father was gregarious. The spotlight attracted William Wrigley but sent his son looking for a quieter spot, like his weekend home in Lake Geneva, Wisconsin, or underneath a hood anywhere.

William Wrigley was a back-slapper and attention hound who would have loved his own reality show. He was the life of any party and wore his business successes on the sleeves of his finely tailored suits. He loved his slogans— "Nothing great was ever achieved without enthusiasm"—and he came to be seen as a Midwestern Gatsby, riding his wealth to prominence in a city known for meat packers and mobsters.

He so epitomized a generation of brash, self-made men that he was the subject of a *Time* magazine cover story a week before the stock market crash in 1929. His son could have turned out like Jett Rink but instead captured his father's respect while marching to a completely different drummer.

Jerome Holtzman, the Hall of Fame baseball writer whose career took him to both the *Chicago Sun-Times* and the *Chicago Tribune*, described the difference between the two Wrigleys.

"The older Wrigley cut a wide path," Holtzman wrote. "He would strut down Chicago's main streets with his gold-headed cane and a white carnation fastened to his lapel. Cronies referred to him as 'The King.' His son shunned the spotlight. He was never on center stage."[19]

Another longtime Chicago sports writer, Bill Gleason, called William Wrigley "an outrageous hustler," who would have been tough for anyone to emulate. His son was amazingly comfortable in his own skin.

"The young Phil Wrigley knew that he could not follow his father's act," Gleason wrote. "Phil would be himself. Quiet, introspective, kind. He would take no bows. He would bask in the reflected light of his father [and others]....
He would help those who gave off the light."[20]

After high school, Phil traveled around the world before stopping to work in the Wrigley plant in Australia. He enrolled at the University of Chicago to study chemistry when he returned but never planned to stay long enough to get a degree. He wanted some practical knowledge that could help him in the family business, and after he had taken the course that most interested him he stopped going to the other ones. He went into the service in World War I, where he was put to work as a mechanic. He wound up running an aviation-mechanics school at the Great Lakes Naval Air Station outside Chicago.

In working with motors and anything else mechanical, he discovered a passion that was rarely evident in his professional life, both in industry and baseball. He was accomplished in those arenas, and received a second look because of his relentless civility, but when he most stood out was when he was working with his hands.

No engine was too big or too complex for him, no detail too fine. He worked on Rolls-Royces and Swiss timepieces. One longtime associate recalled seeing Wrigley repair a broken wristwatch while watching a spring training game.

Wrigley preferred yard work to golf or tennis. "There's a lot more exercise in running a chainsaw over some logs than there is in a round of golf," he said.[21]

Following a kidnap scare in the early 1930s, Phil abandoned the Lakeview Avenue mansion to move into a high rise on Lake Shore Drive. He would never again live in the old house but went there regularly to work on cars. "You can't park your car in an apartment," he said. "You can't take it apart on the living room rug."[22]

Phil was 31 when he was named president of the Wrigley Company in 1926 and was on his own six years later when William died. Phil proved that an executive could be both successful and generous, surviving the Depression but never forgetting it. He looked after his customers and his employees in a fashion that could be described as loving.

One of the most repeated stories about Phil Wrigley involves the restaurant at the Wrigley Building and a lunch with friends. Designed by William Wrigley to be the most famous office building in the world, it was built on Michigan Avenue just north of the Chicago River with a tower borrowed from the shape of the Seville Cathedral and touches from French Renaissance architecture, including an array of clocks. Built on what had been an ill-kept street of businesses and low-end residences and lighted at night by an outrageous set of floodlights.

One of his companions ordered a double martini, and after draining it casually commented that it did not offer double the pleasure for double the money. Wrigley conducted an immediate experiment, ordering the suitable glasses and pouring water from one glass to another. It quickly became clear that double was a misnomer, as that size glass did not hold twice as much as a regular glass. Wrigley ordered all the doubles glasses destroyed and replaced with glasses that did hold twice at much, even getting them in place for happy hour that evening.[23]

Wrigley was beloved by most of the people who worked for him. And why not?

Shortly after taking over as president in 1934, he went to the board of directors to get approval for a plan which would designated $1 million of the company's surplus to give workers making less than $120 a week something he called "income assurance."

Trying to lessen the load for government, he guaranteed employees up to 30 weeks pay if a downturn in business caused them to be laid off.

"This assures an employee a definite income for a definite period, regardless of conditions beyond his control," Wrigley once explained. "It is a backlog for him, just as the surplus of the company is the backlog for the stockholders. Since the surplus of the company is the backlog for the stockholder, it seemed right that he share some of this assurance with the employee."

Wrigley had each of his lower-paid employees sign a contract accepting his offer. All that he asked of them was that they not go on welfare rolls if they were unemployed.

"It is our idea that a company in a position to do so should assume full responsibility of taking care of the people within the organization in slack as well as boom times," he said.

The Wrigley Company managed to thrive in the Depression. Wrigley awarded everyone in the company a 10 percent raise at a time when most Americans were fighting to get by. "It was an act that made headlines around the world," said an associate. "He thought it would be contagious, that it would get the American economy going again."[24]

>> <<

"All is confusion."[25]

The slogan could be taken as a thoughtful world view or as an inside joke. It was displayed on a placard in Phil Wrigley's office at the Wrigley Building. Especially confusing to many people, in particular fans angry about the Cubs' status as perennial also-rans, was Wrigley's willingness to talk to almost anyone at any time, frequently even without the filter of a secretary to screen calls.

You could dial the Wrigley Company number in the phonebook, ask to speak to Mr. Wrigley, and find yourself almost immediately in a thoughtful discussion with one of Chicago's best listeners.

Wrigley enjoyed the frequent exchanges.

"Generally they start out a little belligerent," Wrigley said in a *Saturday Evening Post* profile in 1972. "'I want to talk to Mr. Wrigley,'" they say. "'Okay, you're talking to him,' I say. They always seem a little surprised."

This was talk radio before its time, with Joe from Evanston or Big Mike from Cicero suggesting ways to help the Cubs catch the Dodgers or the NL frontrunner *du jour*.

"They do have the damnedest ideas," Wrigley said. "'If you only come up with three 20-game winners, you'll be all right.' Well, who the hell wouldn't?"

Ayn Rand finished writing her classic novel *Atlas Shrugged* in 1956. She is said to have created the characters as vehicles to model her idea that society's best hope rests on adopting a system of pure *laissez-faire* economics, and Wrigley carried the best of their qualities—ingenuity, persistence, humility, and compassion.

No one really knows how often Wrigley ventured to the ballpark to watch his baseball team. Holtzman, who grew up on Chicago teams and started covering baseball in the late 1940s, reported seeing Wrigley at only "four or five" games, and never at Wrigley Field—which Wrigley himself always called Cubs Park.[26] But Banks is among those who insist that Wrigley often dressed in overalls and blended in with fans in the bleachers.

Wrigley didn't need to smell the hot dogs to follow his team. He would listen to games on the radio in his office, where he mostly focused on the international business of chewing gum and his other holdings, which included California's Catalina Island. Visitors would be asked to stand during the National Anthem and the seventh-inning stretch.

You couldn't argue with his priorities. After all, in Banks' final season, which was the Wrigley family's 51st running the Cubs, the Wrigley Company was valued at $275 million while the Cubs' assets were $5.4 million.[27]

Baseball fans constantly clamored for Wrigley to dip into his chewing gum fortune to buy better players—either the few established stars who were made available or through a massive upgrading of the farm system—but Wrigley was unmoved.

"There are a great many stockholders in the Wrigley Gum Company who would be the first to complain if any of their money was used in baseball," Wrigley said. "So none of it ever has been used for that purpose, or ever will. We aim to have the Cubs pay their own way, as if they were my only interest. In this the Cubs are no different than any other major league club whose owners have no outside interests."

Before William Wrigley's death, the Cubs had gone to the World Series in 1918 and '29, losing both times. They went three times in the 1930s, again losing every time, but it seemed only a matter of time until they would win. When they met Detroit in 1945, with the overworked Hank Borowy losing Game 7, Phil Wrigley wasn't in the crowd that crammed into the ballpark at the corner of Clark and Addison for any of the four games. Reports said he was in his office at the Wrigley Building, writing letters to fans who were upset they couldn't buy tickets.

What kind of an owner was this?

The late Bill Veeck Jr., who essentially grew up at Wrigley Field when his father was the team president, came to believe that Wrigley's only interest in running a baseball franchise was to make good on a deathbed promise he had made to his father.

"Phil Wrigley assumed the burden out of his sense of loyalty and duty," Veeck said. "If he has any particular feeling for baseball, any real liking for it, he has disguised it magnificently."[28]

Wrigley invested little personal ego in wins and losses but nevertheless wanted the best experience for the fans who followed his team. One season he concluded that fans in box seats needed more elbow room, so he used the off-season to have workers reduce the number of seats in each of the railed sections from 10 to eight, costing himself revenue.

He likewise ordered seats down the foul lines to be taken off their concrete moorings and angled toward home plate, so fans wouldn't have to turn to see home plate. He closed off and covered sections of the center-field bleachers so that the glare of fan's white shirts wouldn't affect his hitters' vision (a concept that wasn't carried over at Fenway Park even after Tony Conigliaro was almost killed when he was hit with a pitch from Jack Hamilton in 1967).

At a time when most ballpark walls carried as much advertising as the side of one of Danica Patrick's race cars, Wrigley decided he could live without that revenue stream. He agreed with club president Bill Veeck's idea to plant ivy at the base of the warning track, covering the park's red brick walls. He steadfastly refused to put in lights, even when they were commonplace everywhere and could have helped increase attendance—the Cubs' franchise attendance record stood from 1929 until '69—and drive down the team's annual operating losses.

Wrigley once told Veeck, "A team that isn't winning a pennant has to sell something in addition to its won-and-lost record to fill in those low points on the attendance chart."[29]

Another assistant, Charles Drake, recalled a conversation that would prove jarring to fans. He said he mentioned to Wrigley that the public had been conditioned to "demand a winning team," but Wrigley had other ideas.

He said he wanted to shift the interest to something more reliable—and generally less expensive. "The fun, the game, the sunshine, the relaxation," he said. "Our idea is get the public to go to see a ballgame, win or lose."

That would be a recurring theme for the franchise for decades to come.

"His solution was to sell 'beautiful Wrigley Field,'" Veeck said. "That is, to make the park itself so great an attraction that it would be thought of as a place to take the whole family for a delightful day. It was no accident that the title of the [Cubs] magazine I edited for him was called *Fun and Family*. We sold 'beautiful Wrigley Field.' We advertised 'beautiful Wrigley Field.' The announcers were instructed to use the phrase 'beautiful Wrigley Field' as often as possible.... The trouble was that I could never get the [the phrase's] creator to take the next logical step...to give the customers what they really set out for the ballpark hoping to find—entertainment and excitement."[30]

With the Cubs becoming what songwriter Steve Goodman would call "the doormat of the National League," a nice ballpark only went so far. By the early

1960s, the team was reportedly losing almost $1 million a year. That total grew as relentlessly as the outfield ivy in ensuing years. Along with estate taxes, the steady outflow would prompt William Wrigley III to sell the team to the Tribune Company in 1981—four years after Phil Wrigley's death. And only seven years later, lights finally went up.

But not on the mechanic's watch.

Wrigley explained his position on night games in the simplest terms. He said he didn't want to impose on the Cubs' neighbors.

"You wouldn't like to live where you have 20,000 or 30,000 people yelling and hollering up to midnight every night," he said.[31]

When the Cubs did finally push their attendance beyond 1.5 million, Wrigley was pleased that they had done it on the strength of Banks, Billy Williams, and Fergie Jenkins instead of the addition of lights.

"What we needed was good baseball," he would say, "not night baseball."[32]

Wrigley was just as selfless in matters involving the National League. He didn't object when Lou Perini moved the Braves from Boston to Milwaukee in 1953, encroaching on his territorial rights. He knew that the Braves had become such a weak sister to the Red Sox and their icon, Ted Williams, that bankruptcy was becoming inevitable. He felt baseball needed strong franchises more than he needed to maximize attendance.

Wrigley likewise could have made it tough for Walter O'Malley to move the Dodgers from Brooklyn to Los Angeles, as that too was Cubs territory. The Pacific Coast League team was aligned with the Cubs, which had allowed Wrigley to become acquainted with West Coast baseball. He had written reports for ownership encouraging a move westward, so he was more than happy to move his Triple A team to Dallas–Fort Worth to accommodate a move.[33]

O'Malley had agreed to pay Wrigley $3 million in the deal, but Wrigley ultimately took less. He put general manager John Holland on a train to New York to settle the deal and instructed him to tell O'Malley the price had dropped.

"Mr. O'Malley was flabbergasted," Holland said about the meeting. "Mr. Wrigley had given me instructions to tell Mr. O'Malley we would agree to the swap for $2 million instead of $3 million. Mr. O'Malley couldn't understand why we were saving him $1 million. So I told him, 'Mr. Wrigley doesn't want you to change your mind. He wants major league baseball in California.'"[34]

When national television arrived in the 1940s, Wrigley was one of the few owners who saw it as a step in the wrong direction. He worried that it would kill minor league baseball, causing fans to stay home from ballparks all across America to watch Joe DiMaggio and Williams from the comfort of their living room couch.

The original television deal paid teams a $30,000 fee when they were featured. Wrigley instructed commissioner Ford Frick's office to take the Cubs' fee and send it to minor league baseball's umbrella organization, the National Association.[35]

When the Braves started to look for greener pastures as their Milwaukee crowds dwindled following the heyday of Warren Spahn and Eddie Mathews, Wrigley objected—albeit privately—about a plan to shift the team to Atlanta. He felt baseball would get a black eye from franchises hop-scotching around the country.

Wrigley wanted his team to win and seemed to never run out of ideas designed to give them an edge over the competition. He bounced between the traditional—bigger and better farm systems, proven managers—and the bizarre—hiring an Evil Eye to hex the opposition, sometimes from behind home plate, sometimes from next to the Western Union machine if the team was playing out of town.[36]

When the Cubs were regularly going to the World Series, he brought in a psychologist from the University of Illinois to test players and determine common qualities that might be used to help select future generations of winning players.

"If you want to make the best knives in the world, you buy the finest steel," Wrigley said. "You can go out and spend $250,000 for a ballplayer, and he may not be able to cut the butter. But if you know what makes a player who does come through in the majors, you have something. It's surprising how many players can play Triple A ball but still not make the majors."[37]

Wrigley once brought Lou Boudreau from the radio booth to the dugout, switching places with manager Charlie Grimm. He designed a way to wire his pitcher's jackets with heat (an idea that never caught on). He hired a man with almost no baseball experience to oversee the operation, terming him his athletic director.

In his best known and arguably least successful innovation, Wrigley invested the 1961 and '62 seasons in an experimental concept known as the College of Coaches. Rather than appointing one manager, he created a 12-man committee that regularly rotated authority and positions, some in uniform and some in scouting and other off-the-field activities.

"If orthodox doesn't work, why shouldn't we try the unorthodox?" Wrigley reasoned.[38]

>> <<

Baseball owners have always been seen as barons using their teams to help the rich get richer. That was one of William Wrigley's motivations for plunging his family into the business, but there were few payoffs until 1981, when his grandson sold the team to the Tribune Company, which was eager to televise games on national cable via WGN.

When the Cubs were winning pennants, the crowds were enough to let the owners divide some profits. But Phil Wrigley and his investors received no dividends from 1948 into the 1970s. Wrigley claimed to have once suggested a $3 dividend only to have a stockholder declare, "We need a shortstop instead."[39]

Yet the team's difficulties didn't affect Wrigley's commitment to doing the right thing, even when he could have looked the other way.

Wrigley underwrote the All-American Girls Baseball League from 1943–45, unknowingly giving Madonna and Rosie O'Donnell a leg up in their entertainment careers. When the Cubs moved their spring training camp to his family-owned Catalina Island after World War II, he invited wives to accompany players and coaches, a gesture that was unpopular with most teams who felt women would get in the way of baseball.

Wrigley was as accessible to his players as he was to the random callers to his office. He didn't preach about the importance of the business unit as a second family, but he put that belief into practice.

One day in 1948, Wrigley received a call from a public official in Baltimore. Hack Wilson, who had driven in a record 191 runs for the Cubs in 1930, was in the city morgue. Wilson was a roustabout who drank himself out of baseball at the age of 34 and would encounter one problem after another in the ensuing years, dying destitute at the age of 48. The men at the morgue knew of no next-of-kin, so they called the man who owned Wilson's old team.

Wrigley made arrangements for the funeral and burial, even building a monument to reflect the future Hall of Famer's accomplishments. He politely declined an offer from commissioner Happy Chandler to split the costs. "I've never seen a half funeral," Wrigley said. "The Cubs will pay all expenses."[40]

No one other than Wrigley ever knew the times that the owner stepped up to help out a player or former player. One such case involved outfielder Lou Novikoff, born to Russian immigrants in Arizona. He was seriously ill and just as broke a decade after his career ended.

Novikoff didn't ask for help, but Wrigley started sending him regular checks after learning of his sad plight. He was embarrassed later when other former players told the tale to a newspaper reporter.[41]

Wrigley never did get used to attention.

While he would happily take calls from reporters at his office, he shunned radio and television interviews. He said he differentiated between print journalists and broadcasters because the former trafficked in "information" and the latter in "show business."[42]

According to Holtzman, Wrigley made only two public speeches. Both came at the baseball writers' annual Diamond Dinner in the off-season and only after the writers had pleaded to let them give him a trophy.

He didn't exactly hog the mike.

"The first time Wrigley said, 'Thank you,'" Holtzman wrote upon Wrigley's death. "The second time he expanded his speech and said, 'Thank you very much.'"[43]

4

MARCH

J.G. Taylor Spink believed in accuracy, not in sensational, attention-grabbing headlines. His baby for 55 years, *The Sporting News*, wasn't known for going out on a limb. It was called "the Bible of baseball" because it covered the sport more thoroughly than any other publication, with features on top players, details of trades, and box scores from every major league game.

It was no surprise then that the cover of *The Sporting News'* 1969 preview issue pictured the St. Louis Cardinals' outfield—Lou Brock, Curt Flood, and the newly acquired Vada Pinson—with one word summing up why they were the pick to win a third straight National League pennant: "Speed."

Reporters who visited the Cardinals' camp at the Busch Complex in St. Petersburg, Florida, saw a team that they expected to stroll to the National League East title. Meanwhile, about 10 miles away at the Payson Complex, the Mets quietly held workouts and relaxed together afterward, little attention paid to them after a 73–89 season in 1968, with perhaps only the players themselves realizing how easily they could have had the franchise's first winning season.

This had been such a period of low-scoring games that owners would opt to lower the height of the pitcher's mound from 15" to 10", hoping to give hitters a better chance. Only six big-league regulars had hit better than .300 in 1968, when the Cardinals' Bob Gibson turned in one of the greatest seasons ever by a pitcher (22–9, 1.12 ERA, 13 shutouts), and the lack of firepower meant a wealth of close games. The Mets played 63 that were decided by one run and had won only 26 of those games.

This was a subject of discussion on the frequent fishing trips that Tom Seaver, Nolan Ryan, shortstop Bud Harrelson, and defense-first catcher Jerry Grote took under the Bayway Bridge in St. Petersburg. They were sometimes joined by Gil Hodges, who was continuing a peaceful recovery from a heart attack suffered late in '68.

On one of those trips, Seaver, who sometimes referred to himself as the Supreme Optimist, declared that the Mets were so flush with pitching "we could win our division if we play up to our potential."[1]

Seaver was only 24, but when he talked, his teammates listened. He set the tone for a team built around the young guns in its pitching staff, which included Gary Gentry (22), Jerry Koosman (26), Tug McGraw (24), and Ryan (22).

Ryan would become one of baseball's icons, with 324 wins, 5,714 strikeouts, and seven no-hitters, three more than Sandy Koufax. But at that point in 1969 he was just a kid who was rushed to the majors because he could throw a ball through a wall. He was from Alvin, Texas, which Koosman said was "so small it didn't even have a last name." Ryan was nicknamed "The Phantom" by teammates because he could not get on the mound often enough to back up the excitement he'd generated since scout Red Murff signed him.[2] His development was slowed because of injuries, including frequent blisters, treated by trainer Gus Mauch with pickle brine and military commitments. Like other players who came and went during seasons, he was in a top priority reserve unit in the National Guard.

Ryan shuttled back and forth to Houston every other weekend. He was on an engineering unit that specialized in laying water lines and putting up storage tanks, with the idea of quickly assembling bases after a full-scale invasion of Vietnam, which would never come. The work satisfied his military obligation but wasn't exactly the best way to prepare to pitch.

"I shouldn't have been in the big leagues," Ryan said. "I should have been down."

Ryan, a country kid, sometimes envied the advantages that Seaver had gained while pitching at USC. "I thought he was a very advanced pitcher for his age," Ryan said. "He had two outstanding pitches. He could throw his fastball where he wanted, and he threw hard, in the mid-90s. His slider was his out pitch."

>> <<

The Mets' fate had turned three years earlier, when Seaver (who would go on to win 311 games and beat Ryan to the Hall of Fame) more or less landed in their laps.

He had grown up in Fresno, California, a huge fan of the Dodgers and a pitcher whose fastball matched neither his ambition nor his understanding of how to use it. He was smaller than most of his high school classmates and wouldn't earn a spot on the Fresno High varsity team until his senior year. He planned to be a dentist and attend USC, but it was his younger teammate, Dick Selma, who interested scouts, not Seaver.

After graduation, Seaver joined the Marine reserves, went through boot camp, and enrolled at Fresno City College. He also added at least 3 inches and 30 pounds to his body. Suddenly he could throw as hard as he had wished to in high school, and after an 11–2 season he had himself a scholarship to USC.

There he joined a fraternity and befriended USC running back Mike Garrett, who would win the Heisman Trophy in 1965. In addition to the normal baseball workouts, Seaver ran wind sprints alongside Garrett and even lifted weights with a regimen designed by Garrett. He would later pass along that piece of his conditioning program to Ryan, who would join Seaver in showing that baseball was wrong in its bias against weight training.

Seaver, who had regularly traveled to Dodger Stadium to see Koufax and Don Drysdale pitch, was drafted by the Dodgers in the 10th round of baseball's first draft after his sophomore season in '65. General Manager Buzzie Bavasi sent a former pitcher named Tommy Lasorda to try to sign Seaver, but he didn't come close. Seaver wanted $50,000 to leave USC, arguing that Selma had gotten $20,000 from the Mets when he signed out of Fresno High, and the Dodgers would only allow Lasorda to increase an original offer of $2,000 to $3,000.

"Good luck in your dental career," Seaver would later say Lasorda told him.[3]

Seaver planned to return to USC for at least one more season, but Major League Baseball held a winter draft in '66, only about six months after the regular one. Seaver was selected No. 1 by the Braves and signed for $51,500, feeling very smart about having turned down the Dodgers and looking forward to playing alongside Henry Aaron. But USC had already begun its spring schedule when Seaver signed, and that made the Braves' contract invalid.

Seaver figured he'd stay at USC until the draft that summer, but the NCAA ruled him ineligible because he had signed a pro contract. He was suddenly a great talent with nowhere to pitch. Commissioner Spike Eckert stepped in, deciding to hold a lottery for Seaver's services. Eckert said that any team could participate as long as it agreed to give Seaver the $51,500 he had forfeited when the Braves weren't allowed to keep him.

Bavasi, then embroiled in highly publicized negotiations to end a holdout by Koufax and Drysdale, failed to submit the paperwork for the draft. The Braves likewise took a pass. The Phillies, Indians, and Mets were the only three teams aggressive enough to risk big money on Seaver,[4] and in a drawing held in Eckert's office, the Mets were drawn out of hat.

Seaver would spend only one season in the minors—Jacksonville manager Solly Hemus declared him to have "a 35-year-old head on top of a 21-year-old body, [rather than the usual] 35-year-old arm attached to a 21-year-old head"— before a Rookie of the Year season with the Mets in 1967.

"Seaver had Hall of Fame written on him when he walked into camp and pitched his first game," outfielder Ron Swoboda said. "He was a finished product when he came there. I don't ever recall the sense of him being a rookie. He came out of the box a big-league pitcher, and there was this golden glow about him. This was clearly big talent—intelligent, capable, controlled, and [with] awesome stuff."[5]

Seaver was an All-Star and a 16-game winner that first season, then he repeated both those accomplishments in '68. He had such a presence that his teammates played harder when he pitched.

"You notice his concentration out there on the mound when he's pitching," Harrelson said. "And playing behind him, you try to match it."

Seaver could have been flattered. Instead he pointed out how such an approach was an insult to the Mets' other pitchers and a sign that the overall expectations needed to be raised.

"There was an aura of defeatism about the team, a feeling of, 'let's get it over with,'" Seaver said. "I noticed that the team seemed to play better when I pitched but...that wasn't right, and I said so. I probably got a few people mad, but I went around and told the guys that if they did that for me and not for somebody else, it was wrong."[6]

>> <<

While Seaver and Ryan fished, the Cubs went about spring training with a confidence that had seemed alien before Leo Durocher's arrival. They knew they should score plenty of runs with Billy Williams, Ron Santo, and Ernie Banks in the middle of the lineup.

After all, they had led the NL with 4.3 runs per game in 1967 and were second to Cincinnati with 3.8 per game in the pitching-dominated '68 season. Their challenge was to give up fewer runs, as only the Reds and Phillies had allowed more the previous season. The starting rotation was led by a trio that had come together in 1966, and Fergie Jenkins, Bill Hands, and Ken Holtzman all knew that Durocher would push them hard. He always did.

"The Cubs are two players away from being a pennant winner," Jenkins said. "All we need is another good outfielder and a starting pitcher who can win about 15 games."[7]

Attitudes in the camp were good, and at least some reporters around the team felt the environment was so positive because GM John Holland had acted quickly to defuse a possible racial divide.

The much-traveled Cubs outfielder Lou Johnson, who had been denied his dream of playing basketball at the University of Kentucky because the Southeastern Conference wasn't recruiting black athletes, sometimes seemed in his own world after Martin Luther King's assassination in 1968.

Wrigley Field was a white man's world, and some bleacher fans waved Confederate flags to honor the Cubs' catcher, Randy "Rebel" Hundley, a Virginia native with a heavy Southern accent. Riding in an elevator with Hundley and some other players shortly after King's assassination, Johnson glared at Hundley before getting out to be by himself. He felt that Hundley was being insensitive, although the catcher worked well with Jenkins and never had issues with Williams and Banks.

Johnson seemed to distance himself from his teammates until mid-season, when Holland shipped him to Cleveland for Willie Smith, who was nicknamed "Wonderful Willie" because of his upbeat presence. Johnson was happy for a change, in part he said because he had fallen into Durocher's doghouse. "The man never talked to me," Johnson said. "He relayed his orders through messengers."

The Cubs' camp was also a happy one because Phil Wrigley had once again rewarded some of his top employees. He was probably just being generous when he handed out two-year contracts to Santo, Williams, and Jenkins on March 6, while also extending Banks' existing two-year deal to run for a third year, but he had spent the winter watching Santo be courted by the so-called Global League.

This was to be a league with teams in cities as diverse as Mobile, Alabama, and Tokyo, Japan, also putting Milwaukee (recently jilted by the Braves) back in the spotlight. It was the brainchild of Walter Dilbeck, who once ran unsuccessfully for mayor of Evansville, Indiana, campaigning on a mule and passing out free barbecue in saloons. He had involved former commissioner Happy Chandler and longtime St. Louis outfielder Enos Slaughter in his plan.

If the Global League became a real threat, Wrigley wasn't going to lose any of his key players.

"This started with Ernie last year when he requested a two-year contract," Holland said of the unprecedented wave of multi-year contracts. "And we feel like it was a contributing factor to the great year that he had. It relieved a lot of the pressure on him. These are the only players we offered two-year contracts. You have to know your players. Not all of them would be candidates for this. You wouldn't give one to a young player—only to established stars. We're just happy to express our gratitude to these men who have contributed so much to the success of the team."

Santo, Williams, and Jenkins received the two-year offers when they went to Holland expecting the usual one-year deals. Banks didn't do much more than sign his name. "I didn't know anything about it until Mr. Holland came out on the field today during batting practice and told me," he said. "What a tremendous thing."

Santo typically overlooked that his franchise was baseball's most perennial also-ran.

"I just wish all players could have a chance to play for this club," he said. "It's the greatest organization anywhere. This contract gives me added security and makes me want to play that much harder."[8]

Center field, surprisingly for Durocher and Holland, was looming as a problem area. The Cubs felt they had secured one of the best young outfielders in baseball when they acquired Adolfo Phillips from Philadelphia in a 1966 trade that also brought them Jenkins, who then was a 23-year-old reliever.

Durocher had gushed about the speedy Phillips, describing him as "one of the most physically gifted players I have ever seen," perhaps even "another Willie Mays."[9] Phillips had been Durocher's center fielder in '68 but couldn't handle being force-fit into the leadoff spot. He batted .241 with a strikeout total topped only by Santo, and he had once been fined $200 for loafing on the bases.

"Adolfo can hit, has the power, and can run, field, and throw," Durocher said. "He lacks desire. He has to show me he wants to play."[10]

Durocher had thrown open the position for all challengers, with the cast of players in camp including 19-year-old Oscar Gamble, glove man Don Young, and minor leaguers Jimmy Qualls, Jimmy McMath, and Jim Dunegan.

Never short of hyperbole, Durocher labeled Gamble, McMath, and Dunegan "three of the hardest hitting prospects you could ever hope to see."[11] But it was Phillips whom Banks and the other veteran players hoped to see standing between Williams and right fielder Jim Hickman on Opening Day.

Those hopes were dealt a blow when Phillips was hit in the right hand in one of the first exhibition games, suffering a broken bone that required his hand be placed in a cast. Durocher wasted no time falling in love with Gamble, who was even less experienced than Brock had been when the Cubs brought him to Chicago in 1961, his first pro season.

The day after Phillips had been hurt, Gamble had two hits, drove in three runs, and threw out a runner at home plate in a win over the Giants. He had been introduced to Willie Mays before the game by Banks. "It was the first time I've seen him so excited," Banks said. "He was so nervous he was shaking."[12]

Durocher indicated he was leaning toward Gamble if Phillips wasn't ready for Opening Day. "[He] is my center fielder," Durocher said. "I'm not going to fool around shifting a lot of players. And what other club is going to give me a center fielder? None. No. Oscar is staying right where he is."

Buck O'Neil seemed shocked. "Oscar's in over his head, but he seems to be doing a good job," said the scout who had signed Gamble. "But do you realize that his high school in Alabama didn't even have a baseball team? There were no little leagues or anything. Including the 34 games he played last year in the rookie league and the ones this spring, he hasn't played in more than 150 games in his life. When I saw him, he was just playing in a sandlot on Saturdays and Sundays."13

Young, 23, had gotten to the big leagues as a 19-year-old, arriving in memorable fashion. He and Byron Browne made their big-league debuts on September 9, 1965, at Dodger Stadium in Sandy Koufax's perfect game—"like losing your virginity to the prom queen," according to author Jane Leavy.

Young had always seemed unsure of himself and socially awkward. He was good enough in center field to generate comparisons to the White Sox's Jim Landis, who won five consecutive Gold Gloves in the 1960s, yet no team had claimed him when the Cubs left him unprotected in the Rule 5 draft after the '68 season. "He could have a great future, but it's up to him," Durocher said. "I don't care what he hits. I want to see more enthusiasm from him. He's got to be more aggressive."14

Center field wasn't the Cubs' only problem on the field. The game Gamble helped win was the one victory between them and a 0–9 start to the spring. So on March 17, Pete Reiser, Durocher's top assistant, called a team meeting to tell players it was time to get serious.

"I've been serious all along, but apparently some people haven't," said Reiser, who announced morning workouts were being moved up from 10:00 to 9:30 AM.15

The meeting fell to Reiser because Durocher was back in Chicago, making a public appearance while visiting his lady friend, Lynne Walker Goldblatt. This would be the first of at least seven times that Durocher would leave the team or simply fail to show up for games during the 1969 season—a pattern that Wrigley and Holland allowed to develop because they seemed to lack the willingness to confront the manager, sometimes forgetting who worked for whom.

Things were running much smoother in St. Petersburg. The Mets sailed toward Opening Day, their hopes growing stronger as they pounded out victories by double-digit margins over the teams that played in the '68 World Series—12–0 over Detroit and 16–6 over St. Louis.

"Most of the guys had a philosophy similar to mine," Seaver said. "Maybe they didn't articulate it, but deep down they shared my attitude. I wanted to be the best ballplayer, the best pitcher Tom Seaver could possibly be. Jerry Grote wanted to be the best catcher Jerry Grote could be, etc. If each of us achieved his goals—a reachable, realistic goal—individually, then we could all reach our team goal, no matter how unrealistic, no matter how impossible it seems to outsiders."[16]

>> <<

While Holland felt the short-lived boycott of camps by players had left no scars on the Cubs, it damaged the tranquility of life at the Cardinals' camp.

Rather than being thrilled that his team had won pennants in three of the last five seasons, beer baron Gussie Busch was enraged that his players had been part of a union action to challenge management. The money involved was of no consequence to Busch, who had always been considered generous as an owner. But John Helyar, author of the *Lords of the Realm*, said that Busch was mortally offended because he had a "need to bestow rather than be dictated to."

Busch had set up Stan Musial in the restaurant business and awarded an Anheuser-Busch distributorship to Roger Maris. He would give Brock a yacht when he retired. Yet on March 22, the only thing he was giving any of the Cardinals' players was a tongue-lashing.

Busch called a meeting of St. Louis players and invited a group of Anheuser-Busch directors to attend, along with the Cardinals' beat reporters.

"Gentlemen, I don't think there is any secret about the fact that I am not a very good loser," he began. "One thing is for sure. I don't like to lose in baseball, and I don't like to lose in the beer business. For that reason, you can well understand that there have been a number of times in the past 17 years when I felt like giving the club away."

Busch recited a string of actions he had taken as owner to help the Cardinals, seeing them all as selfless sacrifices. Then he said how hurt he had been by the holdout and the rhetoric that led to it.

"Baseball's union representatives made all kinds of derogatory statements about the owners," he said. "We suddenly seem to be your greatest enemies. Your representatives threw down all kinds of challenges, threats, and ultimatums.... I do believe I have an obligation to remind you that this year, instead of talking baseball all during the off-season, most fans have had a steady diet of strike talk and dollar signs.... You can bet on one thing—the fans will be looking at you this year more critically than ever before to see how you perform and to see whether or not you are really giving everything you have.

"If you are counting on security at age fifty—or sixty-five—then you have an obligation to help make the people who love the game—who pay to see it played, who listen to it day after day, enjoy watching and listening to it."

Busch was greeted with dead silence when he asked if players had any questions. Writers were given blank stares when they asked players for comment. Heavy was the head wearing the crown.[17]

>> <<

Mario Navarro, owner of the San Juan Senators in the Puerto Rican Winter League, was seeking a manager who could have the impact that Roberto Clemente had brought to the position. With Clemente no longer managing, Santurce's Frank Robinson had been the biggest name running a team in the league, and Navarro seemed willing to spend what it took to top Robinson.

Along with his general manager and Jose Santiago, a Cubs' area scout for Puerto Rico who also worked for the Senators, Navarro sought preliminary meetings with Hank Aaron, Willie Mays, and Banks. Mays had no interest whatsoever, but Aaron and Banks would weigh the possibility for months before ultimately declining.

Banks knew the time was coming when baseball would have a black manager. He was intrigued with the idea that he might be the trailblazer.

"It would be *something* to hold up to black people, wouldn't it?" Banks said. "I'd like that. I think I could do it, too. I think the players would accept me, a Negro, as a manager. I think Chicago, for one, would accept it. It's a tough job, I know. The pressure. But, heck, I can take the winning and losing and the pressure. Wouldn't it be something?"[18]

Durocher, when asked about Banks, provided an interesting take on the modern manager.

"You don't manage with four-letter words anymore," he said. "You're dealing with college kids with money. You have to reach them. It doesn't matter if you're black or what. Half of [the players] are black."

In truth, though, Banks wasn't looking too far ahead. He had gone to the World Series for the first time in 1968 when Jack Brickhouse set him up to serve as a reporter for WGN radio, and there he had seen Al Kaline rewarded for his perseverance.

Kaline, Detroit's great right fielder, had played 2,095 games over 16 years before stepping onto baseball's biggest stage. Banks was entering his 17th season. He had played 2,262 games.

"I honestly hope Ernie Banks gets in one," Kaline said as Opening Day approached. "It tops everything. I know how it feels to keep waiting and hoping year after year. All I can say is it's worth waiting for. You appreciate it more."

It had been easy for Banks to project himself into Kaline's shoes as the perennial All-Star rose to the occasion to deliver a vintage performance and help beat the Cardinals.

"It's incredible how much recognition you get merely by playing in the World Series," Kaline told reporters. "I wish I could show you some of the letters I've gotten. They write and say they always felt I was a good ballplayer, but the World Series proved it to them."[19]

Banks craved the chance to walk in Kaline's footsteps.

"When you're not on pennant-winning clubs, you always have this feeling—'I don't know if I'm a clutch player or not. I've never been challenged to make the big hit or the big play with a title at stake,'" he said in Scottsdale. "That kind of competition and challenge has never been there in my career. I want to see how it feels. I mean, even if I didn't play baseball any more in my life, I would always remember this: 'Gee, I don't know how good I would have been under pressure, real pressure.'"[20]

Were the Cubs good enough to get there?

"This is the most important year of my life," Banks said. "This is my biggest opportunity in baseball. I think if I failed to do the things this year that I really want to do to help the Cubs win the league championship, I would be a most unhappy person the rest of my life."[21]

5

A Friend for Life

On his first morning as a professional baseball player—a semi-pro, really—Ernie Banks awoke in a room at the Mount Olive Hotel in Amarillo, Texas, that he shared with Marvin Hickman, a friend from Dallas who had also been picked for tryouts. They had laughed during the night about a hole in the roof, which allowed them to peer upward and see the night sky. Hickman, Banks remembered, called it the "starlight room."[1]

It was an introduction to the crude conditions of baseball on the game's margins, where both hunger and a healthy appetite could keep players going for decades while traveling in circles. Banks was thrilled to be there and even happier when he was selected as the Colts' starting shortstop after a few days of practice.

Pay would be determined by the size of the crowds, but it was usually about $5 per player, sometimes less, sometimes more.[2] It didn't take long for Banks to ease anyone's doubts that a 17-year-old kid could survive in a league filled with hardened men, many in their 30s and some even in their 40s. He hit a home run to left-center on his third at-bat in his first game, breaking up a scoreless tie and earning him an immediate reward.

Bill Blair, the Negro Leagues veteran who had taken him to Amarillo, rushed up to Banks in the dugout and told him to "get up in the stands and pass your cap." Banks didn't know the custom, which was quickly explained to him, but he wouldn't have to be told twice after he sheepishly moved through the crowd of about 500 fans, who dropped pennies, nickels, dimes, and an occasional quarter into his cap. He would count it after the game—it totalled more than $6.

"I had never made money so easily and so quickly," Banks wrote in *Mr. Cub*, an autobiography published in 1971.[3]

Never mind that the skinny kid hadn't wanted to play baseball, that he had to be bribed by his father to even play catch. He was now on the path of the athletic mercenary and would stay on it for 25 years, interrupted only by a two-year hitch in the Army.

"I didn't understand anything about playing baseball," Banks said. "I started playing, and it was enjoyable. Most of my life I played with older people on my team, in my league. I learned a lot about life. Every day in my life I learned something new from somebody."

The Colts spent the summer traveling through Texas, New Mexico, Oklahoma, Kansas, and Nebraska, playing local teams at every stop. There were frequent bus breakdowns, after which the team's owner, Johnny Carter, would miraculously produce friends with automobiles to get the players to their next stops. When there were no hotels or restaurants in communities where such services were only for whites, Carter would arrange housing with black families.[4]

Carter was promoting Banks and Hickman as the Colts' top attractions, and fans in Hastings, Nebraska, were intrigued by a game between the Colts and Mickey Owen's All-Stars.

Owen was a story in himself. He played with the Cardinals and Dodgers before World War II but jumped to the Mexican League after his military service, which did not amuse commissioner Happy Chandler. Owen was handed a three-year suspension and responded by creating his own barn-storming team. This was the last stop of the summer, and Banks received $12.50, his best pay day of the tour. He took it home to his mother, Essie.

Banks returned to the Colts the following summer after his junior year at Washington High. Record keeping from that period is sketchy, but you couldn't say the same about Banks' play. The kid hit around .350 and had about 15 chances to pass his hat.

One of his best days came against the Kansas City Stars, a feeder team of the legendary Monarchs, in a game played in Lubbock, Texas. The Stars' player-manager was 45-year-old outfielder James "Cool Papa" Bell, who was probably the first to realize Banks' potential.

"He was a wonderful guy," Banks said. "A wonderful, pleasant human being. All my life I've had people like that. … I learned a lot from him."

During that first meeting, Bell had pulled aside the shy shortstop for a quick lesson in Baseball Survival 101. "If you miss a ball, catch the next one," Cool Papa said. "If you strike out, hit the next one out of there."

Bell was struck as much by Banks' calm demeanor on and off the field as his graceful power. "His conduct was almost as outstanding as his ability," Bell said.[5]

Bell told Banks that he'd get an offer from the Monarchs when he had finished high school and would say later that he called first-year manager Buck O'Neil to recommend Banks for a starting position with the Negro American League team. O'Neil, Bell would say, told him that he was happy with his shortstop, Gene Baker.

"Baker was good enough to play several years in the bigs," Bell said, "but he was never Banks' equal."[6]

Somebody was listening to Cool Papa, however.

Shortly after Banks had returned to Dallas to start his senior year at Washington High, the Monarchs sent two representatives to 1723 Fairmount Street to discuss his future. One representative was the stately Dizzy Dismukes, who had begun his career as a submarine pitcher in 1913; the other was one of the current players, infielder Barney Serrell. The men offered the Washington High senior a permanent spot with the Monarchs for the following season, saying he'd be paid $300 a month if he could make the team. It did not take Eddie and Essie long to give their approval.[7]

Banks captained the football team, lettered in basketball, and thrilled his mother by completing his course work. The day after graduation, he was on a Greyhound bus bound for Kansas City and baseball's big stage.

The Monarchs, managed by O'Neil, played in the Negro American League's West Division against the Chicago American Giants, the Memphis Red Sox, the Birmingham Black Barons, and the Houston Eagles.

"It was a new beginning in my life," Banks said. "I was really traveling. I was meeting people from all over. I was seeing other cities. My eyes were opened."

The Monarchs were the New York Yankees of the Negro Leagues, the perennial champions whose roster was loaded with players as colorful as they were talented. Roll call through the years included Satchel Paige, Ted "Double Duty" Radcliffe, Turkey Stearnes, and Jackie Robinson.

But life in the Negro Leagues wasn't exactly life in the major leagues. Consider the supply of bats. Monte Irvin remembers how a good bat sometimes seemed just as important as a good woman. "I had a bat made out of hickory—most of 'em are made out of ash—[and] I used the bat all year, the same bat," Irvin said about his career with the Newark Eagles. "A newcomer came into spring training, and I didn't know he had picked up my bat, and he broke it. I ran him out of the ballpark. They had stopped making them out of hickory. It was tough to get one made out of hickory."

Irvin said players would only get one or two chances a year to select their bats. The concept of a bat representative waiting in the clubhouse to pay players to use their equipment was both decades and worlds away.

"When we came through Louisville, we would visit the factory and you could get whatever model you wanted, at that time," Irvin said. "Of course, you were paying for it. We had to pay for it.... A bat was about $2 at the time."

Baseballs were also hoarded. Irvin laughs at the affinity that the late Abe Manley, who ran the Eagles with his wife, Effa, had for them.

"We had our owner who was in love with baseballs," Irvin said. "He loved new baseballs. He didn't want to give you a ball to take infield practice with. He'd give you an old ball. I'd say, 'Cap, we need a new ball.' There might be 4,000–5,000 people in the ballpark, and he'd hire some kids to chase the foul balls. If the kids didn't show, he would chase the balls himself in a $100 suit. He would sit right behind the driver on the bus, and he had the ball bag next to him. It was the strangest thing. He just loved baseballs."

For Banks, the bus rides and hotel stays were a treasured part of the Negro Leagues experience. He loved listening to the tall tales and fish stories that were exchanged while eating crackers, peanut butter-and-sardines sandwiches, and other portable delicacies.

He loved legends like the one in which Cool Papa Bell was supposedly so fast that he could turn off a light switch and be in bed, under the covers, before it got dark. Was Bell really that fast?

"No," Banks said, laughing. "But most of the guys I played with in the Negro Leagues, they could tell stories that you just believed.... They could tell some stories, I'm telling you, that you'd really have to believe. When I was in Negro Leagues, riding the bus, I'd sit beside Buck O'Neil and all these guys, and they would tell stories. ... I would look around and say, 'Was that true?' I believed it. Everything they said I believed. When you're with an older person who knows more than you, and they're telling you a story about their lives growing up, you believed it. You can't prove it's not true. I couldn't prove that wasn't true. They said a lot about Cool Papa Bell, a lot about Satchel Paige, a lot about Jackie Robinson that I listened to, and I believed it because they told it in a way that you believed it. Most of them could have been great producers in Hollywood because they could tell some stories you just cannot believe were true, but they were."

Banks missed the chance to play alongside Paige, who signed with the Cleveland Indians two years before Banks joined the Monarchs. They would face each other through the years during off-season barnstorming trips, and Banks loved Paige just as much as Bell and the others.

"He was a philosopher," Banks said. "Satchel was very funny and very talented. He had a great sense of humor, a lot of talent, whole lot of talent. He knew about everything in life. He played for just about every team in the United States."

>> <<

Toward the end of his first season with the Monarchs, Banks got an offer he couldn't turn down—an invitation to spend the winter traveling with Robinson's barnstorming troupe, the Jackie Robinson All-Stars, who would be playing a team representing the Indianapolis Clowns. Roy Campanella, Don Newcombe, and Larry Doby were among the players who had committed.[8]

Banks got another surprise when the team assembled in Jacksonville, Florida. It marked his first meeting with Robinson, and Banks was worried about fitting in. That concern was gone when Robinson laid out his plan—Banks would rotate between teams, playing shortstop for the Clowns in one game and then the All-Stars the next game, giving him a chance to serve as Robinson's double-play partner.

Banks traveled with most of the players on the Clowns bus while Robinson, Campanella, and the other major leaguers drove their own cars from game to game, sometimes even arriving by air. He was in Meridian, Mississippi, leaning against the batting cage, when Robinson approached him.

"Young man," Robinson said. "I've been watching you, and you really can pull that inside pitch. You hit very well."[9]

Robinson worked with Banks to help him get rid of the ball quicker on double plays, and by the time the tour ended and Banks headed to Dallas, he felt he had grown to 7' tall. He was rolling with cash after being paid $400 for the tour, so he caught a train, not a bus.[10]

The high didn't last long, however, as Banks was drafted into the army a few weeks after he arrived home. He spent most of 1951 at Fort Bliss, near El Paso, with an all-black battalion of troops from Texas, Louisiana, Alabama, and Mississippi. His reputation as an athlete was well known, and he backed it up with games of all kinds on the base. His prowess led to him being selected to represent the base during a visit by the Harlem Globetrotters.

Banks was just as thrilled as if this was a call to the big leagues. He got to know Marques Haynes and Goose Tatum, but the most surprising turn of events came when Abe Saperstein, the Trotters' owner-coach, waved him over to the bench for a conversation as the game was starting.

Saperstein told him to sit next to him, then detailed the plays that would be run when Banks was in the game. But Banks' thoughts were hardly on pick-and-rolls or water buckets filled with confetti. He was trying to process the encounter with Saperstein as it happened.

Banks was 20 years old, yet this marked the first time he had ever sat next to a white man.[11]

The battalion received orders to report to New Orleans on January 25, 1952, with overseas duty waiting. They traveled by boat to Germany, a miserable 17-day voyage for the land-loving Banks. Banks spent much of his time in the army on kitchen duty, but once in Europe he did get back into the swing of baseball. A six-team league was formed among the units in Germany, and Banks was the star for a team that finished out of the running with him playing every position except catcher.[12]

Black and white troops had rarely served next to each other until General Dwight D. Eisenhower approved the use of black reinforcements (including future big leaguer Hank Thompson) at the Battle of Bulge in 1944, and President Harry Truman had formally issued integration orders for the military in 1948.

But de facto segregation remained the practice until July 26, 1951, when Eisenhower, as the supreme commander of NATO, mandated desegregation.

Thus Germany provided Banks his first real chance to live in a mixed society. It was a confusing period, and letters from the Brooklyn Dodgers and Cleveland Indians expressing interest in his post-service availability somehow only added to the confusion as Banks considered his future.

Banks' overseas assignment ended in mid-January 1953, and he was discharged in March. He returned to Dallas, and instead of calling the Dodgers or Indians, he phoned Buck O'Neil. The Monarchs were training in Atlanta, and O'Neil told Banks he had a "new uniform out and hanging in a locker" if Banks wanted it.[13]

Two days later, Banks was a very happy Monarch again. This time, however, the happiness didn't last.

The Negro Leagues were quickly dying, with fans turning their attention to Mays, Campanella, and the other African Americans playing in the major leagues. Bus rides seemed longer, in part because Banks was conflicted by being apart from his new wife. He had married Mollye Ector, a high school sweetheart, upon his return from Germany—the ceremony was performed at a reverend's house, not in a church.

Banks hasn't often talked about this chapter of his life, which was omitted completely from his autobiography. But he opened up in an interview with the *Dallas Morning News'* Barry Horn on a visit back to his hometown in the 1990s.

"I didn't think it made any sense spending those long hours on the bus and playing all those games that people weren't minding anymore," Banks said. "And then I hurt my ankle in Grand Rapids, Michigan. I was sliding into second base. It was bruised and it was painful and it had no time to heal."[14]

Banks did as he had seen other teammates do when the mood struck them. He hopped on a bus home to Dallas, where he would sort out what to do about his life and the newlywed wife who awaited him in Kansas City. He was making a crazy mistake in O'Neil's opinion, and the Monarchs' manager traveled to Dallas to personally deliver that message.

O'Neil told him that his team needed him, and that was all Banks needed to hear. He would finish that season and then decide if he wanted to continue playing.

O'Neil knew Banks had little real choice. He was about to be in serious demand by the best teams in the world, the ones that O'Neil would have given almost anything to have had the chance to join when he was in Banks' spikes.[15]

>> <<

Ninety-three years old at the time, irrepressible baseball ambassador Buck O'Neil was in Houston for a game at Minute Maid Park in the summer of 2006. The temperature and the humidity were both in the 90s, but there was no place O'Neil would rather have been than at a ballpark.

He had signed autographs and greeted fans before the game, promoting the legacy of Negro Leagues baseball, and he seemed drained to his companion, writer Joe Posnanski. They weren't going to stick around for all nine innings but were enjoying the start of the game.

After the bottom of the second, Houston outfielder Jason Lane tossed a ball in the stands on his way to the dugout. Two fans lunged for it—one a middle-aged man in a sports coat and loosened tie; the other a boy barely old enough for Little League, wearing a Craig Biggio jersey. The reach advantage favored the businessman, and he wasn't shy about using it. He beat the kid to the ball.

In the minutes that followed, the man did what people who grab balls at big-league games do. He made a monkey of himself, showing it to the group sitting around him, getting more excited all the time. He called someone on his cell phone. The kid, who had walked away empty-handed, sat in his nearby seat, looking like he had gotten to the front of the line only to learn Baskin Robbins had run out of ice cream.

"What a jerk," Posnanski said.

"What's that?"

"That guy down there caught the ball and won't give it to a kid sitting right behind him."

O'Neil said nothing as Posnanski continued to stew. He repeated himself, again calling the guy a jerk.

"Don't be so hard on him," said the placid O'Neil. "He might have a kid of his own back home."

Huh, thought Posnanski. He hadn't thought about that. Maybe he was going to take the ball home to give it to his own little Biggio fan. But then another thought struck Posnanski.

"Wait a minute," Posnanski said. "If this jerk has a kid, why didn't he bring the kid to the ballgame?"

O'Neil had an answer for that, too. "Maybe his child is sick."[16]

>> <<

Born in 1911 in Carabelle, Florida, the outback territory southwest of Tallahassee but not quite on the Gulf, Buck O'Neil's family moved to Sarasota when he was about the age of the kid in Houston. He found a job with a cobbler, learning to repair shoes. But he didn't make as much money as he could if he joined his father who worked in the nearby celery fields, so he joined his father in the fields.

It was hard work, but he did his best. Because he was a big kid, he was given the job of box boy. He'd carry out the celery that other hands had cut and packed into boxes. He could carry four at a time, through the muck of the fields, in the heat of a Florida spring and summer.

One day at lunch, standing behind the boxes while the workers were eating on the other side, O'Neil said to himself, *"Damn, it's got to be something better than this."* He didn't think anything else about it until after getting off the truck that night, when his father brought it up. He told O'Neil he'd heard what he had said. He also had an idea.

"There is something better than this, but you just can't get it staying here," his father said. "You got a friend. Why don't you say something to him, and maybe you'll get a chance to go up to Edward Waters, and you can play baseball up there or something. This is your chance to get out of here because it's not coming to you. You know what's here."

O'Neil was a good baseball player, good enough that he had been playing first base for the Sarasota Tigers—a town team filled with older kids and young men—since shortly after his family arrived in 1924. His friend Lloyd Haisley had attended the all-black Edward Waters College the previous year, and Haisley took him back in the fall. He was given a scholarship, which is really just a three-syllable synonym for *chance*.[17]

For O'Neil, this was a door opening to a lifetime in baseball. He was a talented hitter and had a good head on his shoulders. Edward Waters would then land O'Neil a job on the Miami Giants, who traveled as far north as New York playing teams like the Homestead Grays, Black Yankees, and New York Cubans. O'Neil's skills were obvious to anyone, and he worked his way up the ladder, even when he had little money in his pockets or food in his belly.

One fall, O'Neil and another player from Sarasota decided to head home from Wichita, Kansas. They called O'Neil's father, who wired them train tickets, but they had less than $1 between them for a trip that would take three days. They pooled their money to buy day-old bread, but O'Neil remembered that by the time they got home, "Our day-old bread was two days gone." He said he ate so much when he got home that his mother cried.

O'Neil played for the Shreveport Acme Giants and the Memphis Red Sox. But the need to earn a living put him in a grass skirt playing for the barnstorming Zulu Cannibal Giants at one point.

"I was making $100 a month with the Red Sox, and the Giants offered me a lot more, so I jumped," O'Neil said. "Abe Saperstein owned the team, and we didn't think that much about wearing the costume. This was show business. At least I didn't have to put on the war paint like some of the guys. Besides, we had trunks on underneath our skirts. A first baseman in a stretch would have been pretty vulnerable without those trunks."[18]

After four years playing all over, O'Neil was spotted by J.L. Wilkinson, the only white owner in the Negro Leagues. It got him an invitation to join the Kansas City Monarchs.

That was the height of success for a Negro Leaguer.

"I was making $100 a month," O'Neil said. "The Monarchs stayed at the Street Hotel at 18th and Vine. That was actually the best black hotel in Kansas City at the time. Being a Monarch gave you a little prestige. Just being a Monarch added something to you. And you actually were hobnobbing with the 'Bullet' Joe Rogans, the Frank Duncans, the Newt Allens. You were actually thrown right in the limelight in that time, and that part of town was really jumping."

O'Neil would play alongside Satchel Paige, Hilton Smith, Turkey Stearnes, Ted "Double Duty" Radcliffe, and Willard Brown, and he played against Josh Gibson, Cool Papa Bell, and other legends.

"We were like the New York Yankees," O'Neil said. "We had that winning tradition, and we were proud. We had a strict dress code—coat and tie, no baseball jackets. We stayed in the best hotels in the world. They just happened to be owned by black people. We ate in the best restaurants in the world. They just happened to be run by blacks."[19]

Buck hit .350 in 1946 to win a batting title and took over as manager in 1948. In that role, he shepherded 14 of his players, including Ernie Banks and Elston Howard, into the majors in the years after 1947 when Jackie Robinson broke the color barrier.

O'Neil's sunny-side-up outlook and resourcefulness made him a problem-solver in a world that could be confusing, one where some rules were changing but most were not, one where injustice was a daily reality and the rhetoric of change could be numbing.

"Buck just makes you feel good," said Hal McRae, who loved to have O'Neil visit the clubhouse when he managed the Kansas City Royals from 1991–94. "You might be blue, you might be in a slump, but a few minutes with Buck and the world is a wonderful place. Do you know what he is? He's the guiding light."[20]

O'Neil would become an invaluable resource for baseball historians and an advocate for the Negro Leagues and the players it produced. He hated the old movie *The Bingo Long Traveling All-Stars & Motor Kings* [1976] because it depicted Negro Leaguers as minstrels and ne'er-do-wells, not as ballplayers and hard-working men. He helped establish the Negro Leagues Baseball Museum in Kansas City to preserve the reality of that era and almost never turned down an opportunity to speak on that subject, whether it was on an ESPN show or at a tiny school a few hours' drive away.

One story O'Neil often told in his later years was about Willard Brown, who was nicknamed "Sonny" because his disposition could be a little bit on the dark side. He was a talented player who grumbled when Negro League teams played town teams made up of disillusioned farmers and bitter athletes who felt they had been abandoned by the fates. But Brown turned into another player, a glorious player, in weekend games against other Negro League teams.

Brown had the misfortune to be signed alongside Monarchs' teammate Hank Thompson to play for the 1947 St. Louis Browns. This was a misfit organization in the southern-most stop in the major leagues, and management wasn't exactly enlightened.

Attendance was down—only 478 for one game less than a week before the signing—and ownership hoped that the addition of black players would cause St. Louis' large black population to flock to the park.

"Naturally we believe these colored boys will help us at the gate, especially in our home city of St. Louis," general manager Bill DeWitt said. "Yet we think of them only secondarily as a gate attraction. We are not hiring these men because they are Negroes but because we hope they can put more power in a club that has been last in the American League [in] batting most of the season."

O'Neil knew better than Brown what he was walking into and wished Sonny good luck when he left Kansas City for St. Louis.

"Won't need no luck, Cap," Brown responded. "There ain't nothing but sunny days in the big leagues."

Never welcomed by his manager and teammates—one developed a mystery illness and stayed away from the park after Brown and Thompson arrived—Brown would last only about a month with the Browns. He hit .179 and returned to Kansas City with his dreams dashed.

In his final days as a big leaguer, Brown made history. Given an unexpected chance to pinch hit in the second game of a doubleheader against Detroit, he didn't have any of his bats nearby. So he grabbed one belonging to Jeff Heath, the team's top hitter, and went out to face future Hall of Famer Hal Newhouser.

Brown smashed a pitch to straight-away center field at Sportsman's Park. He was in a mad sprint when the ball hit the wall and he never slowed down, circling the bases for an inside-the-park home run—the first homer for a black player in the American League.

There were no congratulations when he got back to the dugout, no handshakes or high-fives. Teammates didn't even make eye contact with him, so Brown quietly sat down on the bench. He then watched Heath walk over and pick up the bat Brown had used to hit the home run. He smashed it over and over against a corner of the dugout wall, then left it in ruins.

Imagine the wide eyes of 21st century African Americans when O'Neil told this story.

"What is the lesson of that story?" O'Neil asked. "He hit a home run, and the man broke his bat. What is the lesson of Willard Brown?"

It was clear to O'Neil if not always to his listeners.

"The lesson, children, is that it wasn't easy."[21]

>> <<

As a player-manager, O'Neil was active through the 1955 season. Outfielder George Altman met up with the Monarchs in Indianapolis. He expected to get a thorough tryout, but O'Neil checked him out for a handful of swings in the batting cage, then put him in to play a game. But it was O'Neil who would have the most memorable swing of the day.

"Buck won the game with a pinch-hit homer off the scoreboard," Altman said. "He must have been 45-50 years old at the time ... and he was my manager? He was all business then. He had a booming voice, and you really stood at attention when he spoke."

O'Neil was really only 43. But by then the Negro Leagues were dying, the result of so many of the best players leaving for the major leagues. He had been too old to be considered as a player but was viewed as a valuable resource because of his knowledge of players and his eye for talent.

Cubs personnel director Wid Matthews hired O'Neil to scout for the Cubs after that season—the Cubs' 10th straight without a pennant and 47th in a row without a championship. The two had gotten well acquainted a couple years earlier when O'Neil delivered Banks to the Cubs.

O'Neil led the Cubs to the likes of Lou Brock, Oscar Gamble, and Lee Smith. He also became the first black coach of a major league team, a surprisingly progressive development for the Cubs, who were hardly as progressive as the signing of Gene Baker in 1950 had hinted that they might be.

O'Neil's chance to put on a uniform came in 1962, when Phil Wrigley was experimenting with his College of Coaches concept. His role was mainly as an instructor, spending lots of time with Brock, who had been rushed to the big leagues only one season after O'Neil had signed him off the campus of Southern University.

Vice president John Holland, who had replaced Matthews, said that O'Neil's role was to provide hands-on coaching for players, not to design strategy or suggest pitching changes. This was progress, sure, but it would also turn out to be a limited use of a brilliant mind.

"Buck is a fine instructor," Holland said. "He was perhaps one of the best first basemen who ever played baseball."[22]

Holland spoke of the possibility that O'Neil might one day become the first black manager in the big leagues, but the Cubs weren't prepared to give that idea a real chance. It turned out that Holland and perhaps even the bottom-line-conscious Phil Wrigley preferred to keep O'Neil out of view.

In a 1994 profile for *Sports Illustrated*, writer Steve Wulf said that Charlie Grimm, the old Cubs first baseman and manager, might be the only person in the world against whom O'Neil held a grudge. Grimm occupied a front-office position in 1962, and O'Neil believed Grimm worked to limit his potential impact.

One particularly bad memory came in a game against the Houston Colt .45s when both head coach Charlie Metro (Phil Wrigley went to the term *head coach* over *manager* in that era) and third base coach El Tappe were ejected. O'Neil appeared to everyone there to be a logical choice at least to fill Tappe's responsibilities, if not Metro's, but pitching coach Fred Martin was brought in from the bullpen to man the third base coaching box.

"After 40 years in baseball and 10 years of managing, I was pretty sure I knew when to wave somebody home and when to have him put on the brakes," O'Neil said in the *Sports Illustrated* feature that along with Ken Burns' documentary on baseball gave O'Neil new-found prominence. "Later I found out that Grimm had ordered the other coaches never to let me coach on the lines."[23]

It would be 13 more years before the major leagues had their first black manager (Frank Robinson at Cleveland). O'Neil, while not as well known, easily could have had that distinction but returned his uniform and went back to scouting talent when Wrigley broke off the College of Coaches, announcing that Bob Kennedy would be the so-called head coach for at least the next two seasons.

"They missed the boat by not allowing Buck to [have more authority]," said Altman, a former Monarch who followed Banks to the Cubs. "He had that booming voice and commanded players' respect."[24]

As a scout, O'Neil's work was legendary. The future Hall of Famers he touched included Banks, Billy Williams, and Lou Brock. He should have had at least one more notch on his belt, but Holland and his scouting director, Vedie Himsl, didn't listen when O'Neil pushed hard for Andre Dawson in his scouting reports after being a regular visitor to Dawson's games for the Florida A&M Rattlers.

The Cubs had taken another player recommended by O'Neil in the second round of the 1975 draft—Louisiana high school pitcher Lee Smith, who would go on to rack up 478 saves, which stood as the all-time record until Trevor Hoffman passed it—and had other scouts to satisfy. So they left Dawson on the board until the 11th round, when Montreal claimed him.

"I used to run into [O'Neil] at some banquets," Dawson said. "He told me that he had seen a lot of my games [in college]. He said he pushed the Cubs to take me, but they didn't. That would have been something."

In the case of Billy Williams, he was signed by Ivy Griffin, not O'Neil. But O'Neil was a natural choice for Holland to call after Williams bolted his Texas League team in 1959. Williams was in his third full minor league season and was fed up with being treated like a second-class citizen outside the ballparks.

The last straw came when he and teammate J.C. Hartman were seated in the kitchen of a restaurant at the Ambassador Hotel as their white teammates happily ate in the dining room, recalling details of a game that the San Antonio Missions had won on a ninth-inning double by Williams. The kitchen staff never even acknowledged the black teammates, making them feel even more foolish, and Williams told Hartman he couldn't take it anymore. He was gone in the morning.

The orders to O'Neil were brief. "Go get him," Holland said.

O'Neil hopped in his Plymouth Fury and drove to Williams' family home in Whistler, Alabama, arriving in time for dinner. His pursuit did not seem to surprise the family, who invited him to eat with them. But after a pleasant evening of small talk and news—anything except baseball—Williams' parents were startled when O'Neil excused himself, saying he needed to go to his hotel for rest. He asked if it would be okay to come back the next day.

He again arrived just before dinner and said nothing about baseball or Williams' decision. When she was alone with him in the kitchen, Williams' mother asked if O'Neil planned to talk some sense into her son. "Billy's a smart man," O'Neil said in a voice loud enough to be heard in the next room. "He can make his own decisions."

O'Neil then returned to the table and looked at Williams. "Billy, I want you to come with me somewhere. Will you take a ride with me?"

Williams went outside and into the passenger seat of the Fury, and the two were off to a nearby park where a bunch of kids were playing ball. Williams was well known in his hometown, of course, and the kids stopped their game to go see him.

They asked questions about life in the minor leagues and told him how they hoped to grow up to be like him. Williams embraced the attention, playing catch with the kids and answering all their questions. When the sandlot game resumed, Williams said to Buck, "All right, I'll go back."

O'Neil called Holland with the news later that night. "Put Billy on the first plane in the morning," he was told.

"Plane?" O'Neil asked. "No, sir. I'm driving him back to Texas myself."

Williams, who would go on to have 2,510 hits for the Cubs (and 2,711 overall), credits O'Neil's low-key intervention for changing his life.

O'Neil impacted more lives than can be counted. Banks, like so many others, carried O'Neil with him always.[25]

>> <<

Historian Kermit Eby sees Chicago as a complex city that is impossible to explain simply.

"Chicago is a paradox," said Eby, a Chicago native who grew up in the 1960s, rooting for Ernie Banks and the Cubs. "[It's] a city of broken dreams, unfulfilled ideas, tremendous neighborhoods, compassion, progress, filth, fight, and beauty."

Martin Luther King described it in 1966 as perhaps the meanest city in a mean country. "I have never seen such hate, not in Mississippi or Alabama, as I see here in Chicago," said King,[26] who chose Chicago as a city in which to show that the struggle for minority rights was an issue north of the Mason-Dixon Line after winning civil rights battles in the South. He was drawn to Richard J. Daley's city largely by a local fight over schools that were separate but hardly equal, with the overcrowding and poor quality of black schools spawning the Chicago Freedom Movement, led by activist Al Raby.

This had long been an issue for the *Chicago Defender*, the newspaper that had once pushed hard for integration in baseball and kept raising the issue in Chicago until the Cubs introduced Banks and Gene Baker. The object of its disaffection was Benjamin Willis, the Chicago school superintendent, who by 1963 was being referred to as "the Governor Wallace of Chicago" by the *Defender*.

In 1940, the black population of Chicago was listed at 277,731 and accounted for 8 percent of city residents. But a migration from the south, created by factory jobs and the thriving black community on the South Side, in the area known as Bronzeville, contributed to that figure tripling in two decades. The 1960 census listed the African American population of Chicago at 812,637, which was just more than 22 percent of the city's population.[27]

This was a badly underserved and increasingly dissatisfied population, which was denied housing opportunities outside the city's South and West sides that were already home to comfortable neighborhoods for blacks with money and large and overcrowded ghettos for those without money. The huge burst of growth meant that working-class whites like those in Irish and Italian neighborhoods were feeling crowded by the suburbs and the expanding ghettos, creating tension. The African Americans likewise felt squeezed and threatened by Daley's efforts to rebuild the central city and hostile white communities that were closed to blacks and often violent toward blacks.

As Banks was arriving in Chicago, whites were beginning to flee to the suburbs, with a reported 270,000 moving from 1950–56.[28] In the city, there were clashes between the groups, including small race riots over public spaces such as beaches and parks, setting the tone for the 1960s—Chicago's most turbulent decade.

None of this was really new, of course. From 1917 to 1919, there were 26 reported bombings of black residences in what had been all-white neighborhoods, and most of these were along the lakefront east of Bronzeville.[29] And the city exploded when 600 black workers reported to replace striking white workers at the Argo Corn Products plant just southwest of the city. The fuse was set, and the explosion came when a 16-year-old black drowned after being hit in the head with a rock while floating on a raft in Lake Michigan.

When blacks lashed back in anger, white ethnic gangs quickly mobilized and terrorized blacks. Seventeen people died in one day of rioting that summer, and black snipers guarded the ghettos to keep away large, armed white gangs.

This was the setting for Joe Jackson, Eddie Cicotte, and the 1919 White Sox, who won the American League that summer then succumbed to inducements from gamblers to throw the World Series to Cincinnati, just as the resumption of these hostilities would mark Banks' era with the Cubs.

The federal government and the Daley administration would deal with overcrowding in ghettos by constructing public housing—first the Stateway Gardens Project in 1958 (two 10-story buildings adjacent to State Street and six 17-story buildings along the Rock Island Railroad tracks to the west high-rises) and then the Taylor Homes in the early 1960s. This collection of high-rises off South Michigan and State Streets was as ambitious as it was flawed, as more than 28,000 almost all black residents were jammed into a 95-acre parcel of land, with the units themselves taking up less than 10 acres.[30]

It quickly became apparent how the realities of life were far different than had been advertised during construction. "The world looks on all of us as project rats, living on a reservation like untouchables," one resident said in 1965, almost 40 years before the Taylor Homes were torn down.[31]

Rev. King spent so much time in Chicago in 1965 and '66 that he leased an apartment in North Lawndale. He led marches for better schools and open housing, and they were targeted by angry whites who screamed epithets and threw rocks and bottles. King himself was once hit in the head by a brick. He did not back down, but neither did he achieve much. In the end, Daley (himself an early advocate for civil rights as he tried to cultivate black voters) agreed to various reforms but then did little, if anything, to enforce them.

Chicago came apart at its seams at the end of the 1960s, with protests against the Vietnam war adding to the city's underlying tensions. King was an opponent of the war, addressing that cause and civil rights when he visited Memphis in April 1968. His assassination by James Earl Ray triggered riots on Chicago's West Side that quickly spread across the city, as well as the nation.

Cities burned all across the country as blacks expressed their outrage, but Daley took the fight personally. With army troops and 4,200 members of the National Guard (including Cubs pitcher Ken Holtzman) joining the Chicago police attempting to stop arsonists and looters, Daley issued an infamous shoot-to-kill order that—mercifully—his police superintendent ignored. But the order itself marked Chicago as a place where the in-power whites had no compassion and next to zero tolerance for the frustrated, angry blacks.

Historian Dominic A. Pacyga said Chicago "resembled an armed camp" when the Democrats arrived for their national convention in August 1968, an event Daley hoped would propel him to prominence in a party that was grasping for leadership after Lyndon Johnson's decision not to run for election a second time. This time the authorities took on young, white peaceniks, not the blacks they had trained against, and Chicago was again marked as a city desperately opposed to change, one that was willing to fight to preserve a status quo that suited one segment of its population at the expense of others, most notably African Americans.

Even though the so-called Walker Report labeled the conflicts at the Democratic convention a "police riot," Daley tried to extract his view of justice against the event's organizers. Black Panther co-founder Bobby Seale (born in Dallas five years after Banks), who arrived in Chicago at the behest of Abbie Hoffman and others and had seemingly done little to incite a riot, was charged and was eventually tied to a chair and gagged in the court room when he repeatedly raised loud, angry objections in his trial—an action that prompted Graham Nash to write the song "Chicago," with its haunting refrain, "We can change the world, rearrange the world, it's dying—if you believe in justice, dying; and if you believe in freedom, dying, let a man live his own life, dying."

Yet Seale's barbaric handling was a minor offense compared to the treatment of a local Black Panther leader. In the fall of 1969, apparently while he was sleeping alongside his pregnant girlfriend, Chicagoan Fred Hampton (an honors graduate from Proviso East High School who once dreamed of playing center field for the Yankees) was brutally gunned down by Chicago police acting on orders from Cook County State's Attorney Edward V. Hanrahan.. The police team termed their action a shootout, but investigators found only one bullet hole leaving the apartment where Hampton stayed with other Panthers and hundreds of bullet holes entering it from outside.

This was the Chicago that Ernie Banks and the other black ballplayers, men like Billy Williams, Fergie Jenkins, and the White Sox's players like Carlos May and Walt "No Neck" Williams, navigated their way through. It could be a paradise one day and a hellacious riddle the next, and there were no GPS systems or road maps to help one find his way.

6

APRIL

Nightly mob scenes at home plate became *de rigueur* elements of big-league baseball at some point in the 1990s, when steroids and other performance-enhancing drugs fueled late-inning comebacks, and ESPN was there with *Baseball Tonight* to make the clinching game of every June series seem like Game 7—maybe not Game 7 of the World Series, but definitely Game 7 of some series.

Excessive jubilation reigned on a nightly basis, with players diving into piles at home plate like Jack Black crowd surfing in his film *School of Rock* and issuing more pies in the face than Soupy Sales. The Florida Marlins' Chris Coghlan went on the disabled list in 2010 after tearing a ligament in his knee when he landed badly on a hit-and-run pie-facing shortly after the Los Angeles Angels' Kendry Morales had his season ended when his leg was somehow broken in a home-plate scrum after a game-winning home run.

It's hard to say now how much of such exuberance is genuine and how much is manufactured for the cameras. But when the Cubs began the 1969 season, the only propellant for the sequence of celebrations at Wrigley Field—on the field and in the stands where the Opening Day Cubs had their biggest crowd in 40 years—was pure human emotion. There may never have been a better day at the venerable ballpark that opened in 1914.

The details of the 7–6 victory over Philadelphia mattered at the time, of course—especially Leo Durocher's hunch to pinch hit Willie Smith instead of Al Spangler against Barry Lersch in the 11th inning—but what remained when it was time to sweep the stands was the lifelong memory, the knowledge that the emotion of the day was like the liftoff of a moon shot from Cape Canaveral.

Ernie Banks homered in his first two at-bats, and by the count of *Chicago Tribune* reporter George Langford, received nine different standing ovations.[1] Phillies rookie Don Money countered those blows with two home runs of his own, forcing 40,796 to squirm in their seats, but Smith's pinch-hit homer triggered a period of pure ecstasy for everyone not associated with the visiting team.

Smith was mobbed at home plate in a dogpile that made Durocher's mind flash to 1951 and the Polo Grounds when Bobby Thomson's ninth-inning homer off Ralph Branca gave the Giants the National League pennant. Smith hobbled to the clubhouse afterward, having been spiked by a teammate. But it would be quite a while before any of the Cubs' players showered to head home.

For the longest time, Banks, Don Young (who had wound up with the center-field job when Adolfo Phillips wasn't ready and Durocher decided 19-year-old Oscar Gamble needed more time in the minors), and their teammates gathered in the middle of the small room, listening to Vince Lloyd replay highlights from the game.

"We knew right there that this was the season we were going to win it," Ron Santo said.[2]

Eddie Banks, wearing a coat and tie with a Cubs cap on his head, was escorted into the inner sanctum by his 38-year-old son.

"This is a great life, ain't it daddy?" Banks said.

Eddie, at a loss for words, just nodded.

"Thanks for making me a ballplayer," Ernie said.

"You're welcome, Ernie," Eddie said. "Just keep it up."

As was his custom, Banks talked to reporters until there were no questions left.

"Most people think I'm crazy when I predict every year the Cubs are going to win the pennant," Banks said. "Well, even before we moved into the first division two years ago, we had started strong in several other seasons. We just couldn't keep up the pace in the second half. Now we have the unity. There's a mutual respect among the players. And we have a dandy manager."

When there was nothing left to say, Banks turned to song. "Those were the days, my friend," he warbled, using the 1968 hit by Mary Hopkin to sum up his feelings.[3]

Across Waveland Avenue at Ray's Bleachers, fans partied for hours after the game. Some of the heaviest drinkers were bragging about how they had tormented Phillies left fielder Ron Stone, who complained that he had been pelted with eggs, ice, and even one salt shaker.

≫ ≪

While the twice-defending champion Cardinals were getting swept by the Pirates in a three-game series at Gussie Busch's three-year-old stadium under the Gateway Arch—with the much ballyhooed outfield of Lou Brock, Curt Flood, and Vada Pinson going 7-for-40—the Cubs won their first four games and steamed to an 11–1 start.

This was a continuation of how they had finished spring training, as they had gone 12–7 after coach Pete Reiser notified them it was time to start winning. There were some ugly wins in the fast start, for sure—in a 7–6 win over Montreal the teams committed six errors, leading to 11 unearned runs, including the Cubs' three in the ninth, when Banks capped a rally with a bloop single—but out of the gate it was the big hitters who were serving notice.

Billy Williams tied a major league record with four doubles in the second game of the season, an 11–3 win over the Phillies, after which he declared that he wouldn't mind a little more attention.

"I'm a label man," Williams said. "They always label a player when he first comes up to the majors, and I was labeled quiet. You say I haven't gotten the publicity I deserve over the years and that I'm an underrated ballplayer. Well, that's up to you guys. I can't write about myself."[4]

Banks empathized. "It's too bad that a lot of things Billy does are overlooked," he said. "He is a tremendous asset to this team.... He loves the game just as much as any of us. He just has a different way of expressing it. Some guys like me go around hollering, but he quietly does it all."

Williams' complaints were not entirely in vain. The *Tribune*'s David Condon waged a successful campaign for the Cubs to recognize Williams with his own day later that summer, where the future Hall of Famer was showered with gifts between games of a doubleheader sweep over the Cardinals on June 29. But when *Sports Illustrated* twice placed the Cubs on 1969 covers, it was Ron Santo and Banks who were featured.

Santo's two homers were the building blocks toward a 6–2 win to finish a season-opening sweep over the Phillies, and Williams broke up a scoreless tie against the newborn Montreal Expos with a 12th inning single the next day, giving the Cubs a 1–0 victory.

"Every day someone different—that's what it takes to be a winner," Santo said. "And we are the three who have to produce if we're going to win it."[5]

Durocher was sometimes with the team, and sometimes either with himself or his girlfriend, to whom he proposed in early May. He skipped the Cubs' late spring trip to Yuma, Arizona, and then remained in Chicago when the team traveled to Milwaukee to face the White Sox before the opener. The Midwestern weather was miserable, like usual in the early spring, and Durocher wanted to make sure he was healthy when the season began for real. Apparently, Durocher's plan didn't work. He turned over the team to pitching coach Joe Becker for three games in a row in mid-April, remaining at his apartment to battle the flu.

Durocher opened the season with Bill Hands, Ken Holtzman, and Joe Niekro (who was traded to San Diego alongside pitcher Gary Ross for the Padres' Opening Day starter, Dick Selma, on April 25) following Fergie Jenkins in a four-man rotation designed to maximize the impact of his top starters. This was not the approach that Gil Hodges was taking with the Mets.

Tom Seaver was arguably the National League's best pitcher, but Hodges was planning for a long season. He went with a five-man rotation, lining them up like this: Seaver, Jim McAndrew, Gary Gentry, Jerry Koosman, and veteran Don Cardwell, who had thrown a 1960 no-hitter for the Cubs two days after being acquired from Philadelphia, with Nolan Ryan as his long reliever.

After Seaver allowed four runs in five innings on Opening Day, he had to watch four games before making another start. A generation later, all teams would operate this way. But in '69, only seven of the 24 major league teams opened the season with five-man rotations—and among those seven, only the Mets and Red Schoendienst's Cardinals (with Bob Gibson) had an established ace they could have ridden in old-school fashion.

Starting pitchers weren't the only players used differently by Durocher and Hodges. They ran the rest of their teams the way they set up their rotations.

Durocher opened the season with a platoon of Jim Hickman and Spangler in right field but didn't give another reserve a start until Jimmy Qualls started for second baseman Glenn Beckert in the 10th game. Hodges played everyone. Like Baltimore's Earl Weaver, he was a firm believer in the advantages of platooning left- and right-handed hitters to maximize their chances at production, and he didn't care if players like Ron Swoboda moaned when they weren't in the lineup.

"I was never cool with the platooning," Swoboda said. "But in the end Gil proved that he knew what he was doing."[6]

Hodges rotated Ed Charles and Wayne Garrett at third base, the young Ken Boswell and veteran Al Weis at second base, and used the left-handed hitting J.C. Martin to rest catcher Jerry Grote. Ed Kranepool was his first baseman, but against left-handed pitchers he moved Cleon Jones from left field to first and started one of his rookie outfielders, Rod Gaspar or Amos Otis. Swoboda, a right-handed hitter, shared time in right field with first Gaspar (a switch hitter) and then Art Shamsky.

At the end of April, 12 of the Mets' position players had at least 33 plate appearances. The Cubs had only nine with 15 or more plate appearances, as Spangler was the only reserve who played consistently. Hodges also spread around the load in the bullpen, while Durocher relied on Phil "the Vulture" Regan and Ted Abernathy, the latter of whom would join Hank Aguirre, Don Nottebart, and Rich Nye on the side of milk cartons later in the season.

"I won a game in relief on May 14 against San Diego and lost one in Houston on May 17, and that's all I pitched, baby," Nottebart said years later. "Leo forgot me. He had some guys he would use, and that was all. He forgot Aguirre, Nye, Abernathy, [Jim] Colborn, and me. He tried to win the damned pennant with six guys."[7]

Other than long relievers Nolan Ryan and Tug McGraw, none of Hodges' relievers worked more than 10⅓ innings in April, with Ron Taylor and Cal Koonce the anchors. The Mets lost 3-of-4 to the Cubs at Shea Stadium and finished April at 9–11, but they retained the confidence they had carried into the season.

"Gil defined everybody's role," said Ron Taylor, who became the Toronto Blue Jays' team doctor after his retirement from playing. "I could see it coming.... We sat in the bullpen, Tug McGraw and I, Don Cardwell, Cal Koonce, and we said to each other how good this team could be."[8]

≫≪

Among the Mets, Koonce seemed the most upset by the Cubs' fast start. He despised Durocher.

Koonce had spent the first six seasons of his career on second-division teams in Chicago, and when the Cubs were starting to turn the corner Durocher shipped him to the Mets. This 1967 deal was a tricky, wink-wink one done after the trading deadline—at first the Mets sold end-of-the-line pitcher Bob Shaw to the Cubs, and a week later the Cubs sold Koonce to the Mets.

"Down in the bullpen Cal was always talking about Durocher," Ryan said. "One time I asked him, 'Cal, why do you hate Leo so much?' He said it was what Leo said when he traded him, that he told reporters it was 'garbage for garbage.'"

Koonce, pitching in relief of Gentry, failed to protect a 6–3 lead in the first game of an April 27 doubleheader against the Cubs at Shea Stadium. He served up a go-ahead homer to Randy Hundley before Hodges pulled him, using Seaver to finish the game. The second game was a pitching duel between the Mets' tandem of McAndrew and McGraw and the Cubs' Nye, who was left to work himself out of a jam after a Williams error put the winning run on second base to start the ninth. The Mets avoided a sweep when Jones drove a three-run homer off Nye.

Up in the WGN booth, Jack Brickhouse was trying to wipe a smirk off his face. He had feuded with Durocher, who upon arrival in Chicago seemed to resent anyone whose light shone brightly, especially Banks and Brickhouse, and from Brickhouse's vantage point it was clear that Nye was out of gas.

"You know, when I first knew Durocher he was one of the sharpest riverboat gamblers I ever saw in my life," Brickhouse would later tell Rick Talley. "You didn't have to tell Leo if a guy had thrown 87 pitches. He knew whether a guy was tired or not. In those days, he was a son of a bitch, but he was a sharp son of a bitch. But by the time he was finished in Chicago, he was just an old son of a bitch."[9]

7

Open Doors into a White World

Providence and shrewd scouting have been found in limited supply for the Chicago Cubs. But in regard to the signing of Ernie Banks, the combination of luck and smarts tilted the advantage toward Chicago.

Perhaps as many as a dozen men played roles in Banks winding up with the Cubs instead of elsewhere—some acted intentionally, and others were dragged along through the flow of events. Had the Cubs not needed a roommate for Gene Baker, they may not have been as motivated to stalk the Kansas City Monarchs in the summer of 1953. Had P.K. Wrigley not been as open minded as he was on matters of race, he might have run an all-white team longer than he did. Had the Macon Peaches of the South Atlantic League not feared their fan base wasn't ready for black players, Tom Gordon might not have been the first to recommend that the Cubs pursue Banks.

Put all these events together, and the stars were aligned for Banks and the Cubs.

Wrigley's history on matters of race was clear. Every man who was qualified deserved a shot, no matter his pigmentation. When Wrigley had been continuing the development of Catalina Island, which was started by his more adventurous father, he received a call telling him that an African American was making noise about wanting to live there. Wrigley was asked what he wanted to do about the situation that had alarmed the staff. "See if you can find a history book," Wrigley replied. "And read the Constitution of the United States."[1]

Life wasn't as simple as theory, of course. Wrigley left Baker in Triple A longer than he probably needed to play there, in large part because Wrigley was worried about the reaction of the Cubs' lily-white fan base. Gordon, who had been hired as general manager of the Peaches, the Cubs' team in the South Atlantic League, reacted nervously when he heard that black outfielder Solly Drake was likely headed there to start the 1953 season.

Gordon called Gene Lawing, the Cubs' farm director, and said he was worried that Macon wasn't ready for integrated baseball. He was afraid Drake would be abused or that fans would simply stay away from the ballpark, and Lawing responded by sending Drake to Iowa (Des Moines), not Georgia.[2]

Then an amazing thing happened.

The Milwaukee Braves hadn't been so cautious, breaking the Sally League's color barrier by assigning 19-year-old second baseman Henry Aaron, 29-year-old outfielder Horace Garner, and Puerto Rican infielder Felix Mantilla to their team in Jacksonville, Florida. This was a bold move, as there had never been black players in the Southern or Sally leagues, with baseball executives (and in some cases players) unwilling to test the tolerance of Southern whites in a region where society was run by Jim Crow laws and marred by the ugliness of burning crosses and other shows of racial intolerance. The Braves' decision was made easier by Savannah also adding black players for the 1953 season (outfielder Buddy Reedy and third baseman Al Isreal), but only the slightest bit easier.

Aaron, Garner, and Mantilla were challenged by angry, often-drunk southerners on a nightly basis, and even by some of their fans in Jacksonville. Dick Butler, the league president, shadowed the Jacksonville Braves, constantly observing from the stands to make sure the hatred did not get out of town. "Every park I went in, I was on pins and needles," Butler told Lonnie Wheeler, Aaron's biographer. Joe Andrews, a hulking first baseman who played alongside the three minority players, said he was arrested three times that year for arguing with people on Aaron's behalf.

"We'd walk on the field and they would start up the chants, 'Nigger! Nigger!'" Andrews said. "Places like Macon, they'd come into the ballpark with coolers of beer, and they'd be half drunk by batting practice. I'd say, 'These sick rebel suckers,' and every now and then I'd just wander over to the screen to see what I could do for 'em. It was amazing the way Henry and Horace and Felix could take it. I'd be standing next to Henry in the infield and some yahoo would call him a nigger or something, and I'd turn to Henry and say, 'Did you hear that?' He'd look back at me and say, 'What, do you think I'm deaf?'"[3]

It was a surreal season for Aaron, Garner, and Mantilla, at times horrifying and at times electrifying. "I wouldn't live that summer over again for a million dollars," Garner said. "But I wouldn't trade the experience for a million dollars, either."[4]

When Jacksonville visited Macon early in 1953, Aaron was off to a fast start, and the public responded by packing the ballpark with an unusual mixture of fans. "The colored section was filled up, and they had to rope off more of the white section to get all of the black people in," Aaron said in *I Had a Hammer*. "They had the biggest crowds of the season when we were there, and suddenly the general manager decided that maybe a black player or two wouldn't be such a bad idea."[5]

Gordon, the Macon general manager, called Gene Lawing in Chicago and told him he'd changed his mind about Solly Drake. He said he'd love to have him on his roster, and if that wasn't possible, he'd happily take another black player of similar talent. Lawing had no one to offer and suggested that Gordon should launch his own search.

While they were talking, Lawing pulled out the Kansas City Monarchs' schedule and saw that they were headed to Columbus, Georgia, later that week. He suggested that Gordon go scout the Monarchs and spend time talking to Tom Baird, the team's owner.

Gordon did. He was so impressed with Banks that he tried to buy his contract on the spot. Baird told Gordon that Banks wasn't available "at this time," and that when he was he would deal directly with the Cubs or another big league club, not a minor league team.

Gordon immediately called Lawing, raving about the Monarchs' shortstop. In turn, Lawing alerted the Cubs' scouting staff to watch the Monarchs whenever possible, sending in detailed reports.[6]

The reports that came in were intriguing for a team that hadn't had a quality shortstop in more than a decade and felt it needed another black to fulfill the Noah's Ark theory of integrated baseball.

Ray Hayworth, one of Wid Matthews' top men, filed this report: "Good accurate arm. Fielding ranges from good to outstanding. Sure hands. Moves well with good range right and left. Good running speed. Has good hitting form with quick wrists and level swing. Medium stride. A pull hitter."[7]

Hayworth was more effusive in his praise in conversations with Wid Matthews. "Ray learned Banks was just out of the army, which explained why we'd have no scout reports on him," Matthews said later. "Then I called Tom Baird—the Monarchs owner—to see if the Yankees or White Sox might have first claim on the Kansas City players. Baird told me the Monarch stars would go to the highest bidders."[8]

A second scout, Jimmy Payton, filed another solid report: "Throws well without lost motion. Really floats around shortstop and fields ball well from any position. Fast hands and recovers quickly. Could play any infield position. Will become good hitter. Doesn't swing at bad pitches."[9]

Intrigued, Matthews went to watch the Monarchs play in Des Moines and then traveled to Kansas City with scout Ray Blades. The rumor around Wrigley Field was that the Cubs were interested in Alex Grammas, a shortstop with the White Sox's Kansas City Blues who was blocked from reaching the big leagues by Chico Carrasquel, but instead Matthews and Blades were at Municipal Stadium watching Banks and the Monarchs.[10]

Stories that surfaced after the Cubs signed Banks made it clear that they were lucky no one beat them to him.

The White Sox reportedly ignored pleas from one of their pitchers, Connie Johnson, to pursue Banks. Johnson, who had played alongside Banks on the Monarchs, told Sox manager Paul Richards that Banks was going to be a great player. Richards passed that word up the ladder to the front office, but the Sox didn't act.

"Our scouts had seen Banks and were not impressed," said Frank Lane, who was then the White Sox's general manager. "Cincinnati didn't think much of him. The Yankees had turned thumbs down. So the Cubs got him—and now every time I see he has hit a homer, I get sick remembering how easily we could have had the kid."[11]

Both St. Louis teams had an inside track that they ignored, as well. James "Cool Papa" Bell, who had initially recommended Banks for a spot on the Monarchs, was working as a bird-dog scout for the Browns. He urged the Browns to strongly consider Banks, as had Bill Norman, another St. Louis Browns scout. Owner Bill Veeck would insist years later that he was interested but couldn't afford the asking price, and that was probably true. "The Browns never had any money," said Bud Selig, the Milwaukee Brewers owner who later became commissioner.

Veeck actually takes credit for putting the Cubs onto Banks, which is a version of the Banks' signing story that isn't confirmed elsewhere.

"I first heard of him from Bill Norman," Veeck told *Sports Illustrated* in 1969. "He called me up and said, 'There's a kid here you gotta get. Best-lookin' thing I've ever seen.' So I got hold of Baird and asked him how much he wanted. He said $35,000. I told him I'd call him back. Then I called this banker. I already owed him my life. 'How about $35,000?' I asked him. He said I already owed him my life. 'So what,' I said. 'This kid is so great we'll all get even.' The banker said he did not want to get even that much. I called Baird again and asked him if I could put $3,500 down and I'd give him the balance when he found me. Baird said the trouble was that he could never find me. 'All right,' I said. 'Do me one favor, Tom. Don't sell him to anyone in the American League. I have enough troubles without another one.' I then called up Jim Gallagher and put the Cubs on Banks."[12]

Cool Papa Bell sometimes worked both sides of the street in St. Louis. He said he tried to interest the Cardinals in Banks after the Browns passed. Former Negro Leagues catcher and manager Quincy Trouppe, who was scouting for the Cardinals, also recommended Banks. But in Trouppe's autobiography he said that the Cardinals sent another scout to sign Banks, and that scout sent in a report that said, "I don't think he is a major league prospect. He can't hit, he can't run, he has a pretty good arm, but it's a scatter arm. I don't like him."

Bell blamed Richard Meyer, the general manager of the Cardinals, for not acting on his recommendation.

"Just think what the Cardinals could have done in the races they were close to winning—in 1957 and 1960 alone—when, unlike now, they had a shortage of catching and shortstopping," Bell later told the *St. Louis Post-Dispatch's* Bob Broeg.[13]

Despite his genuine interest, the Cubs' Matthews moved slowly, opening a wide window for other teams. He still had not talked money with Baird when the Monarchs traveled to Chicago in early September. Instead, he ordered Vedie Himsl and Blades to take one last look.

Himsl joined Blades in being sold on Banks and also came away impressed with the potential of pitcher Bill Dickey. They combined to write this report on Banks:

"Good chance he is a major leaguer right now. Very good fielder with good hands and arm. Good runner. Hustles well, and is a good hitter with power. Holds bat rather high, but drops it when pitcher makes delivery. Does this fast enough so we don't think it's a hitch. Outstanding prospect."[14]

Matthews finally concluded it was time to make a deal. He met Baird for dinner that night at the Hilton Hotel on Michigan Avenue, armed with his checkbook.

After dinner, they retired to Baird's hotel room where Matthews made his pitch.

"I like to trade fast," Matthews said, in an interesting choice of words. "We're either going to make this deal now, or it's all off. We want Ernie Banks and that pitcher, Bill Dickey, in a package deal. Together or not at all. Name the price."[15]

Baird said the cost was $20,000 for the two, then offered Banks alone for $15,000. Matthews said the Cubs wanted both, "so you have $20,000." The two shook on the deal, never giving a thought to what Banks or Dickey would think about the transaction.

≫ ≪

While Baird and Matthews did business at the Hilton, a high-end hotel opposite Grant Park, Banks and his teammates were tucked away 57 blocks south at the Pershing Hotel on Cottage Grove Avenue.

According to Eddie Flagg, the former manager of the nearby DuSable Hotel, 1953 was a historically bad year for hotels in Bronzeville because hotels in the loop had begun taking black guests.[16] It was fitting then that the Monarchs, themselves falling apart because the best African American players were in the big leagues, were present to witness another dying piece of African American identity.

Banks sat in the lobby of the Pershing Hotel on Sunday night, September 7, with no idea that his life was about to change. The Monarchs were traveling to Muskegon, Michigan, the next day, a 180-mile jaunt around Lake Michigan. This qualified as easy travel, allowing players to sleep in before heading for the team bus, but Banks' schedule would be altered.

Buck O'Neil approached Banks with unexpected orders. He told him to get in touch with Bill Dickey and meet him in the hotel lobby at 7:00 AM, five hours before the bus was supposed to leave. O'Neil didn't say why, and that caused Banks' mind to race the rest of the evening. He lost interest in whatever he was watching on television and went for a long walk before returning for a restless attempt at sleeping.

The next morning, Banks and Dickey were up early, dressed, and packed. O'Neil greeted them warmly but didn't reveal the reason he needed to see them.[17]

"I've always had this thing that ignorance is bliss," Banks said. "I didn't ask Buck where we were going.... Like I said, my life is like a miracle."

Banks recalled that morning vividly almost 60 years later. "I was surprised [the first time] I came to Wrigley Field," he said. "We got in a cab and started driving. I looked up and saw this big red sign that said Wrigley Field. 'What are we doing here?'

"I was with another guy named Bill Dickey. We got out, walked into the ballpark, looked around, and [I] said, 'What in the world are we doing here?' We came upstairs and started talking to the general manager. He mentioned this to Buck O'Neil, he mentioned this to Bill Dickey, and he mentioned this to me. He said, 'You're going to play here. You'll be back in 10 days to join the Cubs when you get off the road.' I went back and finished the season with the Kansas City Monarchs, then joined the Cubs."

Banks learned that the Monarchs had sold the rights for him and Dickey to the Cubs. He was so shocked that he wouldn't ask O'Neil how much money he would be making until they were in the cab headed south, back to the Pershing.

O'Neil understood how such a detail could have been overlooked. He grabbed hold of Banks' hand and told him he'd be making $800 a month—almost triple his salary with the Monarchs. "After your first full year in the majors, I want you to write me with news that your salary has been doubled," O'Neil said. "It's all up to you now."[18]

When the cab arrived, the *Chicago American's* Jim Enright was standing beside the bus, waiting to confirm the story he had been told by someone inside the Cubs' offices—Gene Baker wasn't going to be the lone African American on the Cubs, he had been joined by Ernie Banks, star shortstop of the Monarchs.

Enright's story was big news in the September 8 *Chicago American*—the headline read "Cubs Sign Banks, Negro Star"—and Banks and Enright began a friendship that would be important to Banks throughout his big league career. He remembers answering mostly yes and no to Enright's questions, but the reporter salvaged one quote in which Banks flashed the kind of swagger he would retreat from throughout the ensuing years.

"Naturally I'm pleased over becoming a major leaguer, and I'll do my best to help the Cubs," Banks said. "I know I can field, and I'm confident I can hit major league pitching."[19]

The *Chicago American* story referred to Banks as baseball's best shortstop prospect since Chico Carrasquel and Billy Hunter. It reported that Banks was 6'1", 180 pounds, married, and hitting .388 with 22 home runs for the Monarchs, whose season was to finish Sunday.

Inwardly, Banks did not know what to make of his new opportunity.

"I really didn't want to come here. Do you believe that?" Banks told a room full of Cubs fans at Wrigley Field in 2010. "I said, 'What am I doing? I'm playing for the Kansas City Monarchs. I'm very familiar with all the players. We got along well.' [But] they said you've got to go to Wrigley Field. I said, 'For what?' They said, 'You are with the team. You have to go.' I said, 'Who are the people on the team?' They said 'Ralph Kiner, Hank Sauer...' Who are those people?"

Sherwood Brewer, a speedster who could play all over the field, was among the Monarchs who tried to assure Banks that he would be fine. He told him to make sure he got to know Ralph Kiner, calling the National League's perennial home run champ a "good man" who would help anyone, even a newcomer from the Negro Leagues.

"Sherwood told me that I had to go, that it was the major leagues," Banks said. "I said, 'What's the major leagues? This is the major leagues, with you guys.' [Brewer] said, 'It's the majors, as high as you can go.' I said, 'I'm already as high as you can go. I'm playing with you guys.'"[20]

≫ ≪

Banks flew from Pittsburgh to Chicago as scheduled on September 13 at the end of the Monarchs' season. He was greeted at the airport by Roy Johnson, one of the coaches on manager Phil Cavarretta's staff. Johnson drove him to the Sheridan Plaza, a 12-story hotel on North Sheridan Road, north of Wrigley Field and, in socio-economic terms, about a million miles from the Pershing.[21]

Designed by architect Walter W. Ahlschlager, the Sheridan Plaza was a $2 million project when it was built in 1919.[22] It competed with the Edgewater Beach Hotel for business from the Cubs and National League teams visiting Wrigley Field.

Banks said he and Johnson talked only about baseball on the ride from the airport, although he did learn that Gene Baker had been promoted from Triple A Los Angeles and that the two of them were to report to Wrigley Field the next day when they would become the first blacks to play for the Cubs.

Banks kept to himself that night, sitting in the lobby a while to see if he spotted any men who looked like they could be his teammates before he spent a night of tossing and turning in his bed. He couldn't sleep, so he went down early for breakfast. Johnson was there and introduced him to two of his teammates, Dee Fondy and Frankie Baumholtz. Then Banks grabbed his gear and headed to Wrigley Field.[23]

He had been there before, earlier in the month, but he hadn't been in the Cubs' clubhouse or on the field. The experience of seeing it all for the first time was surreal. He still insists that a song danced through his head as he floated along.

It was a melancholy song—"Is That All There Is?" by Peggy Lee.

In the song, a girl goes to a circus, takes in the complete spectacle, yet feels there's something missing. She falls in love "with the most wonderful boy in the world," but he goes away. She thinks she might die, but she doesn't. And this was the story in Banks' song?

Here's how Banks remembers his grand arrival.

"I got on a plane, came here, met a guy named Gene Baker," Banks said. "I went upstairs, had a uniform, got dressed, went out on the field, looked around, all the vines were not out at the time. I just looked around. In my mind I was thinking about Peggy Lee…'Is that all there is? Is that all there is, my friends? Then let's keep dancing'…Looking at the bleachers, how close it was, no lights at Wrigley, not many people in the stands. It was just strange to be there."

No doubt it was, but whatever song Banks was playing in his head wasn't actually Peggy Lee's "Is That All There Is?" It didn't hit the charts as a single until near the end of Banks' career in 1969. But who would remember a day like Banks' first in a Cubs uniform with perfect clarity?

His mind had to be racing, his head swirling.

Banks said there were only three Cubs in the clubhouse when he walked in—Sauer, backup infielder Bill Serena, and Randy Jackson, the regular third baseman. Banks said he was still in a daze when Yosh Kawano, the Cubs' equipment manager, unpacked his gear.

Kawano took one look at Banks' spikes, resplendent with bright yellow shoelaces, and knew he had work to do. "Yosh disappeared quickly and returned with a pair of black laces in his hands," Banks said. "Speaking in almost a whisper, he said, 'Maybe you ought to switch to these to conform with the rest of the fellows.' In baseball, at the major league level, those bright yellow laces were for hot dogs. Yosh wanted to be sure I wouldn't be classified as one."

Kawano assigned Banks to a locker next to Sauer, who answered to "Mr. Mayor" as arguably the team's most popular player. When Banks met Kiner, he proved just as friendly as Brewer had said he would be.

"It's good to know you," Kiner said. "It's good having you with the Cubs. If there is anything I can do to help, just call on me."[24]

Broadcaster Jack Brickhouse introduced himself to Banks, then provided unsolicited encouragement. "Ernie, how are you?" Brickhouse said. "You'll be fine. Just go out and play."

In that moment, Banks made a lasting friend. "It was not his broadcasting, it was his feel for people," Banks said of Chicago's busiest sportscaster. "He was like a brother, like a lawyer, like a judge. He was always there for you.... He didn't give a lot of advice but he did share."

Banks says that Cavarretta also welcomed him to the team, but when he looked back at the day years later, the details weren't sharp in his memory. He could recall the feeling, however, like it happened yesterday.

"It was just a shock to me," Banks said. "I was totally lost. That's the way my life has been."

Banks didn't appear lost when it was his turn to take batting practice for the first time. He picked up one of Kiner's bats, a Louisville Slugger R43, and asked if it was okay to use it. Kiner said fine, then asked Banks what model of bat he generally used.

"I had to tell him that where I came from we were happy to have bats, period," Banks said. "If a bat was new, you never worried about the model."[25]

Banks could feel the large crowd around the cage as he stepped in to hit the tosses from Roy Johnson. He knew that all eyes were on him, and with his first swing he sent the ball into the left-field bleachers.

"I just stepped into the bagging cage, they threw me the ball, boom, I hit it out of the park," Banks remembered. "Is that all there is?"

With the Cubs 23 games under .500 and long since mathematically eliminated in the National League race, this was one of the many Septembers when Phil Wrigley's club was trying to build enthusiasm for the next season, its only goal to remain ahead of Pittsburgh and out of last place. The Brooklyn Dodgers were in town, finishing a series and trying to clinch a pennant.

A tiny crowd watched the Cubs' Johnny Klippstein beat the Dodgers 3–1 in 1 hour, 55 minutes that day, with both Banks and Baker watching from the bench. Baker had befriended his younger teammate during pregame infield, telling Banks to watch him to see how the Cubs did things. Banks had also crossed paths with Jackie Robinson, whom he had first met on the barnstorming tour after the 1950 season, when Banks was one of the few Monarchs invited along.

Robinson was 34 and in his seventh big league season. He asked Banks to remind him where he was from. "I said Dallas, and he answered, 'Some great athletes come from Texas,'" Banks said. "'I'm sure you'll live up to the true Texas tradition.'"[26]

Robinson also gave Banks a piece of advice. "He said, 'If you listen, you will learn,'" Banks said. "And for four or five years in the majors, that's all I did."

Cavarretta left Banks and Baker on his bench for three days. Before the final game of a series against Philadelphia, in a September 17 game that marked the end of a 13-game homestand, Cavarretta finally put Banks in the lineup, facing left-hander Curt Simmons, an All-Star in each of the last two seasons.

When Banks trotted out of the dugout to take his position at shortstop, there was an audible murmur in the crowd—if a crowd of 2,793 is big enough to cause a murmur. The Cubs were finally breaking the color line, with Banks chosen for the job as Baker continued to get rest and treatment for a bad back that had sidelined him at the end of the Triple A season.

Banks asked Kiner for a rundown on Simmons before the game and received a lesson that would stick with him through the years.

"Don't worry too much about one particular pitch," Kiner said. "Just go up there confident that you'll get your pitch, and try to make contact. Hitting, good hitting, is confidence. Forget about his pitch, and concentrate on getting your pitch."[27]

Banks, batting seventh (between Serena and longtime backup catcher Clyde McCullough), was hitless and charged with an error. But he hadn't gone down easily, putting the ball in play three times and drawing a walk. He scored one of the runs as the Phillies rolled to a 16–4 victory.

When the Cubs headed to St. Louis on Banks' first road trip, traveling by train, Bob Lewis, the team's traveling secretary, advised Banks to stick close to Baker. He realized why after they arrived at Union Station. The white players and the rest of the party headed to the Chase Hotel. Baker and Banks were put in a cab to the Olive Hotel in a black neighborhood. Lewis called later to make sure they were doing well and to remind them of the time to report to Sportsman's Park for the next day's game.

Banks had no complaints, noting that they had access to a "big icebox filled with food." But he and Baker were turned away when they tried to kill some time with an afternoon movie downtown, waved away by the ticket taker. They took the snub in stride, with Baker telling Banks, "I hope you enjoyed the show we aren't going to see at this theater."[28]

On the field, Banks picked up where he had left off with the Monarchs. He had two hits in his second game, both singles, and he hit his first home run off St. Louis' Gerry Staley in his third game. He continued to open eyes until it was time to go back to Dallas, finishing his 10-game run with a .314 average, two home runs, a double, and a triple. He had only one fewer walk (four) than strikeouts (five)—pretty heady stuff for a 22-year-old kid who was a long way from home.

>> <<

Monte Irvin, a Hall of Famer who ended his career with the Cubs after playing for the Newark Eagles of the Negro National League and the New York Giants, said that in his day, "You had to learn to duck before you could learn to hit." This was true to some degree for all hitters, as pitchers felt free to throw at hitters for a variety of reasons, but it had special meaning for black players.

As he established himself as a big leaguer, Banks would be challenged by pitch after pitch that either knocked him down or hit him. He did not let it anger him.

"They knock him down, he wouldn't complain," Irvin said. "Go on to first base. At that time they would [throw at black players]. Somebody else on the Cubs might hit a home run to beat a pitcher, but they waited until Ernie came to the plate before they knocked anybody down. That happened to me, too. That's just the way it was. They did that with [Gene] Baker and Ernie. On our team they used to do it to Sid Gordon, who was Jewish and played third base. That's the way it was then. But things got better."

In his first big league spring training with the Cubs in Mesa, Arizona, Banks suffered one of the worst beanings of his career. He wasn't able to duck a Don Elston fastball in an inter-squad game, which struck him in the head with such violence that he was hospitalized and ultimately missed about a week of work.

This was the kind of incident that could have brought drama. But it was no big deal in those times, apparently unintentional, as Banks harbored no ill will toward Elston, and Banks used only three sentences to describe it in his 1971 autobiography. The last of those was a four-word sentence that dismissed the event. "Luckily," he wrote, "I recovered quickly."[29]

A spring-training injury could have been significant, especially one that potentially could have affected Banks' performance when he returned. He wasn't promised the shortstop's job. He alternated time with six-year veteran Roy Smalley, who had hit .249 the season before. But Banks' skills were clear to those who watched the team.

Fred Lindstrom, the Chicago native who was only 18 when he played with the New York Giants in the 1924 World Series, gushed about Banks during a pregame interview with Bob Elson, the White Sox's radio play-by-play man.

"The Cubs have themselves a great shortstop, and one who'll hit!" Lindstrom said. "See him at the plate? He has the reflexes and wrist action to wait until the ball is almost by him. Then he gets that club around like Eddie Mathews. He's born to be a star."[30]

Wid Matthews hoped that was right. He traded Smalley to the Milwaukee Braves for pitcher Dave Cole on March 20, handing Banks the regular spot in the lineup that he would hold onto for the next 16 years.

>> <<

Six years is a long time in baseball. The schedule can seem endless. Games come out at players and the people who work in the game like exits for a long-haul truck driver, one after another after another, often through the night and often a long way from home.

Mark Prior's career with the Cubs lasted five years, the same time it took the Florida Marlins to go from inception to World Series parade (the Arizona Diamondbacks did them one better, making that blessed journey in just four years). Six years can be a lifetime in baseball.

For the Cubs, that's how long it took to integrate after Jackie Robinson's arrival—six full seasons, all of them second-division seasons. Who needed help, anyway?

Phil Wrigley, who was not a racist, didn't look to black players to help his perennial also-rans. There was little outcry from his fans or Chicago's newspapers, and in the late 1940s attendance was good at Wrigley Field, where 99 percent (or more) of fans were as white as the chalk outlining the batter's box. Wrigley did not want to tamper with a business model that was working.

But he did not want to be perceived as regressive. So in the spring of 1949, he told general manager Wid Matthews that he was open to having black players— well, at least one black player—in the farm system, just not at Wrigley Field. Scouts were sent to watch the Kansas City Monarchs, and the player they were sold by manager Buck O'Neil was Booker McDaniels, a hard-throwing, fast-living pitcher who was then 36 years old.[31]

McDaniels, who stood 6'3" and weighed around 200 pounds, had never been a real star, largely because he was just as likely to walk 10 batters as he was to get 10 strikeouts. Sometimes he'd do both in the same game. But he threw hard enough that he would, according to Negro Leagues legend, sometimes masquerade as Satchel Paige or Connie Johnson when the stars were tired or unavailable and the team was barnstorming to areas where Paige and Johnson were known mostly by reputation.

McDaniels was assigned to Los Angeles, becoming the first black player in the Pacific Coast League. He only lasted two seasons and was let go shortly after another black player arrived. The second would have staying power.

Gene Baker, a right-hand hitter and infielder who sometimes wore glasses, was a star athlete growing up in Davenport, Iowa. He spent two years in the navy after high school and then started playing semi-pro ball. He was about to turn 23 when he landed with the Monarchs and quickly established a reputation as one of the best fielding shortstops—some say *the* best—in the Negro Leagues.

Perhaps because they knew McDaniels couldn't last much longer, the Cubs bought his rights from the Monarchs for $6,500 on March 8, 1950.[32] Baker was initially assigned to Des Moines (Iowa) in Class A ball but showed he was ready for better competition. He passed through one of the Cubs' two Triple A teams, Springfield (Illinois) on his way to a long stay with the Los Angeles Angels.

Baker played 100 games for the Angels in '50, hitting .280, earning a spot on the PCL All-Star team, and starting to have serious dreams about playing in Chicago. But he would spend three more seasons in Los Angeles—living proof that the Cubs and their white fan base weren't oblivious to the impact that black players were having all over the major leagues, yet it was also a means of delaying the awkwardness and discomfort of integration.

In a bizarre chapter in the Cubs' long history of dubious approaches, Matthews established a hands-off policy toward all players on the Angels' Triple A roster, looking only to Springfield for help once a season had begun. Huh?

Matthews confirmed the policy in a *Los Angeles Times* story at the end of the 1950 season. "For the past several seasons, [we] have refrained from picking off Angel stars," Matthews said. "We will not take any player from the Angels during the season without the express approval of President Don Stewart of the Angels and the Los Angeles baseball writers."[33]

Matthews said the Cubs could have used first baseman Frank Baumholtz at one point during that season but "laid off him" because the move would have hurt the Angels more than it would have helped the Cubs.

From a competitive standpoint, this made no sense. But it would give the Cubs cover if anyone ever asked why Baker was a fixture with the Angels rather than with the Cubs, who stuck with light-hitting shortstop Roy Smalley as if he had been confirmed as a Supreme Court justice.

The White Sox traded for Minnie Minoso early in the 1951 season and brought black catcher Sam Hairston to Comiskey Park for a handful of games later that year. But it wasn't until 1951, Baker's second year at Triple A, that the Cubs signed another black player. That was 20-year-old outfielder Solly Drake, who was considered more of a long-term project than a player who could make an immediate impact.[34]

Few hard questions were being asked in Chicago, so Baker just bided his time as Smalley hit less than .250 every season.

"I started getting edgy in '51," Baker said in a 1993 interview. "But in those days, you didn't ask. I was getting impatient, and it got me down. I saw other players from other teams going up."[35]

In August 1953, the Cubs' hand was finally forced. The *Chicago American's* Jim Enright, an aggressive young reporter, decided to poll the PCL's managers to see what they thought of Baker. Enright talked to seven whose teams had played against Los Angeles, and all of them felt Baker deserved a big-league opportunity.

"Purely on playing ability, [Baker] is a big-league player," Hollywood's Bobby Bragan said. "He is a big-league fielder, big-league base runner, and can do it sufficiently to play there. If I was managing a club in the American and National League, I would definitely want this guy on my club."

Portland's Clay Hopper said the only question about Baker was how he would react under the most intense pressure. "Baker has every qualification a major leaguer needs," he said. "Fast. Good arm. Good pair of hands. Good power. Erratic at times. If he is right inside, he is ready."

Sacramento manager Gene Desautels said his team had played Los Angeles 22 times that season, with Baker a consistent thorn in the Solons' side. "In those games, he has been good to sensational," Desautels said. "Therefore from his performance against us, if I were a major league manager, I would consider him ready for an immediate opportunity to play in the major leagues."[36]

Journeyman Tommy "Buckshot" Brown had provided momentary hope for the Cubs by hitting .320 in 61 games in 1952, but the following season he dipped to .196. He and Smalley were regularly booed at Wrigley Field, and an anonymous Cubs player asked, "Are they more interested in finishing third at Los Angeles than they are winding up seventh in Chicago?"

In an interview with the *Chicago American*'s Wendell Smith (a black journalist who was honored posthumously with the baseball writers' highest award), Matthews insisted that Baker had never been window dressing. He sounded defensive in trying to explain why Baker had been left on the vine in Los Angeles.

"We have not brought him up, however, because there has been some question as to whether he could stay up here at this time," Matthews said. "We did not feel he was ready in 1951, nor did we feel he was ready last year. He has been playing very good ball this season for the Angels, and it appears now that he may be able to make the grade without any question. We'll probably find out for sure in spring training."

Baker had done a mini–Cal Ripken at Los Angeles, playing 420 consecutive games from July 8, 1950 to August, 31, 1952. But Matthews cited Baker's tendency to wear down late in seasons and said that because the Cubs thought so highly of him they paid him *not* to play at one point.

"Baker wanted to go to Puerto Rico and play winter ball," Matthews said, referencing the end of the 1951 season. "He said he needed the money. I didn't want him to go because I am against a player playing winter and summer. It's too exhausting. Baker was a skinny kid who needed to rest and put on some weight during the winter. At the end of the Pacific Coast League season, he was a very tired young man.

"At the same time, I couldn't tell him he couldn't go to Puerto Rico and play. After all, he had to support his family. But I was so set against him playing winter ball that I violated all the principles of good business and paid him $300 a month not to go. He was on our payroll for $300 per month from September until it was time to go to spring training...if we didn't like Baker, if we didn't think he had something, we certainly wouldn't have put him on the payroll for doing absolutely nothing, nor would we have cared if he had gone to Puerto Rico and tired himself out."

Baker came to Mesa, Arizona, for spring training with the Cubs before the '53 season. Matthews said that manager Phil Cavarretta had the authority to make Baker his shortstop if he wanted but that Baker hadn't hit well enough to justify the promotion.

"At the end of the spring tour, Phil decided Baker needed a little more time at Los Angeles," Matthews said. "He explained it to the players, and Baker was satisfied that he had been given a fair trial. At least that's what he told Phil."

Matthews did say he hadn't promoted Baker during the PCL season because he was valuable to the Angels and popular with fans.

"Don't forget that under the open classification [that] now governs the Pacific Coast League, if we had brought him up early and he had failed, we couldn't have sent him back to Los Angeles," Matthews said. "As a result, Los Angeles would have been without him, too."[37]

>> <<

Baker was on his way to Chicago shortly after the ink dried on the stories by Enright and Smith. Perhaps he would have been anyway, but it never hurts to hold someone's feet to the fire.

"He's playing fine ball, hitting well, and seems much stronger," Matthews told Smith. "I don't think he'll fade at the end of the season this year. He has matured. I think he's probably ready for big-league ball now.... As for people saying I'm holding him back purposely, that's farthest from the truth. Don't forget that when I was Branch Rickey's assistant at Brooklyn, I had a very important role in Jackie Robinson's case. I was all for him coming up. I think any player who is good enough should get his chance. I think that way about Gene Baker, too."[38]

There were forces at work other than Baker's play and public scrutiny over the Cubs' glacier-like movement toward integration. Money is always part of the story, and that was true here, as well. In a 1953 story in the *Chicago Daily News*, Phil Wrigley had said his baseball team had generally operated at an annual profit of 4–5 percent and had lost money only twice since it had been under his control—in 1942 and '50. But attendance was down in '53, the team's seventh straight in the second division, and Wrigley claimed he would lose nearly half a million dollars.

The outlook was made even dimmer by developments to the north and the south. Kid third baseman Eddie Mathews was well en route to hitting 47 home runs in Milwaukee, where the Braves had just relocated from Boston in a move that Wrigley did not attempt to block. Black center fielder Bill Bruton had built his own fan base there by leading the National League in stolen bases. But perhaps even worse for business at Wrigley Field was the White Sox assembling a consistent winner around Billy Pierce, Chico Carrasquel, Nellie Fox, and Minoso.

Wrigley had reason to start worrying about the hole at shortstop.

Baker's promotion to Chicago was announced on September 1, effective at the end of the PCL season for Los Angeles. He and two of his Angels teammates were expected to report to Chicago on September 14, when the Cubs would have 11 games left.

One problem remained. The practice at the time was to think of black players in pairs so they would have a roommate who could help them navigate the difficult waters outside the ballparks. The Cubs had no one to bring up alongside Baker, so Wid Matthews ordered his scouts to go check out Ernie Banks and the Kansas City Monarchs, who were about to visit Comiskey Park for a series against the Chicago American Giants.

"They knew we were going to bring Baker to the Cubs, and they knew he'd need a roommate," said Lennie Merullo, a former infielder for the Cubs who headed the scouting department in the 1950s. "[That's] one reason they signed Banks—so Baker would have a roommate. That's true. You had to have a couple on the ballclub. You couldn't isolate a guy."[39]

It fell to Matthews to explain the situation to Wrigley, who did not seem to understand the two-at-a-time policy. In one of their regular phone calls, Matthews told Wrigley he had taken on another "Negro player" from the Monarchs.

"Who?" Wrigley asked.

"Fellow named Ernie Banks."

"Gee whiz," Wrigley said. "We are bringing up one Negro player. Why go out and get another one?"

"Well, we had to have a roommate for the one we've got."[40]

By rights, Baker should have been the first African American to play for the Cubs. He was probably as skilled as at least half of the Cubs in 1950 when he signed, and he had waited patiently for three seasons in Los Angeles, playing hard, never complaining publicly. Yet after his promotion was announced he was sidelined by a back injury—a development reported by Enright on September 9.

Baker might miss another 10 days, according to Enright. And when Baker did arrive in Chicago, he was examined by the Cubs' team doctor, L.L. Braun. Cavarretta confirmed that Baker was going to have to wait a little longer to get in a game. "He can field and throw, but he can't swing a bat without it hurting him," he said.[41]

Banks had blown away the Cubs with his play at shortstop for the Monarchs and how he swung the bat the first time he stepped into the box at Wrigley Field. He drove the ball out of the park on his first swing in batting practice, and he kept hitting the ball hard.

Matthews quickly realized he had a new problem, except this was one of the good kind. You can't play two shortstops, and with Baker and Banks he had two deserving of playing time. One would have to move, and it was Baker who was asked to make the sacrifice.

"Ernie had a better arm than Gene," Monte Irvin said. "Gene had a second baseman's arm."

Matthews told Baker he was being moved from shortstop to second base.

"When we brought Baker up to the Cubs, I sat down with him and explained the situation," Matthews said. "I told Gene that Banks might be a truly great shortstop, that we couldn't use two shortstops but that we needed a second baseman. I explained that I felt Gene, because of his greater experience, could make the switch to second base more easily. In addition, he could help coach Banks if he was out there alongside him all the time."[42]

Banks debuted for the Cubs on September 17, the last day of a 13-game homestand. Baker got in his first game on September 20 in St. Louis, striking out as a pinch hitter against Gerry Staley. He was in Cavarretta's lineup at Cincinnati two days later, and played alongside Banks the next three seasons.

The following spring, Cavarretta went to Matthews with an assessment of his team that was so candid in its bleakness that it would cause Cavarretta to become the first manager ever fired before Opening Day. He said later that he told the general manager that Baker "may be able to do the job" but that Banks was "my star of the future."[43]

While Banks had a booming bat and bigger arm, Baker, six years older, was more of a well-rounded, polished player. He also was a communicator who worked especially well with all his teammates.

"Gene Baker was bright, knew the game well, the fundamentals," said pitcher Jim Brosnan, who made his big-league debut with the 1954 Cubs. "He had good range but not great range. He had a second baseman's arm and he could bunt, hit, and run, and do the little things a No. 2 or a No. 7 or 8 hitter could do. And he was very consistent at what he did. No one ever expected him to be a star, but he was a professional. He gave that impression right from the start."[44]

Baker hit .275 with a surprising 13 home runs as a rookie, playing 135 games under former Los Angeles Angels manager Stan Hack, who replaced the too-honest Cavarretta on April 1, less than two weeks before the season opener. Banks matched the .275 average with 19 homers and 79 RBIs, second to team leader Hank Sauer in the latter category.

Banks made 34 errors that season but knew he would have had a rougher time in the field had he not been able to talk to Baker during games, both on the field and in the dugout. Baker would encourage him and correct him if he got confused about his positioning on relay throws or in rundowns.

"Gene has been a tremendous help to me," Banks said. "He's coached me and advised me on lots of things and helped correct my mistakes. Without him, things would have been much more difficult."[45]

Banks' career took off in 1955, the first of his eight consecutive years as an All-Star, and Baker slipped slightly although his durability showed up, too. He and Banks joined Stan Musial, Gus Bell, Johnny Logan, and Wally Post in playing all 154 games.

After the season, Matthews set the two players' salaries for 1956. He called Banks in first and rewarded him with a nice raise. He then summoned Baker and gave him his new contract, paying him exactly the same as Banks.

"I thought he'd faint when he saw the figures," Matthews later told reporters.

This was classic Phil Wrigley, taking care of employees who had served the company well. It acknowledged Baker's value to Banks.

Before the following season, the *Chicago Daily News'* Howard Roberts praised the teamwork of Banks and Baker as they entered their third year playing alongside each other.

"Banks and Baker today are as much of a team as Burns and Allen, Martin and Lewis, or Scotch and Soda," Roberts wrote. "They're together off the ball field as well as on it. And on it they're the best double-play combination in the league."[46]

Sportswriters weren't alone in noticing how much of an impact the two had. Brosnan, who had pitched for the Triple A Angels in '55, was taken aback by the duo's development when he again played beside them in '56.

"All of a sudden, they were the key guys on the ball club," Jim Brosnan said. "Hell, Baker to me was just as good for our club as Gene Mauch had been for the Los Angeles Angels the year before. Pitchers would pay more attention to what Mauch would say than the catcher or our manager. Baker was the same way. Gene always sounded like he knew what he was talking about. He knew the game well. Gene Baker had become a leader. He didn't get any press, and I don't think he got a lot of support from the other guys on the club, though I can't think of anyone who minded that Baker and Banks were on the team. They weren't accepted socially, but since they were both rather quiet men who didn't need to be gregarious, all they needed was each other."[47]

Unfortunately for Banks, Baker would be traded to Pittsburgh during the 1957 season, and it was there that he established his lasting legacy. Baker was a backup infielder on the Pirates team that won the 1960 World Series on Bill Mazeroski's Game 7 homer. He became the first black to manage an affiliate of a big-league club the following year, taking over at Batavia in the New York–Penn League.

Baker joined Danny Murtaugh's coaching staff in 1963. The Cubs' Buck O'Neil had beaten him to the National League, becoming the first black to coach in the big leagues, but Baker was given the third-base coaching assignment that O'Neil had been denied. When he filled in for Frank Oceak, who left the Pirates because of a death in his wife's family, Baker was the first black to coach on the base lines.[48]

>> <<

Banks had spent the winter at home in Dallas with his wife, the former Mollye Ector. They were sweethearts from Washington High. Mollye's family had moved to Dallas from the East Texas town of Marshall, which was where Eddie Banks had been raised.

"Ernie and I both played on softball teams," Mollye told the *Chicago American*'s Enright. "One summer a park recreation director introduced us at a social. Ernie walked me home. Early that winter we met at high school, and Ernie asked me to a movie. We went out regularly from the time he was a senior."

Given Banks' schedule, the two were forced into a long-distance courtship. Mollye and Ernie traded letters often during his two years in the army, and in one written in Munich, Germany, Banks proposed.

"It took me five minutes to write back that I'd marry him when he got out of the service, and we were married on April 6, 1953, at the home of Rev. Ira Loud in Dallas," Ector said. "Then Ernie went to spring training with the Monarchs. But he was home again in a month to do something for a knee he'd hurt in football. The knee got better, we found an apartment in Kansas City, and I finally saw him play.... One morning early in September, I was surprised by a long-distance telephone call and it was Ernie, asking if I'd mind living in Chicago. He said I'd better not mind because he had just signed with the Cubs. Since then everything has been wonderful for us."[49]

For Banks, one of the highlights of that winter had been an invitation to join his manager, Phil Cavarretta, for dinner at Cavarretta's home. It was a significant gesture, as races didn't often mix in Dallas in the 1950s, and it helped Banks to feel even better about the upcoming spring training.[50]

But things weren't well for the Cubs. After finishing 1953 with a 65–89 record, they opened the exhibition schedule 5–15. Cavarretta had given P.K. Wrigley an honest assessment of the team, saying that Banks was one of the few players he was genuinely excited about, and that it was going to take help from outside if they were to avoid an eighth consecutive losing season.

"The only one I could see who had great potential was Ernie Banks," Cavarretta said. "He was a shortstop, and Gene Baker was also a shortstop.... I moved him over to second because I wanted him to play. I saw ability there. But I could see Ernie Banks with the quick wrist action. I said, 'This guy has to play.' I knew he had very little experience. I didn't think we were going to win many games, so I figured we'd better play this kid because this kid was going to be great. You don't have to be an Einstein to see it. And his fielding was good. He was a good fielder. We were playing and playing [games that spring] and not winning."[51]

To everyone's surprise, especially the inexperienced Banks, Cavarretta was fired before Opening Day. With the Cubs in Dallas for two games near the end of spring training, a personal showcase for a 23-year-old shortstop who had just been handed a starting job, Wrigley did what owners always do when they don't know what else to do. He fired the manager.

Matthews delivered the message, telling Cavarretta he was being replaced by Stan Hack. It marked the first time that a big-league manager had been sacked in spring training.

Welcome to the big leagues, Ernie Banks.

Yet with their first big-league season in front of them, not much would bother Banks and his double-play partner, Baker. The two formed a combination that somehow earned them the nicknames "Bingo" (for Banks) and "Bango" (for Baker).

They were inseparable on and off the field, experiencing more things together than either did individually. The Cubs traveled to Birmingham on their way back to Chicago that first spring, and Banks and Baker were forced to stay on the bus when their teammates went into the hotel to dress. Banks understood that he and Baker would be housed apart from the team, but he didn't understand how little status they held.

He hopped off the bus and wandered toward a Greyhound station to buy some candy. "Want any?" he asked Baker.

Baker knew Banks was walking into trouble but just smiled and said, "Oh, yeah, bring me a piece."

Banks went in the front door of the bus station, and suddenly everything inside just stopped. One man approached, telling him he was supposed to be around back. "You can't buy any stuff in here," he said.

Banks went around the back of the station and into the door marked "colored," then made his purchase. Baker was laughing when he climbed back on the bus.

"Man, why didn't you tell me I couldn't go in there?" Banks asked.

"I wanted you to get the experience and to know what's going on," Baker answered.

Banks told Baker he had never thought he would be turned away. "I thought, well, I'm playing for the Cubs," he said. "I mean everybody knows the Cubs, you play for the Cubs, and you can go anywhere. It gave you a free pass. But Gene already knew that wasn't the truth."[52]

Once when the Cubs were playing the Brooklyn Dodgers, Banks and Baker were walking toward the Commodore Hotel from Ebbets Field when the Dodgers' Roy Campanella stopped to give them a ride.

Campanella, born to an Italian father and an African American mother, was a Negro Leagues legend and had arrived in Brooklyn one year after Jackie Robinson. He was in the first class of black All-Stars, joining Robinson, Don Newcombe, and Larry Doby in the 1949 game at Ebbets Field. A catcher, Campanella was revered for his wisdom about the game and life.

Even though rush-hour traffic was heavy after the matinee game, Campanella insisted on giving Banks and Baker a ride all the way from Brooklyn to the Cubs' hotel in Manhattan. He talked all the way, telling them stories from his career and offering advice on how to act as both rookies and pioneers. He spoke about the responsibility carried by the players who had climbed above the Negro Leagues.

"Just remember this, fellows," Campanella said. "And at your age it's easy to forget. The higher you climb in baseball, the greater your responsibility will be all up and down the line, both on and off the field."[53]

Baker, in many ways a mentor for Banks, had passed along some advice of his own to Banks as the two were launching their careers.

"It was a big, big adjustment for me to come [to the Cubs]," Banks said decades later. "He had more experience than I did. I came here, it was like, 'Wow, what do I do?' Do I keep quiet? That's what I did."

Baker had formulated the see-everything, say-nothing strategy during his three seasons with the Los Angeles Angels when he wrestled internally, trying to find the best way to fit into a society that had excluded African Americans. Baker felt it had worked for him in the Pacific Coast League, and now it was time to try it in the National League.

"Gene told me just keep your mouth shut and play baseball, that's it," Banks said. "I didn't talk to anybody. They thought I was deaf and dumb."

No one much cared what was behind Banks' façade. Both Chicago fans and management were thrilled with what they saw on the field.

In his rookie season, Banks played in all 154 games, missing only one inning. He hit .275 with 19 home runs and six stolen bases. His fielding was an issue, however, as he was charged with 34 errors and suffered some mental lapses.

"It just goes to show how much I have to learn," Banks said after the season. "In one game, the Cardinals had a runner on third. We moved the infield in on the grass to head off the run at the plate. Rip Repulski—I'm sure he was the batter—hit a hopper to me. I glanced at the runner to make sure he'd hold his base, whipped the ball to Gene at second, and he fired to first to nail Repulski. A double play? Nope. There never was a runner on first. It was the fanciest one-out play you ever saw."[54]

Banks finished second to the Cardinals' Wally Moon in Rookie of the Year voting, receiving four first-place votes (three more than Hank Aaron). He was even named on some MVP ballots. But it was the following season, 1955, when the enormous nature of his talents presented itself.

Surrounded by a thinner cast with Kiner gone and the ageless Sauer suddenly playing like a 38-year-old, Banks must have felt all alone in many games during a 72–81 season—the Cubs' ninth consecutive losing year. He was developing the selfish focus that great hitters from Ted Williams to Albert Belle and Albert Pujols have spoken about, boiling down his day to the 5-10 minutes that he stood in the batter's box, facing a pitcher.

"What I learned is I played the game like there was nobody there but me," Banks later said. "I didn't think about the fans because we didn't have any. I didn't hear them, didn't see them. I just played the game, me and the ball. I don't care who's throwing it, I'm going to hit it. I'm going to catch it. I'm going to throw it. I'm going to do the things as if I'm playing by myself."

Banks raised his batting average 20 points and cut down his errors in his second full season, but those weren't the reasons his value soared. He began to drive the ball like no Cub had since Hack Wilson, Gabby Hartnett, and Rogers Hornsby had played for Joe McCarthy at the end of the 1920s, when they shared the city's spotlight with Al Capone.

Still built as slightly as when he signed with the Cubs, Banks delivered 82 extra-base hits, tying for the most in the NL. He put himself into a home-run race with prototypical musclemen Ted Kluszewski and Duke Snider, along with the ascending Willie Mays, who was then in his fourth season with the New York Giants.

Banks had gotten off to a solid but not stunning start, with eight homers in the Cubs' first 40 games. He would hit 29 in the next 72 games, getting his fourth grand slam off the Pirates' Dick Littlefield on August 2 and then delivering a three-homer barrage against the Pirates two days later. Banks had five homers and 13 RBIs in that magical four-day, five-game series at Wrigley Field and somehow had put himself on the pace that Babe Ruth maintained when he hit 60 homers in 1927.

When the Cubs visited Brooklyn in late August, the *New York Times*' Arthur Daley explored the sensation that was the young Banks.

Daley wrote that "eyebrows were raised"—a good thing in the pre-steroids era—when the "seemingly fragile Banks" passed Kluszewski and Snider in the home-run race.

"The popular conception of the home run slugger is of a big guy like Babe Ruth, Lou Gehrig, or Jimmie Foxx—or maybe even compact little powerhouses like Hack Wilson and Mel Ott," Daley wrote. "Banks just didn't appear to fit the description at first glance. A second glance, however, indicated that the situation could be as misleading as love at first sight. Ernie isn't a frail little boy at all. The Cub shortstop is 6'1" and a wiry 175 pounds. His weight has gone as high as 185 between seasons, and since he's only 24 years old, he's a growing boy. He'll get bigger and better."

Asked where he got his power, Banks tried to shrug off the question. "I dunno," he told Daley.

But the esteemed columnist, who would become the first sportswriter to win a Pulitzer Prize a year later, wasn't one to drop a subject once he had hooked into it. He asked the question a second time, with a different approach, and this time Banks gave him an answer. He said the only explanation that he had was having switched to a lighter bat early in the season—going from a 34-ounce model to a 31-ounce bat he borrowed from the Giants' Monte Irvin.

"I never deliberately tried to hit a home run in my life," Banks said. "I swing no differently than I did last year. The only way I can attempt to explain it is the bat. I was using a 34-ounce bat last season, and the pitchers were stopping me on outside pitches. I just couldn't get my bat around.

"Then one day in Chicago late last season I picked up Monte Irvin's bat and hefted it. 'Hmmm,' I said. 'This feels good.' It had a thin handle and weighed only 31 ounces. I could hit the outside pitches. I got one for spring training, and I've been using it since. It whips better than a heavier bat, especially for a wrist hitter like me."[55]

Daley reacted as if the idea of a lighter bat was like letting Mark McGwire, Barry Bonds, or Sammy Sosa go to the plate with an aluminum stick during the height of baseball's steroid-fueled era of unprecedented power.

"If the modern buggy-whip bat had been invented earlier, the Bambino might have hit 100 homers a season, his blistering line-drive singles going all the way to the fences—and beyond," Daley surmised.

But he didn't write that to downplay Banks' accomplishments or potential. In the column of August 24, he made it clear he was quite smitten with Banks by wondering if the second-year Cub could become the greatest shortstop ever because of his power.

"A strange thing about shortstops, as distinct from every other position, is that one man has towered above all others down the years as the leader," Daley wrote. "He is Honus Wagner. No one else has been mentioned in the same breath with him. But in 10 or 15 years the fabulous Flying Dutchman may have his first challenger, Ernie Banks."[56]

Banks hit his record fifth grand slam on September 19 at St. Louis with only five games remaining in the season. It came off the Cardinals' Lindy McDaniel, a hard-throwing Oklahoman, who was making his first start after receiving a $50,000 bonus.

Banks would have been happy to share the record but instead had taken one record away from Ruth and Lou Gehrig, among the others who had hit four in a season. "I never dreamed it could happen to me," said Banks, who told reporters he had never hit a grand slam at any level before the '55 season. "Then the kid gave me a fastball that was a bit outside, and I knew it was gone as soon as I hit it. It was one of the best pitches I've hit all season, but it's still hard to believe."[57]

Banks did have one regret—that baseball's Hall of Fame had requested the ball be shipped to Cooperstown as part of its collection.

"Gee, I hope they don't [do that]," Banks told Enright. "I'd like to keep it. I have all four of the other baseballs, and this would really be a prize souvenir to add to my collection, especially when you consider how lucky I am to have it. The bleacher fan who ran down the ball was kind enough to throw it back on the field [to return it to me]. I don't know [his name], but I'll find out some way, somehow, before we leave St. Louis. Whatever the name is he's got a gift coming from ol' Bingo—and he'll get it if I have to personally conduct the search."[58]

Banks finished the season with 44 home runs. No shortstop had ever before hit 40 homers in a season, the distinction for most at the position previously belonging to Vern Stephens, who hit 39 in 1949. A legend had been born.

Pants Rowland, then 38 years removed from managing the White Sox to a World Series championship and employed as a Cubs' vice president, declared Banks the best shortstop in the franchise's history.

"When anyone talks of Cub shortstops, they bring up Joe Tinker of Tinker-to-Evers-to-Chance," Rowland said. "Joe was great. I saw him. But Ernie Banks fields equally well and is much stronger at bat. And you just guess how Tinker would have reacted with today's rabbit ball. Banks handles it well. He plays those half-hops like ordinary grounders. You have to be enthusiastic about Banks—he's just a baby, and everyone is talking about him."[59]

Frank Lane, who had moved from the White Sox to the Cardinals' front office, was still lamenting the scouting reports that he said had stopped him from following Connie Johnson's recommendation to sign Banks when he was with the Monarchs. Early in the 1956 season, Lane said he'd take Banks over any player in the game early, even if it cost him $500,000—a level that wouldn't be reached in baseball salaries until the Phillies signed Mike Schmidt in 1978.

Lane had seen many of Banks' games first-hand during his breakout '55 season, riding Chicago's "L" trains to Wrigley Field regularly when the White Sox were out of town.

"You must see Ernie every day to appreciate him," Lane said. "Through a whole series, Ernie might not be impressive because he is so businesslike. But in checking back, you almost always find he has done something with his bat or glove or both to help win the game.... You know, for a good shortstop you'll sacrifice hitting ability—Leo Durocher and Marty Marion stayed up with weak batting. But Banks is a good fielder and a good hitter. He has the knack of waiting until the ball is there, then he flicks that 31-ounce bat and there goes the ballgame."[60]

>> <<

Cool Papa Bell, Buck O'Neil, and others who had helped Banks get the chance of a lifetime were thrilled by how well the skinny kid from Dallas had taken advantage of the opportunity. Bell frequently visited with Banks during the Cubs' trips to St. Louis, his home, but always felt he had been cheated out of his rightful finder's fee.

Bell said that Monarchs' owner Tom Baird had promised him 33 percent of the purchase price of any player he recommended who was subsequently sold to a big-league club. Furthermore, he was sure that the Monarchs had received $35,000 from the Cubs, not $20,000 as had been publicized.

"When the Cubs bought Ernie, they gave O'Neil a lifetime scouting job," Bell said. "The Monarchs suffered from a convenient lapse of memory. Instead of something close to $12,000 for my share when they sold Banks to Chicago, they sent me a gift—a basket of fruit."[61]

A basket of fruit for discovering a player who revolutionized the shortstop position? These were the sacrifices that the older generation of Negro Leaguers would make while creating opportunities for younger men, including the great hitters like Mays, Aaron, and Banks.

8

May

Nolan Ryan once talked baseball with the ageless Satchel Paige. The two men were separated by more than 40 years in age. They were both Southerners—a reality that Texans like Ryan always resent, as part of them still generally believes they come from an independent republic, not the western extension of the land mass including Louisiana, Mississippi, and Alabama—but their experiences couldn't have been more different.

Ryan, the country hardballer; Paige, the Negro League icon. Yet the first time they met, they spoke the same language, with Ryan soaking up Paige's legendary skills as a storyteller. At one point, Paige asked Ryan if he knew the best pitch in baseball. Ryan hesitated, then shook his head. It didn't sound like a trick question, he would say later, but he didn't want to embarrass himself by saying something obvious and being wrong.

"The bow tie," Paige said.

Ryan was puzzled. "I never heard of it, Satch," he said. "What kind of pitch is that?"

"That's when you throw a fastball right here," Paige answered, running his hand across his Adam's apple.

Ryan grinned. He knew that pitch. He just didn't know its name. But for the rest of his long career, whenever Ryan knocked down a hitter—frequently Hall of Famers like Reggie Jackson, George Brett, and Rickey Henderson—he would come back to the dugout and tell teammates that he'd decided to "give him a bow tie." And Ryan would smile, just like he had on the day that Paige expanded his vocabulary.[1]

When Ryan first got to the big leagues, he loved to watch the game's intimidators work. Hitters dug their spikes into the dirt at their own risk against men like Don Drysdale, Juan Marichal, and Bob Gibson.

Drysdale hit 154 batters, a National League record. He once knocked down Rusty Staub because a Dodgers teammate told him that Staub had been poking around in Drysdale's shaving kit in the clubhouse at the 1968 All-Star Game. "That's for looking in my damned shaving kit!" Drysdale shouted as Staub picked himself up.[2]

College men, like the Mets' Tom Seaver, weren't known for being tough guys. But Ryan learned early that the kid from USC could hold his own among the NL's cadre of old-school assassins.

In one exchange, Gibson and Seaver knocked each other down with head-high fastballs. Seaver, retaliating after Gibson knocked him off the plate, threw a 99 mph fastball that caused Gibson to bail out so quickly his batting helmet went flying. He stood up, brushed himself off, and glared at the mound. "I know you got better control than that, Tommy," Gibson said.[3]

This was a tough era, and these were tough men. "This game isn't played with gingersnaps," was how Leo Durocher put it.[4]

Under Seaver, with a staff loaded with young power pitchers, the Mets became a team known for following baseball's machismo codes, some of which they were willing to amend on the fly. This was made clear to the Cubs when the teams met in early May at Wrigley Field.

The Cubs won the opener 6–4, but Mets leadoff man Tommie Agee had gone 4-for-4, including a ninth-inning home run off Phil Regan. Fergie Jenkins was facing Ryan the next day, and his first pitch "flipped" Rod Gaspar, who was filling in for Agee. Ryan's own control was unusually sharp that day. Perhaps because he was starting for the first time that season and thus focusing hard on simply throwing strikes and perhaps because he hadn't yet become a true headhunter, he didn't hit anyone.

Ryan had to face a special set of nerves every time Banks came to the plate. As a kid, he had watched the legend from Dallas at Colt Stadium, where the expansion Houston Colt 45s played from 1962–64. He had pitched to him only once before, serving up a home run at Wrigley Field the previous September.

"Obviously growing up as a kid you knew who Ernie Banks was," Ryan said. "You knew the player he was. I saw him at old Colts Stadium a couple times, then to pitch against him was an honor and a challenge.... What you knew about Ernie was his passion about the game. He was always talking to everybody who came to first base. When you actually played against some of your childhood idols, it made it even that much more special and intriguing."

Ryan retired Banks the first two times in this game, once with a strikeout. But Banks' leadoff single in the seventh inning helped turn a 2–0 deficit into a 3–2 win for the Cubs.

According to Ryan, there was talk after that Saturday game that Durocher had ordered the Chicago pitchers to throw "at our best young hitters, especially the blacks, Cleon Jones and Tommie Agee." Seaver was starting the first game of a doubleheader on Sunday, and it was clear to Ryan he was going to set a tone.

Seaver routinely retired Don Kessinger, Glenn Beckert, and Billy Williams in the first inning. But when Ron Santo led off the second, Seaver's second pitch almost hit Santo in the head. Ryan recalls the pitch sailing between Santo's batting helmet and his hair.

"Nobody told Seaver what to do," Ryan said. "Gil Hodges hadn't. But as a young team struggling to gain a toehold, we had to fight back. Tom knew what was expected, and he was the one who had the ball. Any of us would have done it, especially after we lost the first two."

When Seaver came to the plate in the top of the third inning, Bill Hands hit him on his left wrist with a pitch. Seaver would end the inning stranded on second base. When he jogged in to the first-base dugout to get a drink and collect his glove, Hodges delivered a specific set of orders.

Hands was due to lead off for the Cubs, and Hodges wanted immediate payback. "You hit him," he told Seaver. "I don't care if it takes four pitches. Hit him."

Seaver did, firing a fastball that left a bruise on Hands' leg. "That," Ryan said, "was called sending a message."[5]

Seaver pitched the rest of that game with an aching wrist, at one point calling catcher Jerry Grote to the mound to tell him to stop throwing the ball back to the mound so hard. "Grote could really sting you," Ryan said. "Sometimes he just wanted to keep you alert, but more often he was so emotional he didn't realize he was punishing his own pitcher."

Seaver went the distance to beat Hands 3–2. The Mets won the nightcap by the same score, this time with Tug McGraw beating the Cubs' newcomer Dick Selma, whom San Diego had traded to the Cubs after selecting him from the Mets in the expansion draft.

"That was my first really satisfying game," Seaver told reporters afterward, feeling so good that he freely discussed the pitch that sent Santo sprawling.

"I tried to brush him back in New York, but I didn't do much of a job," Seaver said, referring to an April 25 loss to Jenkins in which Santo had hit a home run. "He was hitting me well. Possibly he's taking the bread out of my mouth.... I had to make sure he respects me. You can't let hitters dominate or intimidate you.... I had to let Santo know I knew what he was doing to me. Then Leo had Hands hit me. What do I do, throw a bat at Leo? I had to do what I did. It's a part of baseball. It's a good hard game."

Seaver said there was nothing wrong with that day's exchange.

"There's a fine line between throwing at someone or brushing him back," he said. "It's the difference between good hard baseball and dirty baseball."

Santo, the focus of Seaver's attention when the day began, was 0-for-6 in the doubleheader. More importantly, the Mets had put the brakes on a 9-14 start that had made Hodges look silly for predicting they could win 85 games.

"You would have thought it foolish to throw at us when we had Tom and myself and the other guys, who could throw hard, but we weren't that well known yet," Jerry Koosman would say later. "But [the Cubs] helped get the fire going. They generated a lot of energy. That was one club you loved to beat."[6]

>> <<

Ernie Banks knew something about being knocked down and getting right back up. He'd been doing it his whole career. In many ways, he was the anti-Drysdale. He didn't take anything personally, at least not publicly. He could smile about Durocher's frequent attempts to kick him to the curb in favor of a younger, less threatening first baseman.

Banks was now a decade removed from his back-to-back MVP seasons. He had battled knee problems on and off since his short hitch in the army, and they had limited his mobility long before 1969.

"He had slowed down considerably, couldn't run anymore," Ryan said. "He could catch a ball, and he could still hit. He hit home runs. He was still an effective hitter. The way we viewed him was he was still a fastball hitter, and if you made a mistake he could hurt you with the breaking ball. We wanted to keep the breaking ball down, stay in on his hands. That's the way we pitched him, pretty typical of guys toward the end of their career."

Banks wasn't exactly Methuselah, but sometimes he must have felt like it. He had driven in 100-plus runs seven times in his career, but those days seemed gone at this point. His RBI totals the previous three years were 83, 95, and 75, and only in 1967 had he gotten the 600-plus plate appearances he was used to in the era when he played every day.

Yet Banks had generated so much power in the second half of the '68 season—homering once every 14.9 at-bats, a ratio almost as good as the 13.1 pace of 1958–59—that *Sports Illustrated* took notice. "I've retired him three years in a row," Durocher told *Sports Illustrated*. "But I guess he just gets tired of seeing those young kids I keep putting in his place."[7]

Banks wasn't the first player to produce in his late thirties. Tris Speaker hit .389 at age 37, and Babe Ruth hit 41 homers and drove in 137 runs at the same age. But Mickey Mantle retired at 36, and Willie Mays slipped into a steady decline after turning 35.

Banks, seemingly always a step ahead of Durocher, credited his longevity partly to his manager. He didn't like Durocher—what player could?—but he respected his authority. Some said that was just Banks' natural way—that he was seeking rewards by deferring to his white boss—but to those around him every day it seemed more method than madness.

What could Durocher say if Banks always responded by raising his game? And he was hardly the only member of the Cubs who had realized the value of paying Durocher a compliment. Selma had quickly praised his new manager for spotting a flaw in his delivery.

Banks generally referred to Durocher as Leo, but when he was his most serious he described him in a more formal manner, just as Derek Jeter would do in referring to Joe Torre.

"Mr. Durocher is always saying, 'Give me a little bit more,'" Banks said. "That's what has made me a better man—just being around him. I kind of marvel at people who have this knack of leading. The young guys on this team respect Mr. Durocher. They do what he wants them to do, and they feel like they are going to benefit by it."

Banks said he wished he had played for someone like Durocher earlier in his career. "You might resent his efforts in the beginning, but all of a sudden you realize he has made you a better ballplayer—no, not only a better ballplayer, but a better man," he said. "He's made me go for that little extra you need to win."[8]

Banks didn't hit another April home run after the two on Opening Day, but still finished the month batting .276 with 17 RBIs, second to Santo for the first-place Cubs. He went 4-for-15 in that early May series against the Mets, continuing a slump in which he was 7-for-43 over a span of 15 days.

Durocher dropped Banks from the lineup only once during this run, starting Willie Smith against the Giants' Bobby Bolin on May 9. But after an 0-for-3 effort on May 12, Banks' batting average was down to .254. That changed quickly in a 19–0 victory over the expansion San Diego Padres the next day, the most one-sided shutout in the National League since 1906.

Banks pounded homers off Dick Kelley and Leon Everitt—the latter would be sent to the minors the next day and never get back to the big leagues. Banks drove in seven runs overall, adding a run-scoring double to the pair of three-run home runs, and his relief was obvious afterward.

"Sure, I had gotten a little worried, but Billy Williams came to me the other day and said, 'Don't rush it, Ernie. It will come back,'" Banks said. "That helped me a lot…. I've been changing my stance in the last couple of weeks, spreading out a little bit more and trying all kinds of things. But my big problem is that I was swinging too hard. I started swinging too hard when we were in Philly [in late April], and I'm not that type of hitter. I've got to swing easy and just try to meet the ball."[9]

Banks terrorized the unfortunate Padres, going 10-for-24 with four homers and 16 RBIs in six games against them during the next two weeks. The Cubs were 7–0 overall against San Diego, a big chunk of a 16–9 month in which they extended their lead in the NL East to 7½ games over Pittsburgh.

The Cardinals were a distant fourth at 21–25. They were a full 10 games back and would never cut that deficit to less than 7½ games.

"Everywhere you go people say, 'Hey, what's happened to the Cards?'" Ken Holtzman said. "We're what's happened to the Cardinals."[10]

9

A Hitter and a Bullshitter

Wade Boggs piled up base hit after base hit in his Hall of Fame career. He only generated power in his later years, but in his peak seasons he could hook an outside pitch into the right-field corner at Fenway Park toward the Pesky Pole or use an inside-out swing to power a line drive off the Green Monster on pitches that seemed certain to get in on his hands and shatter his bat.

Boggs was a disciple of Ted Williams' highly technical approach to hitting, calling *The Science of Hitting*, Williams' 100-page manual, "a major influence" behind his success. Both of those Boston greats consider hitting major league pitching a task almost as difficult as producing peace in the Middle East.

"Hitting a baseball—I've said it 1,000 different times—is the single most difficult thing to do in sport," Williams wrote. "I get raised eyebrows and occasional arguments when I say that, but what is there that is harder to do? What is there that requires more natural ability, more physical dexterity, more mental alertness? That requires a great finesse to go with physical strength, that has as many variables and as few constants, and that carries with it the continuing frustration of knowing that even if you are a .300 hitter—which is a rare item these days—you are going to fail at your job seven times out of 10?"[1]

There's no doubt hitting a baseball is very, very difficult.

Michael Jordan, one of the greatest athletes of his era, took a season off from his run of championships with the Chicago Bulls to play baseball, which he called his first love. He worked daily with hitting guru Walt Hriniak and in the end learned that he was a .202 hitter—in Double A ball. Maybe he should have studied the career of Jim Thorpe. An Olympic gold medalist in the decathlon and one of America's first great football players, Thorpe played six major league seasons, hitting above .248 only once and rarely even receiving regular playing time.

But not all great hitters viewed hitting as complicated.

Filmmaker Ken Burns once asked Willie Mays what he was thinking when he went to the plate. Mays replied that he tried not to think, that what he wanted to do was to empty his mind.

"This is a game that we celebrate being present in a moment that you and I could not parse for our lives," Burns said. "To make a decision within a few thousandths of a second to swing at the ball because you are recognizing it's spinning a certain way, and to adjust to the fact it's actually doing something else, and to not fail 11 times out of 10, which is what every one of us would do? It's an amazingly cerebral thing at the same time it's also about not thinking."

All of his life, Ernie Banks knew he could hit. He didn't need to spend a whole lot of time thinking about exactly how he hit—beyond trying to imitate Hank Thompson, the machine gunner/Negro Leaguer he had seen playing softball in Dallas—and was blessed in having come out of the gate hitting in Chicago. Batting between .275 and .313 in his first five full seasons in the big leagues kept coaches away from Banks in an era when other young hitters, including future Hall of Famer Lou Brock, would regress from the attention they received.

Banks said he rarely analyzed his swing—although he would occasionally look at videos (home movies, really) to compare his form from one year to another—preferring a "very simple" approach to hitting, as well as everything else in baseball.

"Just hit the ball, catch the ball, throw the ball, run to first," Banks said.

Life was rarely clearer or simpler for Banks than when he settled into the batter's box, 60'6" away from a pitcher armed with a baseball and a lifetime's experience in the many ways to throw it.

"It didn't matter to me about who was pitching," Banks said. "I guess ignorance is bliss. I didn't want to know who was pitching. It was just somebody throwing a ball."

Banks' approach was so simple that it sometimes seemed he wasn't really trying. He sometimes seemed unprepared, which could grate on those who, like Ted Williams, believed that every at-bat was like a prize fight, if not a battle between two armies aligned against each other with certain known strengths and weaknesses.

Rogers Hornsby, one of baseball's greatest hitters, spent two years as one of the Cubs' hitting coaches. Years later, he was still fuming because Banks had once returned to the dugout asking who the pitcher was after twice striking out against Lew Burdette, a veteran All-Star who would be a 20-game winner that season.

Did Banks really not recognize Burdette? Hornsby couldn't believe he had been that lazy, that ignorant.

"If I was managing today, I'd beat the hell out of him," Hornsby said about Banks in a 1963 feature story in the *Saturday Evening Post*. "All these kids in the stands know who's pitching, and here's a guy making $40,000 a year and [he] ain't got the desire to look at the program."[2]

But for Banks, hitting was never about the pitcher. It was about seeing the ball and hitting the ball.

"I asked Willie Mays this one time, 'Willie, what do you think about when you're at the plate?'" said Banks, whose question would later be repeated to Mays by Burns, the filmmaker. "He said, 'I don't think about anything except hitting the ball. That's it.'"

Banks could relate. "That's what I did," he said. "I know pitchers threw curves, change-ups, all that kind of stuff. I didn't pay much attention to it. All I wanted to do is hit the ball."

Lou Brock said that Banks helped him become a hitter. They often discussed hitting when they roomed together, as Brock was learning on the job after being moved to the big leagues too quickly. Banks kept his instruction both simple and positive.

"When you walk up to the plate, there's really only three factors involved— you, the pitcher, and the ball," Banks told Brock. "Once the ball is released, there's only two factors—you and the ball. And hell, Lou, the ball is just a round, hard piece of horsehide, but you are a man with a bat in your hands and good eyes in your head. So whaddaya mean, you 'can't hit Koufax?'"[3]

Knuckleballer Phil Niekro was no different for Banks than facing Bob Gibson, Don Drysdale, Juan Marichal, or another of the power pitchers of that era.

Whether at 99 mph or 59 mph, the baseball was eventually going to pass in front of Banks, who had a soft, almost elegant presence in the right-hander's batting box. If the pitch was over the 17-inch plate above the knees and below the armpits, Banks would reach for it with a swing that was frequently timed perfectly to flick the ball toward the ivy growing on the walls at Wrigley Field.

"I knew how I was going to pitch him, just like he knew what was coming," Niekro said. "You just hoped when you pitched against him you made good, good pitches. You make a mistake on him, you're watching that ball fly into the bleachers."

Monte Irvin, then a teammate of Mays' with the Giants, admired Banks from afar in 1953–55, then played alongside him in '56. He boiled down Banks' greatness as a hitter to five words.

"Good reflexes," he said. "Lightnin-fast reflexes."

Banks doesn't disagree.

"My hitting was just the way I did it," he said as his 80th birthday was approaching. "I picked cotton. I don't know if you know anything about this… [but] I picked cotton when I was quite young. My dad used to take me to the cotton fields, tell me to pick cotton. It taught me how to use my hands. I would grab [as quick as I could to get as much as possible in my sack]. When I started to play baseball, I just had the natural quick hands. That was my extra advantage, my slight edge over anybody else. I had quick hands. I could wait to the last minute and hit the ball. Nobody could understand it. But I had those quick hands which I developed by picking cotton."

Banks was also blessed with fighter-pilot eyesight. It tested at 20/13 when he first joined the Cubs (although it would later become a concern and would always be suspected as an explanation when his batting average dipped).

Banks had a habit of hitting home runs at the points in time when he was the most focused—his first ever game as a semi-pro player with the Amarillo Colts; his first batting-practice swing at Wrigley Field; and twice in his first nine games as a big leaguer. But he did not profile as one of baseball's great power hitters.

"I didn't expect Banks to be a slugger because of his wiry build," said Stan Hack, who managed the Cubs from 1954–56. "The power he gets from that wrist motion—and our tests proving his eyesight is far better than average— explain his ability to lash out a homer at the last minute. But he's so calm and businesslike when he comes back to the bench you couldn't tell whether he hit a homer or struck out."[4]

Banks reportedly weighed only 170 pounds in 1957, which would be the second of his five 40-homer seasons. But future Hall of Famer Robin Roberts said, "From the elbows down, he's got the muscles of a 230-pounder."

Banks knew how to use what he had been given.

"Some fellows have those bulging muscles, and it seems right that they should hit homers," Banks said when he hit for almost unprecedented power in the spring of 1958. "As you can see, I'm not one of those muscle guys. I must concentrate on [timing] and keeping my wrists strong. I can't overpower the ball. I must wait until the last minute and then depend upon my wrists and reflexes to do the trick."[5]

Irvin—whom Banks would refer to as a "father figure"—contributed to Banks' emergence as a power hitter by loaning him his bat during batting practice one day late in the '54 season. It was a Hillerich & Bradsby's Louisville Slugger S-2 model, weighing only 31 ounces and featuring an unusually thin handle.

Banks immediately started driving the ball better than he had been, saying he "found that I could whip it through there better than the 34-ouncer." He placed an order for himself the following spring.

"He loved that bat," Irvin said. "That's when he became really a good pull hitter. It had a big butt and a small handle. He could whip it. He could pull that outside pitch to left field. He was already a good fastball hitter; he became a good curveball hitter, as well."

Strikeouts were a part of Banks' game. He never led the National League in whiffs but did rank in the top 10 three different times (72 in 1955, 85 in '57, and 87 in '58), albeit with pedestrian totals on a scale when compared to Sammy Sosa. Yet he was always confident enough to spit on the first pitch, even if it was a strike.

"Lots of kids are afraid to take a strike to see what the pitcher has," Cavarretta said. "But not Ernie."[6]

Irvin said that Banks would take the first pitch "nine out of 10 times," using it for surveillance purposes. "When you take a strike, you can see what a fastball looks like, what a curveball looks like," Irvin said. "Then when you're ready to offer, you have an idea what the ball is going to do."

As Banks waited for the pitcher to deliver the ball, his fingers were always in motion on the bat handle. He'd hold it between his palms and then constantly grip and ungrip it with his fingers and thumbs, tightening them around the handle only after the pitcher had kicked his leg to start his windup.

"I thought I was Van Cliburn," Banks said. "I was playing the piano."

Banks didn't realize he had developed that habit until television cameras began to focus on his hands, prompting commentary by Jack Brickhouse. Hitting coaches refer to such movements as "triggers" that set a swing into motion, but Banks dismissed his as "one of those unconscious-type movements I made."

Banks did almost no baseball-specific training between seasons.

"I swing a bat for about 15 minutes every day during the winter, and I spend some time squeezing a hard rubber ball," Banks said in a 1958 interview. "It helps keep my fingers loose and strengthens the wrists."[7]

He became a low-handicap golfer while he was with the Cubs but believes he may have benefited from another hobby—handball.

"[Handball] developed my hands, my wrists, my hand-eye coordination, and all of that," Banks said. "In spring training 1958, I hit about 15 home runs. Everybody was looking at me, saying, 'What is this guy doing?' I hit against Warren Spahn. He threw me a screwball outside the plate, and I hit it to left field. After the game he came and said, 'What are you doing? To hit a pitch like that to left field?' I didn't say anything. I just had quick hands. My hands were just quick, naturally quick, from picking cotton."

Banks, a dreamer by nature who could easily crawl into his own world, also had the ability to focus on whatever task he had been given, whether it was picking cotton or hitting in the clutch.

At Wrigley Field, Banks would chatter to everyone he saw before games— teammates, opponents, fans, the Andy Frain ushers, PA man Pat Pieper, and reporters. He grew to know many fans by their names.

"I had a wonderful time playing there," Banks said. "I said, 'Let's play two.' I didn't want to go home. I just loved it, enjoyed it. We didn't draw a lot of people to the ballpark—2,500, 5,000, like that. I knew a lot of the people. I'd get to the ballpark early. 'How you doin' Sara? How you doing Susan? How you doing Carmen?' It was just wonderful. A lot of people brought their children to the park. It was a friendly place. They had Ladies Day every Friday, ladies got in free.

They had senior citizens day. Mr. Wrigley had days for special groups of people. I really enjoyed it."

Once he settled into the batter's box, Banks was like a contestant on *Quiz Show*, seemingly locked away in his personal isolation booth.

Banks says he never lost sight of the crowd surrounding him but tuned them out audibly, hearing little beside an umpire calling balls and strikes and the thump of the ball either into the catcher's mitt or off his bat. "I never heard the crowd," he said. "They call that focusing."

When they played together, Irvin says that Banks, who had married so young, was having trouble maintaining his marriage to Mollye. It was common for such a situation to detract from a player's performance, but Banks seemed to somehow check his troubles at the door.

"He was having some personal problems," Irvin said about the 1956 season. "His marriage was on the rocks, but it never affected his play on the field. He was always happy-go-lucky, let's play two, always upbeat. You never knew he was having a problem."

Banks was also immune to the attempts of pitchers to intimidate him with beanballs and knock-down pitches. "They knock him down, he wouldn't complain," Irvin said. "Go on to first base."

Henry Aaron said that he often hit better after a pitcher had buzzed him. "I had to," Aaron said. "In those days, if the pitchers found out you could be intimidated, you were finished."[8]

Banks' toughness was never in question. He won a job with the Cubs in 1954 after being hospitalized when he was hit in the head by a pitch thrown by minor leaguer Don Elston in an intrasquad game, and said he knows of only three times when a pitcher deliberately hit him. Each time, after being beaned by Jack Sanford, Bob Purkey, and Bob Friend, he hit a home run the next time up.

He had one of the greatest games of his career after Moe Drabowsky beaned him on May 25, 1962, in Cincinnati. This was a Friday night, and Banks was hospitalized until Sunday morning. He traveled with the Cubs to Milwaukee but didn't face Warren Spahn on Monday.

He returned to the lineup Tuesday, smashing three home runs and a double in five at-bats. He came up in the ninth inning with a shot at a four-homer game but grounded to shortstop Roy McMillan. Sadly, but not stunningly, the Cubs somehow lost 11–9.

"It would've been nice if we could've won it," said Banks, who otherwise didn't want to make too much of his sensational return. "I wasn't unconscious like the reports said. I was dazed, but I was conscious.... I've had headaches all along. They come and go. I usually get them when I bend down. I made up my mind when I got to the park today that I could play but still had a little headache. I took two aspirin in the third inning and pretty soon it went away."[9]

Banks did make one adjustment, however. He returned wearing a plastic batting helmet for the first time. He had spent most of his first decade in the majors wearing just a plastic liner under his cap.

Tough game. Tough man.

>> <<

On a summer day in 2010, one of baseball's true nobles was having a breakfast of scrambled eggs and scones at a table in the dining room of a retirement home in Houston. Monte Irvin was talking about baseball, as usual, and at age 91 there was little he had forgotten.

He had certainly not forgotten Leo Durocher. How could anyone forget "The Lip?"

"He was a real good manager," Irvin said. "You wouldn't want your father or your brother to be like him, necessarily, but he was a real good manager. He knew when to give you the needle, when to pat you on the back. He made arguing with an umpire an art. He'd go kick dirt on his shoes. That's when you could talk to an umpire, you could argue with an umpire. Today it's, 'You're out of here.'"

Few players grew to know Durocher better than Irvin. The pride of Abe and Effa Manley's New Jersey Eagles—a man who Negro League owners were pushing to break baseball's color barrier before his stint in the army contributed to that assignment falling to Jackie Robinson—spent seven of his eight major league seasons with the New York Giants, where he would serve as a mentor to Willie Mays and participate in one of the most remarkable season-ending runs in history.

When Irvin and 23-year-old second baseman Hank Thompson arrived at the historic Polo Grounds on July 8, 1949, becoming the Giants' first black players, Durocher welcomed them in a way that Irvin would remember warmly for a lifetime.

"Listen," Durocher barked. "We got a couple of guys who just came in we think can help us win the pennant, maybe a World Series."

Then Durocher turned his look on Irvin and Thompson. "If you can play baseball, I don't care what color you are," he said. "You can be purple and play on this team if you can play good baseball. That's all I'm going to say."

Durocher had plenty of credibility with Irvin and Thompson. He had been supportive of Robinson as his manager with the 1947 Brooklyn Dodgers before Commissioner Happy Chandler hit him with a year-long suspension for associating with gamblers.

Durocher had let the Dodgers' veteran players know that he would not stand for them abusing Robinson, who was treated cruelly by opposing players and many white fans.

"I don't care if the guy is yellow or black or if he has stripes like a zebra," Durocher said. "I'm the manager of this team, and I say he plays."

Durocher respected Robinson for his aggressive play and hustle, paying him a compliment that he would direct toward Ron Santo when he later managed the Cubs. He called Robinson "a Durocher with talent," which to him said an awful lot.

>> <<

Born in West Springfield, Massachusetts, in 1905, Leo Ernest Durocher was only 20 years old when he debuted for the New York Yankees. He spent 17 seasons as a big-league player, changing teams three times along the way. Durocher was a solid shortstop but only a .247 career hitter, which caused Babe Ruth to nickname him "The All-American Out."

To describe Durocher as feisty would be like calling the Grand Canyon massive or to say that Bruce Springsteen is a self-starter. He had been raised poor—his mother was a hotel maid and his father worked in a low-paying job on the railroad—and after going to church every Sunday but never having a Christmas tree in his house, Durocher determined early he was going to make a different life for himself.

Leo worked paper routes and shoveled driveways in his neighborhood. But by his teenage years he had fallen into some regular work that would shape his life. He worked in a pool hall that was in the same building as the barber shop where he went for haircuts every Saturday morning. He cleaned up and prepared the tables for the day ahead and generally found an hour or so where he could shoot pool uninterrupted. He became one of the best players in town and was known as the "house man" by the time he was in high school. Local money backed him against hustlers from out of town. He saved his winnings to buy himself $75 suits, displaying a surprising bit of vanity.

His sense of style and self-confidence, along with a lack of respect for authority, carried over to his baseball, where he was just as precocious as he had been at the pool hall.

Miller Huggins, the Yankees' dugout wizard, had taken an interest in the young Durocher because of his passion and his intelligence, seeing in him the seeds of a future manager. But he certainly wasn't a by-the-books sort of man, angering Yankees management with his outspokenness and habit of bouncing checks, which he used to underwrite a lavish lifestyle and an unquenchable taste for nightlife. He was once accused of stealing a watch that belonged to Babe Ruth.[10]

The young Durocher relished his bigger-than-life persona, helping the Yankees win a World Series in 1928, playing an important role for the Cardinals' "Gashouse Gang" championship team in 1934, and marrying actress Laraine Day after a notorious affair.

Durocher was 33 when the Brooklyn Dodgers named him as a player-manager. He served as a manager for 24 of his next 34 years, winning a pennant in 1941 behind center fielder Pete Reiser and two more pennants after he had moved from the Dodgers to the Giants.

Durocher craved attention and received plenty of it from reporters. He pushed his players hard and staged a daily war with opponents and umpires. Irvin offered a story that explains what it was like to play for him. "We were playing the Reds, and Ewell Blackwell was probably best pitcher in game then," he began. "He was a right-handed Randy Johnson. They had us beat 1–0 in the seventh inning, and Alvin Dark said, 'Leo, maybe if you didn't get on him he wouldn't throw the ball so darn hard.' Leo said, 'That's all right. I know what I'm doing.' He goes out and calls Ewell everything in the book—'You long, tall drink of water, you lucky bastard, you this, you that.' Blackwell got mad and charged Leo, who was coaching third base.

"Next inning Blackwell goes out and got wild. Man on first, man on third, and I'm the hitter. He threw me a fastball inside, and I hit a home run [to the opposite field] down the right field line, 262', hit the foul pole, and we beat 'em 3–1. Leo says, 'See, I told you.' While I was rounding the bases, Blackwell was following me. You just don't hit a home run off Blackwell. If you swung hard he'd knock you down. He said, 'You lucky bastard, you this, you that, you'll never hit another home run off me.' When I crossed home plate I said, 'I might not hit another one, but I hit that one.'

"Now next time we play them I thought he had forgotten about it. He got me 3–0. He hit me here," he said, pointing to his left side, "and the ball came out here [on his right side]. I'm down on the ground, moaning and groaning, and Durocher comes up and says, 'Show 'em up, Monte, don't rub.' I said, 'But Leo, it hurts.' He said, 'Yeah, that's okay.' They worked on me a little bit. I took first base. He hollers out again, 'Show 'em up again, steal it.' I took one step and fell on my face. I was out three weeks—broken ribs."

Durocher's crowning achievement came with the 1951 Giants, who would prompt the best-known call by a baseball announcer, Russ Hodges' immortal "*The Giants win the pennant! The Giants win the pennant!*" That followed Bobby Thomson's home run off Ralph Branca in the bottom of the ninth inning in the deciding game of a three-game playoff against the Dodgers.

Lost in many recollections of that historic playoff was that Durocher somehow guided a team featuring a rookie named Mays into a season-ending tie after trailing the Dodgers by 13 games on August 11. They went 37–7 to the wire, finally catching the Dodgers of Roy Campanella, Duke Snider, Pee Wee Reese, Gil Hodges, and Robinson on the penultimate day of the season.

"Durocher's probably the only manager we could have done that under," Irvin said. "He had unbelievably good luck. Every move he made was the right move. We were playing [the Braves] one night. He took out a hitter who had two strikes on him and put in Bill Rigney. Bill Rigney hit a home run, and we won the ballgame. He pulled the same thing with Sal Yvars—probably the only home run he hit for us. He won a game, you understand. He would always say, 'Just stay close, even though we're behind I'll think of something and we'll be all right.' We'd just say, 'Okay, Leo.'"

Baseball men are superstitious by nature. Durocher would forever believe that the down-the-stretch success of his '51 Giants was preordained because of a spring training visit to a numerologist arranged by Laraine Day and Coach Freddie Fitzsimmons' wife. They sat and listened to the predictions of the woman, which Durocher said he would never forget.

"She told Fred to change the number of his uniform from 6 to 5. And also that he should wear something purple," Durocher said in his autobiography. "And then she got to me. I was going to get off to the worst start I had ever had, she told me, and she was right. We didn't lose our first 11 games, as I keep reading; we won our opener and then lost 11 straight. The first half of the season was going to be so bad, she said, that when I came up to my birthday we would be half a step from falling into last place. She was right. On July 27, we were half a game out of the cellar. After my birthday, she said, things would change and I would go on to have the greatest season of my life and end up winning everything.

"Freddie and I went up, laughing at the girls. How could we have that miserable a start with this good a team? Well, the 11-game streak came to an end when Freddie changed his number and started to wear purple shorts. From there, it was like we were following a script."[11]

Durocher and his editors were a little off on their facts, as often happens in baseball stories. The '51 Giants won two of their first three, then lost 11 in a row to fall to 2–12. They were in last place as late as May 15 but finished that month in fifth place and had climbed to second by June 12. From there on, it was just a question of whether they could catch the Dodgers.

It took until the next-to-last day of the season to do that—tying the standings when Sal Maglie beat Warren Spahn 3–0—and the teams both won on the final day to force a playoff. The rules at the time called for a two-out-of-three playoff. The Giants won the first game at Ebbets Field and came home needing only one more win to complete one of the greatest comebacks ever. But Jackie Robinson and Clem Labine led the Dodgers to a 10–0 win in the second game, and Brooklyn scored three in the top of the eighth in the deciding game to take a 4–1 lead. There was gloom in the Polo Grounds when the Giants came to bat in the bottom of the ninth, three outs away from elimination.

"As I started out of the dugout to go out to the coaching lines, I could see Laraine standing up in her box at the end of the dugout with tears in her eyes," Durocher said. "She shook her fist at me, and I knew she was telling me, 'Don't be down on yourself. You've done a great job, and I want you to walk out of here with your head high.'

"So I stepped back down and waited for the players to come in. 'Fellows, you've done just a hell of a job all year long,' I said. 'I'm proud of every one of you. We've got three whacks at them, boys! It's not over yet. Let's go out there and give them all we got, and let's leave this ball field, win or lose, with our heads in the air.'"[12]

Thomson proved the spring-training seer correct with the "Shot Heard 'Round the World."

>> <<

Durocher managed the Giants through 1955 but then was deemed largely unemployable by major league owners. He worked as a broadcaster and a radio host in addition to time on Walt Alston's Dodgers staff while waiting for another chance to run a team. It came when Phil Wrigley finally decided he was tired of losing.

Herman Franks, who was then managing the San Francisco Giants, had recommended Durocher to the Cubs' John Holland as the perennial doormats searched for a way out of last place. Wrigley agreed to take him on, and the withdrawn owner and the 60-year-old manager began one of the strangest partnerships imaginable.[13]

"I never called him anything except 'Mr. Wrigley,' and he never called me anything except 'Leo' or 'son,'" Durocher said. "That's right, 'son'. Mr. Wrigley is 12 years older than I am, and so if I was 60 in my first year in Chicago, he had to be 72. Still, he could understand that whatever it might say on my birth certificate, in my mind I was 28."[14]

Durocher had been rumored to be on the Cubs' short list for manager as far back as 1956 but he was hardly Wrigley's kind of guy, and the owner dismissed the idea as "ridiculous."[15] But a decade of losing later, the Wrigley family was tiring of criticism over the Cubs' continuing spiral toward irrelevance in the National League.

Durocher's hiring was announced in a news conference at the Pink Poodle, a banquet room at Wrigley Field. Wrigley was at his Lake Geneva home and welcomed the new manager with a press release.

"This is Leo's day," he said in a statement. "There is no immediate announcement as to Durocher's title. We have found from long experience that it doesn't make any difference what title a team leader has as long as he has the ability to take charge. We have a man whose record shows he knows how to take charge."

Durocher, however, had a quick answer when a reporter asked about his title.

"I just gave myself a title—manager—not head coach," he said, officially putting Wrigley's College of Coaches era in the rear-view mirror.

When a reporter asked whether Durocher or Holland would be making trades, Durocher had another quick answer. "It'll be a 50-50 thing," he said, grabbing half of Holland's authority.

Durocher was clear about his mission. "I know the Cubs have been second division," he said. "That's why I'm here. I'm gonna change things around here. If my own brother is on this club, and I've got somebody better, then I'd tell my own brother, 'Go home! We can't use you!' I won't be running any popularity contests."[16]

Catcher Randy Hundley, acquired from the Giants shortly after Durocher's hiring, has a clear recollection of Durocher's arrival as the man in charge. He said players were intimidated by Durocher's reputation for a sharp tongue and willingness to hold others accountable, and that Durocher only underscored that in a meeting early in spring training during 1966.

"The first thing he did, he kept [former manager, current front office man] Charlie Grimm from coming into the clubhouse and being around the players," Hundley said. "He reamed him out. And then he got all over Ernie Banks. The point was that he was showing everybody who was the boss. He was going to be the boss, and it was going to be his way, period, 'and don't fool with me because I'm serious about it, and this is the way it's going to be.' And that toughened the ballclub up, and from there it began to go from a country club to, 'Hey, we're going to play with a Leo Durocher–type attitude on this club, or else we'll see you later.'"[17]

In Durocher's first season, the Cubs did what they had become accustomed to doing—they went backward, going 59–103 to finish last.

"That first year under Leo, we finished tenth, but we started playing Leo's brand of baseball," second baseman Glenn Beckert said. "He wanted to get that losing attitude out of there, that .500 attitude. And he made us believe in ourselves. He ran the team like we were men. He said, 'You're all mature guys. I'm not going to lay down any rules. I'll lay the rules at the ballpark. You're mature enough to learn what you should do on the outside.' He put the responsibility on the players for their conduct.

"Every now and then he'd run a room check, but it was a very loose room check, if you know what I mean. Spring training was great once the team got together. He said, 'Okay, men.' He never called us boys—it was, 'Men, here's what we have to do individually to get in shape.' He taught us to be responsible. But he was tough on that field, man. You better play your ass off and give 120 percent on that field or you're history."[18]

There was little tougher duty than being a part-time player for Durocher. "Leo liked veterans, didn't have patience with rookies, couldn't stand mediocrity," said Gene Oliver, who was a backup catcher and utility man with the Cubs. "Leo is such an intimidating person, and he can belittle you so easily and make you feel so inferior, you learn to play in fear when you play for Leo Durocher.... You knew he'd rip you behind your back. He'd rip you to your face.... If you were an extra man who produced, Leo loved you, but if you were unproductive, he could bury you, too. Leo could do it verbally. I have to be candid—he could embarrass his extra men."[19]

Oliver recalled one time when Durocher singled out Lee Thomas for humiliation. "We were trailing with Kess [Don Kessinger] coming up," Oliver said. "Pete Reiser, one our coaches, was sitting there, and Leo said to Pete, 'Get me Lee Thomas.' So Pete said, 'Lee, get a bat.' Lee got his helmet, his bat, his resin, the pine tar, and he went out to the on-deck circle. Here was Lee within earshot, and Leo said to Reiser, 'Why am I going to hit that fucker? He's going to go up there, and he's going to jerk the first two pitches foul, and the third one he's going to foul straight up in the goddamned infield.' Now Lee could hear this. As fate would have it, he stood in there, foul, strike one; foul, strike two; and Leo says, 'Heeeeere it comes,' and just as Leo predicted, Lee hit it right up the chute.

"So Mad Dog came in, and he was hot because he had heard Leo second-guessing him, and our bats were right in front of Leo. Mad Dog intended to take his bat and swing at the bats in the rack and break all the handles off the bats, and he swung and missed, and Leo said, 'Jesus Christ, you can't even hit anything that's sitting still.'"[20]

Oliver rarely played as a backup to Randy Hundley.

"I was sleeping on the bench one day, 'cause I knew Randy was going to catch, when we had another pinch-hit situation," Oliver said. "I was kind of dozing, and we were trailing, and all of a sudden Leo yelled, 'Ollie, get a bat.' Christ almighty, I ran and got my helmet, and I started to walk up the steps to go to the on-deck circle, and I thought I was going to hit for Hundley. Leo said, 'Where are you going?' I said, 'Don't you want me to hit for Hundley?' He said, 'No. Hundley cracked his bat. He needs another one.' That's how cruel he was. Oh, man."[21]

>> <<

Durocher's nasty, sometimes cruel nature could carry over even to franchise icons.

Banks was well on his way to the Hall of Fame by 1966, of course, having won the back-to-back MVP awards in 1958 and '59 while showing that a player could be both agile enough to play shortstop and powerful enough to hit 40-plus home runs. But age and a series of knee injuries had taken a toll, pushing Banks to first base, where he would eventually play more games than he did at shortstop.

Rather than praise Banks for his long career and continuing run production, his willingness to play through injuries, and his quiet leadership style in the clubhouse, Durocher chafed because he didn't have as much range as younger first basemen and had become a station-to-station runner on the bases, often having to be held at third base on singles to the outfield.

Durocher never seemed to know what to do with Banks or how to handle him. In his memoirs, the Lip summed up his experience with Banks in two neat sentences.

"He was a great player in his time. Unfortunately his time wasn't my time."

In *Nice Guys Finish Last*, the 1975 book written with Ed Linn, Durocher pulled no punches about Banks. He said that one of the first things he had done after getting to know the situation in Chicago was to convince Phil Wrigley that the Cubs would be better off if they traded Banks and Ron Santo.

"I gave Mr. Wrigley the whole routine about, 'Our arrow is going down. What we have to do is reverse the arrow,'" he said. "What he had to do, I felt, was trade Banks and Santo for some young players who would turn our arrow around and get it pointed upward."

Durocher didn't get his way—instead he built the Cubs' most consistently successful team since the 1930s around Banks and Santo along with Billy Williams and Fergie Jenkins.

"I couldn't trade either of them," Durocher said. "I couldn't trade Banks because he was a civic monument in Chicago, and Mr. Wrigley's favorite. I couldn't trade Santo because nobody would give us anything for him that wouldn't have looked like a joke to Chicago fans. So I tried to get my young players by trading Billy Williams. I still shudder whenever I think about it."[22]

Durocher loved the potential of Houston's young third baseman, Doug Rader, a Chicago native who had started his life in an orphanage run by the Children's Home and Aid Society. He tried to get him in a trade for Santo but said Astros GM Spec Richardson "just laughed at me." He did not have as much flexibility with Banks.[23]

"Where Banks was concerned, I could never get permission to even try to trade him," Durocher said. "Except for once, very briefly, after I had been there for three years. And even then, not really. During spring training, Mr. Holland said in the course of a casual conversation, 'You can trade any player on this team if you think it will improve us, and you have Mr. Wrigley's permission.' I took that to include Ernie Banks. Within the week, I was told it didn't. Ernie was too popular with fans."[24]

Durocher took Banks' consistent run production for granted, unable to see beyond the physical limitations that Banks had after more than two decades of giving everything he had.

"As a player, by the time I got there, there was nothing wrong with Ernie that two new knees wouldn't have cured," Durocher said. "He'd come up with men on the bases and if he hit a ground ball they could walk through the double play. To do me any good he'd have had to hit 70 home runs and knock in 2,000 runs. In the field he was very good at one thing. I never saw anybody who could dig a thrown ball out of the dirt any better. But that was where it ended. If the ball wasn't hit right at him, forget it. He'd wave at it. Two feet away from him?

Whoops—right under his glove. But did anybody in Chicago ever write that Mr. Cub couldn't get off a dime? Never. Criticizing Ernie Banks doesn't sell papers; the best it's going to get you is a ton of abuse.

"I'd tell Holland and Wrigley, 'He can't do it anymore. I love him as well as you do. I love him as much as the fans do. But I've got to have someone there who can play. Balls are going by there this far that should be outs or double plays.'"

Durocher saw failings in Banks that were routinely overlooked by sympathetic fans and sportswriters. "He couldn't run, he couldn't field; toward the end, he couldn't even hit," Durocher said. "There are some players who instinctively do the right thing on the base paths. Ernie had an unfailing instinct for doing the wrong thing. But I had to play him. Had to play the man or there would have been a revolution in the street."[25]

Durocher claimed that Banks consistently missed signals from the third-base coach. It got so bad, he said, that he had to simplify them for the perennial All-Star. "With every other player, we had the usual signs—an indicator followed by a combination," Durocher said. "With Ernie, we had to have flash signs. One sign. Like the Little League. 'Ernie, you're always hitting unless we flash something at you.'"[26]

Durocher had been used to being the biggest name on the teams he managed, even when he had players like Jackie Robinson and Willie Mays. It was clear to everyone that he resented Banks' relationship with Chicago reporters, especially Jim Enright of the *Chicago American* and *Chicago Today*.

"How does he do it? You could say about Ernie that he never remembered a sign or forgot a newspaperman's name," Durocher said. "All he knew was, 'Ho, let's go. Ho, babydoobedoobedoo. It's a wonderful day for a game in Chicago. Let's play twoooo.' We'd get on the bus and he'd sit across from the writers. 'A beaooootiful day for twoooo.' It could be snowing outside. 'Let's play three.'

"I don't know why it is, but where Ernie is concerned everybody [was] always ready to fall over and play dead.... His time wasn't my time. Even more unfortunately, there was not a thing I could do about it. Ernie Banks owns Chicago. He's Mr. Cub. All the players on the Cubs have said it themselves. Ernie Banks could come to bat and make a gesture telling everyone in the grandstand where they could go, and they'd rise up as a man and give him a standing ovation."[27]

10

JUNE

A must-see sensation in Chicago since the Opening Day fireworks from Ernie Banks and Willie Smith, the Cubs went national in early June with a spread in *Sports Illustrated* with Ron Santo gracing the cover. The story by Robert H. Boyle ran 3,886 words, about twice as many as Martin Luther King Jr.'s "I Have a Dream" speech, and joyfully told the Cubs' story with everything except Banks delivering a punchy ending.

Given the baseball struggle Banks had endured, it wouldn't have been hard to picture him shouting, "First place at last! First place at last! Thank God Almighty, we are in first place at last!"

The *Sports Illustrated* treatise was required reading all around Chicago and on farms scattered throughout the Midwest. Because of its length, however, some teenage boys were using squirreled-away flashlights to finish after their lights-out time.

Boyle didn't just speak to the usual suspects during his stay in Chicago. He even sought out backup catcher Gene Oliver, a 10-year veteran who had played on five different teams. "This is the finest piece of baseball machinery I've ever seen," Oliver told the reporter. "It's a fantastic, synchronized mechanism."

Boyle, like Oliver, spared neither simile nor metaphor to tell America about Chicago's new darlings. He wrote:

> *To anyone accustomed to what used to be known around Chicago as "the friendly confines of Wrigley Field," the screams of the*

Bleacher Bums and the winning ways of the Cubs must come as a shock. For years the Cubs and Wrigley Field symbolized Chicago's aspirations to respectability. In a city with more than its share of gangsters, ward-heeling politicians, and numbers runners, the Cubs appeared as so many bishops of the Protestant Episcopal Church and Wrigley Field was Chicago's answer to the Boston Athenaeum. One could lay claim to gentility by rooting for the Cubs. There was a certain air of snobbishness even about going to Wrigley Field. The Mob might dump a dozen bodies in the Chicago River, the cops could shake down motorists on the Outer Drive, and the stink from the stockyards could corrode any sinus in town, but all was right in Chicagoland as long as the Cubs played daylight ball in ivied Wrigley Field and took yet another pasting. They knew how to lose nobly, like Adlai Stevenson.

But Wrigley Field has changed. The Bleacher Bums and fans yell and scream. The Cubs look like a winner. They bunt, they take the extra base, they hit home runs. Their manager is Leo "The Lip" Durocher, who, a dozen years ago, was considered too rambunctious for the job by Phil Wrigley, the Cub owner. The Cubs have a truly exciting team. Suddenly a number of younger players—Don Kessinger, a brilliant shortstop, second baseman Glenn Beckert, catcher Randy Hundley, pitcher Ken Holtzman—are coming into their own, and the old standbys—Ernie Banks, Ron Santo, and Billy Williams—are on their way to knocking in 100 runs apiece. The bullpen of Ted Abernathy, Phil Regan, and Hank Aguirre is among the best in baseball. Spurred on by Durocher and buoyed by the Bums, the Cubs are doing a job.[1]

The Bleacher Bums really didn't need national encouragement. They were in the process of becoming semi-celebrities around Chicago, identifiable both by the yellow helmets they wore and the viral treatment they gave visiting left fielders.

They verbally harassed opposing players, sometimes using racial, ethnic, and sexual slurs—for instance, Cincinnati's Pete Rose was razzed and teased with cries of "Rose is a fairy, Rose is a fairy." But the issue that made Wrigley Field a place that teams didn't want to visit was the one that had been raised by Philadelphia's Ron Stone on Opening Day. Fans were throwing things at players, and nobody seemed to be doing anything about it.

When the frustrated Cardinals visited for a four-game series, Lou Brock became a target. He had an orange roll between his legs as he awaited one pitch and a battery whiz past his ear in another slow moment. As he made a leaping, one-handed catch of a Don Young line drive, an apple flew past his head.

St. Louis pitcher Mudcat Grant was struck in the face by a hard rubber ball in the bullpen, and he retaliated by firing baseballs into the bleachers. "Somebody's gonna get hurt out here, and it's too bad," Brock said. "The Cubs are going great, but the fans may spoil it."[2]

Durocher had never walked away from a fight or even a riot. Unlike the tempered comments by Dusty Baker and Moises Alou after the Steve Bartman mess in 2003 when Wrigley Field fans turned on the fan who got in Alou's way chasing a foul pop in Game 6 of the NLCS, Durocher did nothing to try to restore order at Wrigley.

In fact, he did what he could to help create a daily frenzy.

Dick Selma, who had only recently arrived from San Diego, had headed from the bench to the left-field clubhouse to use the bathroom late in a game on May 14. The Padres were leading 2–1 when he headed back to the dugout for the bottom of the ninth.

"You could hear a pin drop," Selma said. "Absolutely no noise. So I scream up to the bleachers, 'Start yellin!' and I start waving my arms. Well, the next thing I know, Ernie Banks hits a home run and the place explodes."

Banks' game-tying homer off a 36-year-old Johnny Podres (who would retire a month later) set the stage for Willie Smith's game-winning single four batters later. Durocher had looked toward the bleachers after the eruption when Banks went to the plate, seeing Selma serve as a spontaneous conductor. A light bulb went off in his head.

"The next day I'm back in the dugout, which is where I like to sit because I can check information with the hitters," Selma said. "But Leo makes me go down into the bullpen. 'Get those Bums goin', he yells, so I go down and start waving a towel around. From then on, when I wasn't pitching, that was my job."[3]

On June 22, Durocher had a similar interaction with Santo. The Cubs were on the verge of losing a second straight game to the Expos before a two-run single by Banks and a two-run homer by Jim Hickman, both with two outs. A 6–3 deficit had been transformed into a 7–6 victory, and Santo was so thrilled that he did his own little celebration as he headed into the clubhouse to get ready for the second game of a doubleheader.

"I was always an emotional player," Santo said. "I carried my emotions on my sleeve. I ran down the left-field line to our clubhouse and didn't realize I had clicked my heels. That night it was all over television. The next day, when I got to the ballpark, Leo Durocher called [me into his office for] a meeting. He says, 'Can you click your heels again? We ought to make that our victory kick, but only at home when we win.'

"So from that moment on, when we won at home, I would run down toward our clubhouse doing it. The fans really got into it. I actually got telephone calls from friends on other teams saying, 'Our pitchers don't like that.' My response to them was, 'Too bad.' I ended up getting knocked down a lot, but it didn't matter."[4]

No team would take the heel clicking as personally as the Mets.

"We didn't think much of that," Nolan Ryan said. "In those days, people just didn't do those kinds of things."

>> <<

Twenty-two games over .500 on June 14, the Cubs were basking in the limelight. One of the daily visitors to the Wrigley Field clubhouse was Jack Childers. His Skokie, Illinois–based company, Talent Network, Inc., had become an unofficial promotional arm of the players.

Childers had used a friendship with Banks and Ron Santo to get a meeting with Phil Regan, the Cubs' player representative. Childers pitched his plan to manufacture items like Cub Power T-shirts, posters, and autographed balls, and also to run a clearinghouse for paid player appearances with him taking 15 percent of the revenue and the rest going to the players to be split equally.

"Regan loved it," Childers would later tell Rick Talley. "He saw it as a 'one-for-all, all-for-one' endeavor [that] would help draw the players together. Instead of the superstars like Santo and Banks making all of the money and being deluged with requests they couldn't handle, this plan would include everybody and take away some of the pressure, which would surely grow."

Childers met with the team before a game in May, and by June he had free run of the clubhouse. His endeavors would eventually bring most of the players about $4,000, which was a lot for the rank-and-file guys making near the $10,000 minimum.

When International Harvester wanted to manufacture a Cubs tractor, Childers involved Regan and Hickman in promotional activities, with both of the players getting free tractors from the deal. He once hired an armored truck to carry autographed baseballs from Wrigley Field to area Walgreens stores, with TV coverage as players loaded balls into the Brinks truck.[5]

Durocher and GM John Holland did little, if anything, to slow down the players' exploiting the team's early success. "The team was starting to lose sight of things," Coach Joey Amalfitano told Talley in 1989 for the book *The Cubs of '69*. "Instead of looking down the road, we were looking at the end of our noses."

Childers' lasting contribution would be a recording of "Hey, Hey, Holy Mackerel," with Willie Smith and the two Olivers (Gene and backup second baseman Nate Oliver) providing some of the vocals. It played through the night at Ray's Bleachers, with its simple chorus becoming the team's war cry.

> *Hey, hey, holy mackerel*
> *No doubt about it*
> *The Cubs are on their way*
> *They've got the hustle*
> *They've got the muscle*
> *The Chicago Cubs are on their way... Hey, Hey.*

≫ ≪

Phil Wrigley was one of the few people in Chicago not visibly caught up in Cub Mania. He was never seen at the ballpark, instead watching games on a television at his office in the Wrigley Building. He had almost never sat in his family box at the ballpark, as he didn't enjoy the attention, but Banks said that during the lean years he'd see Wrigley wandering the bleachers during games.

By 1969, Wrigley said he hadn't been to a game in three years. "I just get so nervous, and I've gotten to be a pretty old man, you know," said Wrigley, then 74. "You get pretty good coverage on television."[6]

Wrigley worked in his office Monday-Friday but spent the weekends at his estate at Lake Geneva—there he was generally too busy to bother watching games. This was the summer that he personally dug postholes for some new fencing, about 5,000 in all.

Wrigley said he celebrated all victories with a highball, and that when the Cubs lost he suffered "quietly, in my insides." He was rooting for his team to win it all, of course, but said he did not plan to attend the games if the team reached the World Series.

>> <<

Durocher, married three times previously but single since 1960, couldn't wait to wed his fiancée, Lynne Walker Goldblatt. They had become engaged only in early May but scheduled the ceremony for June 19, a Thursday when the Cubs were off, at the Ambassador West Hotel.

The plan was for Durocher to manage a series in Pittsburgh Monday-Wednesday, tie the knot on Thursday, and be back at work Friday afternoon at Wrigley Field. But when the Cubs got to Forbes Field for the Wednesday game, having lost four one-run games in the previous three days, there was no Durocher. He had caught a flight to Chicago that morning, apparently so he wouldn't miss the rehearsal dinner, and made his own travel plans rather than going through the team's traveling secretary, as was the protocol.

There was confusion in the clubhouse, and ultimately Coach Pete Reiser was put in charge of the team. When reporters called Holland to ask what happened to Durocher, he didn't try to hide his surprise. "If he isn't with the club," he said, "I don't know where he is."

The Cubs lost in 10 innings that day, with Reiser's questionable calls getting Al Spangler (who had stolen two bases since 1965) and Don Young thrown out stealing in the same inning. Wrigley seemed as befuddled as Holland by his manager's arrogant disappearance, but instead of confronting Durocher, Wrigley merely congratulated him at the wedding.

Ernie Banks takes a full swing at Ebbets Field in Brooklyn, New York. This photo was taken in late August 1955 when Banks was among the league's home run leaders. He finished the season with 44 homers. (AP IMAGES)

Ernie Banks holds his bat and the game ball after homering off the Cardinals' Lindy McDaniel on September, 19, 1955, in St. Louis, Missouri. It was the fifth bases-loaded home run of that breakout season for Banks (and his 44th homer overall), breaking the previous season record of four grand slams, which had been done 10 times previously. (AP IMAGES)

National League president Warren Giles (left) presented Ernie Banks with the first of his consecutive MVP awards on May 18, 1959, at Wrigley Field. The plaque is known as the Kenesaw Mountain Landis Memorial Baseball Award after one of baseball's early commissioners. (AP IMAGES)

Ernie Banks (right) received two awards on January 18, 1959, at the Diamond Dinner sponsored by the Chicago chapter of the Baseball Writers Association of America. Jim Enright of the *Chicago American* presented Banks with the Will Harridge plaque for achievement of the year and the award for Chicago player of the year. (AP IMAGES)

An agile shortstop, Ernie Banks leaped over Gino Cimoli (22) of the St. Louis Cardinals while throwing to first to complete a double play. (AP IMAGES)

Still hoping to rally after being passed by the Mets, Ernie Banks delivers a single to center field off St. Louis' Bob Gibson on September 19, 1969. It was the 2,500th hit of his Hall of Fame career, but like too many others this hit came with no one on base, and the inning ended with Banks stranded on third base. (AP IMAGES)

"Mr. Cub" Ernie Banks in April 1969. (AP IMAGES/RHH)

Ernie Banks still enjoys getting on the field to play ball and has made several appearances at the All-Star Legends & Celebrities softball game. The exhibition game is played annually as part of baseball's All-Star break on the day before the Home Run Derby. Above: U.S. Olympic team softball player Jennie Finch shows Banks her underhand pitching motion before the game started at Comerica Park on Sunday, July 10, 2005. (AP IMAGES/AMY SANCETTA) Below: Football Hall of Famer Jerry Rice holds the game's MVP award as he poses with Banks after the July 8, 2007, game at AT&T Park in San Francisco. (AP IMAGES/KEVORK DJANSEZIAN)

Hall of Famer Ernie Banks poses with his newly unveiled statue in front of Wrigley Field during ceremonies on Monday, March 31, 2008. (AP IMAGES/CHARLES REX ARBOGAST)

"I don't like the way that Leo walked away from the team without saying anything in advance," Wrigley said. "But we'll just have to forgive him this time."[7]

More than 200 relatives and friends attended the wedding, which lost its maximum luster when Frank Sinatra couldn't get out of his engagement in Las Vegas to attend. The entire Cubs' team attended, which had to be awkward. It would have been more so had "the next Willie Mays" been there, but Adolfo Phillips had been traded to Montreal a week earlier.

Phillips, who didn't start any games in his last two weeks with the Cubs, shook hands with everyone after the trade except Durocher, who he said hadn't talked to him in a month.[8]

Broadcaster Jack Brickhouse was notably absent from the Durocher nuptials. "Leo never invites me to his weddings," he cracked.[9]

>> <<

Gil Hodges had no weddings on his calendar. He was focused on a team that was still sputtering just before Memorial Day, with an 18–23 record that would have been worse if not for Seaver's 6–3 start.

While Durocher attended to last-minute details and Childers made money for himself and the Cubs' players, striking while the proverbial iron was hot, the team with a five-man starting rotation, deep bullpen, and rotating regulars found itself. Jerry Koosman threw 10 shutout innings in a 1–0, 11-inning victory over the Padres on May 28, and the Mets went on an 11-game winning streak.

On June 15, Johnny Murphy and Whitey Herzog made an important move, acquiring power-hitting first baseman Donn Clendenon from Montreal. Bud Harrelson, the shortstop, saw him as a piece that the team had been missing.

"For the first time we had the kind of player who could hit three-run homers," Harrelson said. "If we were losing a game by two runs, we suddenly had a winning chance."[10]

The Mets quickly won seven times in a stretch of eight games, climbing to 38–28, only five games behind the Cubs, after sweeping the Phillies in a June 24 doubleheader. Seaver won the opener 2–1, raising his record to 11–3. The team's confidence seemed to grow with each win. "The sense was, 'We're in this, we're beating people we never beat before,'" Harrelson said. "And suddenly we're watching teams play against us, making the mistakes that the Mets always used to make—mistakes that we were no longer making."11

>> <<

Banks was friendly toward everyone, but some fellow players counted as good friends, like Lou Brock. Roberto Clemente was another. They had been playing against each other since 1955, when Clemente arrived in Pittsburgh, and they had bonded together in the National League clubhouse at All-Star games.

Banks was among those who felt Clemente was cheated out of the MVP award in 1960, when Pirates shortstop Dick Groat won after winning a batting title even though Clemente (who inexplicably finished eighth, four spots behind Banks) scored more runs than Groat and drove in almost twice as many. Banks told Clemente that he should have been the one to end his run of back-to-back MVPs. Clemente treasured that show of respect.

Banks once visited Puerto Rico on an off-season vacation. He had not told Clemente he was coming, but word spread that Mr. Cub was staying at a San Juan hotel. Clemente phoned Banks and insisted that he come to his house on the top of a hill in nearby Rio Piedras for a visit. His home was a source of pride for Clemente, as it had been designed by a famed local engineer, Libertario Aviles, and it had an unusual openness and a series of trademark features, including Aztec symbols on the bricks and a bridged walkway leading from the street over a series of shallow ponds to the front door.[12] Its view down the hill and toward the Atlantic was as spectacular as the view of the Pacific from Willie Mays' home in San Francisco.

Vera Clemente, Roberto's wife, prepared a special meal—roasted pig, Banks could still recall four decades later—and the two families had a relaxing evening together that was as memorable as it was spontaneous.

The evening meant a lot to both men.

"He was an amazing person," Banks said. "A very smart guy.... I wanted to help him a lot. He was a right fielder and didn't get a lot of publicity. We had Hank Aaron playing right field and some of the great right fielders. Willie Mays playing center. They didn't give him a lot of credit for what he could do and the way he could play. He was a tremendous baseball player."

When Banks talked to Clemente, he did not "jabber," as one fellow Hall of Famer had described his conversational style. They could conduct serious conversations, seeking genuine insight from each other.

Banks would do that when the Cubs visited Pittsburgh in mid-June. He asked Clemente if this was the year the Cubs were finally going to win.

Clemente pondered the question and then gave a long thoughtful reply, emphasizing the large number of question marks he felt the team had.

"You have some very good pitchers, but you need more. It is a long season, and Leo Durocher will wear them out. You have too many players who have not played under the kind of pressure you will face in August and September," Clemente said, noting that only former Dodger Phil Regan had played on championship teams and naming center fielder Don Young and middle infielders Don Kessinger and Glenn Beckert as guys who could not be counted on at crunch time. Groat and Bill Mazeroski had been rock-solid for Pittsburgh in '60, and Beckert was no Mazeroski at the top of his game, much less battling injuries as he had been this season.

Pittsburgh swept the Cubs in that series, including one-run victories in a doubleheader sweep on June 17, as Banks slipped back into another mini-slump. He had homered twice in Cincinnati on the second leg of a three-city trip but then went 2-for-18, playing only as a pinch hitter in the second game of the doubleheader.

Banks, already obligated to do interviews for Jack Brickhouse on the Cubs' pregame show, had started writing a weekly column for the *Tribune* earlier that month. He promised in the first installment that he was going to write "through rose-colored glasses" because there's enough trouble in the world without looking for "hassles" in baseball.

"When I come to the ballpark, I leave all the world's troubles and mine behind," Banks said. "I enjoy baseball so much, and the enthusiasm of the fans, that I'd be happy to stay nights in Wrigley Field if they'd roll out a cot for me near first base."[13]

But with the biggest season of his life not even half over, Banks had begun bringing baseball home with him. Rather than enjoying the view from the top, he was waiting for the other shoe to drop.

When Rick Talley interviewed Ken Holtzman for his book *The Cubs of '69*, Holtzman remembered a conversation with Banks from the series in Pittsburgh.

"It was late after a game, and I was walking down the corridor, and Ernie Banks called me into his room," Holtzman said. "Ernie and I were very close. 'Kenny,' he said after we had a few drinks, 'we had a nine-game lead, and we're not going to win it.' This hit me hard. This was Ernie Banks talking, and he was saying we weren't going to win. So I looked at him and said, 'Why?'

"'Because we've got a manager and three or four players who are out there waiting to get beat,' Ernie said. He told me right to my face. I'll never forget it. It was the most serious and sober statement I'd ever heard from Ernie Banks. And you know what? He was right."[14]

11

It's Okay to Be Black
If You're Willie Mays

E rnie Banks was a member of arguably the greatest team of all-time.
This is true, even if it seems it can't be given his career-long tie to the
Chicago Cubs. He played shortstop for Willie Mays' All-Stars, a team of black
major leaguers that traveled throughout mostly southern cities to provide a
second income in an era when baseball salaries were small enough that players
needed off-season jobs. Teams had been built around Jackie Robinson and then
Roy Campanella but Mays, who had won a batting title and an MVP Award in
1954, moved into the headliner role after his 51-homer season in '55.

They played the best local teams in the areas they visited, frequently the
remnants from the dying Negro Leagues. They officially split the gate receipts
between the teams, but the opponents usually received only 10 percent and a
shot at bragging rights at the local tavern. The six-week tour in '55 earned the big
leaguers an estimated $3,500 apiece—about half of what each of them would
have received for the six-month major league season.[1]

As the BoDeans sang, it was good work, if you could get it.

How good was the team that Mays put together? It had one more Hall
of Fame outfielder than it could play, for starters. Mays played center field,
employing the same reckless style that allowed him to run down Vic Wertz's
long fly ball at the Polo Grounds in the '54 World Series. He was flanked by
Henry Aaron in right field and a combination of Larry Doby and Monte Irvin
in left.

Campanella caught, and the infield around Banks included Junior Gilliam, Joe Black, and Big George Crowe, who was a year removed from a celebrated 34-homer 128 RBI season at Triple A Toledo. Don Newcombe, who would go 47–12 for the Dodgers in the season before and after the tour, and Sam "Toothpick" Jones, fresh off an All-Star season and no-hitter for the Cubs, were the 1–2 combination on the mound. Their load was lightened by the lesser known Brooks Lawrence, who would win 19 games for Cincinnati the following year.

Traveling in cars, with Aaron riding in Mays' Cadillac at the head of the convoy, the All-Stars cut a swath across America. They started in New York, drove south through the Carolinas and into Georgia, then southwest to Texas and all the way to Southern California. They drove by day and obliterated the competition by night.

Mays played so hard that at one point Irvin, his longtime teammate in New York, lectured him to be careful not to do anything that would affect him when the '56 season began. "Willie was playing his usual reckless game, and Monte reminded him to take it easy, that his career with the Giants was more important," Banks said. "Willie said, 'This is the only way I can play.'"[2]

Almost every night the opponent was sadly overmatched, but baseball is a sport where the best team doesn't always win. Sometimes you run into a pitcher having the night of his life, sometimes you hit line drives right at fielders. Fatigue is sometimes a factor and would have figured to be a major obstacle for wandering players who operated on the theory that sleep is overrated.

Yet the Willie Mays All-Stars went 28–0 that fall, stopped only by five rainouts. "I don't think it would have mattered who we played," Aaron said. "That might have been the best team ever assembled."[3]

Aaron, an Alabama native like Mays, was with Mays when he went shopping for clothes in a Birmingham men's store. The clerk was about to call the police after Mays pulled a roll of $100 bills out of his pocket at the cash register, but all was forgotten when Mays identified himself.

Mays never mentioned the incident, but Aaron has laughed about it through the years, saying the moral is it was okay to be black as long as you were Willie Mays.[4]

Ballparks filled with crowds to see the All-Stars, most of whom were just names in box scores and radio reports, as this was before the TV age. A game in Longview, Texas, had to be delayed as local officials worked to find ways to accommodate an oversized crowd. In all, more than 100,000 fans, mostly African Americans, watched the '55 tour.[5]

Barnstorming was in Banks' blood. He loved hanging around with his peers, and he never forgot what Jackie Robinson had done for him with the invitation to join the Indianapolis Clowns for games against the Robinson All-Stars after 1950, his first year with the Monarchs.

"It was a real joy to me, a lot of fun," Banks said. "I learned a lot from these guys, what they did."

Banks felt a debt because players like Robinson, Doby, and Campanella had encouraged him about his ability. He always felt that Doby and Robinson were behind the letters he had received from the Dodgers and Indians when he was in the army, offering him a chance to try out.

"They all said one thing to me, 'Ernie you can play in the major leagues, we're going to recommend you,'" he said. "I thought they were kidding, but they did. Recommended me to the owners, managers of their teams. I went into the army, and they were waiting when I came out—Jackie Robinson, Campy, Larry Doby, all of them. They were friendly. They wanted to see me and other young black players make it to the major leagues."

Banks would never need more than an invitation to pack up for another month of baseball after the Cubs' season. He was there for another Mays-led team in '56—this time with Frank Robinson joining the cast of stars—and again it was like the Harlem Globetrotters vs. the Washington Generals. The All-Stars stretched their winning streak to 49 before a loss in Victoria, Texas, when Mays was sidelined by a shoulder he had hurt the night before in an awkward slide.[6]

Barnstorming was delivering severely diminished returns. With more games on television and the novelty of black big leaguers wearing off—as well as the team lacking Brooklyn players, who were favored by the southern blacks that had embraced Jackie Robinson—there were empty ballparks and tight wallets from '56 through '60, when Aaron, Robinson, and Banks trudged through a tour minus Mays, who had gone to Japan with the Giants. That team lost money, and there would be no tour in '61.[7]

But the end of barnstorming didn't mean an end to the bond that had been built between the pioneers—hardly.

For Banks and the other African Americans on National League teams, the All-Star Game became an annual opportunity to be on a field together. There were blacks in both leagues, but teams in the American League were not as successful in signing stars from the Negro Leagues or finding younger counterparts elsewhere.

Banks played in his first All-Star Game at Milwaukee's County Stadium in 1955. The cast of African Americans on the NL team included Aaron, Mays, Campanella, Newcombe, and Banks' teammates Gene Baker and Toothpick Jones, and they looked cooked after six innings, trailing 5–0. But Mays started a two-run rally off Whitey Ford in the seventh, and singles by Aaron and Mays contributed to a three-run inning in the eighth, tying the score. The NL won on Stan Musial's leadoff homer in the 12th.

Banks played in 13 All-Star Games and went home a loser only four times. Most years, every third NL All-Star was black, while Yankees catcher Elston Howard (a former roommate of Banks' with the Kansas City Monarchs) was the only African American perennial All-Star in the AL. In the black community, it is not seen as a coincidence that the National League won 19-of-20 All-Star Games from 1963–82.

In a story that appeared in *Ebony* magazine, Aaron claimed the NL was driven by a "spiritual" motivation. He addressed the same theme in his autobiography.

"The All-Star Game meant a lot to us because the big difference between the National League and the American League was that we had the black players.... So it was a matter of pride with us. And we always knew we would win," he wrote. "When people talk nowadays about the National League's domination of the All-Star Game [in that era], they usually say that the National League always seemed to take the game more seriously. But they don't say why. Willie and Ernie and I know why."[8]

>> «

Lou Brock knew he was fast. He wasn't so sure about strong.

The seventh of nine children, Brock was born in El Dorado, Arkansas, and grew up in Collinston, Louisiana, where his mother and others in her family worked as share croppers on a cotton plantation. Brock had flashed his potential as a baseball player at Union High School in Mer Rouge, where he also played basketball and earned good grades, even competing on math and chemistry teams. Yet he had no guarantees about playing when he arrived at Southern University in the fall of 1956, which he was able to attend because the school had a work-study program that was the equivalent of an academic scholarship.

Brock's arrangement required him to maintain a B average, and he found college difficult, receiving a C+ grade average in the fall of his freshman year. That cost him the work-study scholarship, and he knew the only way he could stay was if he impressed the baseball coaches enough in spring tryouts.[9]

Brock didn't rush into anything. Before putting himself on the line, he went out day after day to watch the team practice. He did not think he stacked up. "I sat there scared to death," he said. "The players paraded in front of me with muscles. They looked like athletes. I wasn't sure I belonged on the field with them."

Brock worried about being good enough to handle college pitchers. He'd been gnawing over that question almost every day. His fears seemed on the verge of being realized when he reported for the scheduled tryout along with team members and other hopefuls.

He felt like he was a kid among men, and for a time he wanted to just call the whole thing off and go home. But then his eye fell on a boy who couldn't have been much older than 11 or 12. He was in the middle of the action, acting as if he was 21 or 22. He happily threw the ball around, calling out to the other players like he'd known them his whole life. He put the ball in play at the plate and ran the bases like a stallion.

So Brock asked himself, if this little kid can do this, why can't I? If he has the courage to be on this field, shouldn't I?

The tryout went well. Brock even delivered a long home run off one of the experienced pitchers. He was on the team and in many ways would never again look back.

When that day was over, he looked around for the boy but couldn't find him. He asked his new teammates if they knew his name, and they didn't know what he was talking about. They hadn't seen any little boys. Brock told them he was talking about the guy who was running the bases and happily playing catch with everybody. They told him they hadn't seen any kids on the field.

Brock spent three seasons on the team at Southern, leading the Jaguars to an NAIA World Series championship and landing a spot on the United States team for the Pan American games. He met Katie Hay in a math class and married her. Through it all, he always kept an eye out for the child who had inspired him. But he never saw him again.

Buck O'Neil was nearby once when Brock told the story.

"You think that boy was an angel?" O'Neil asked.

Brock just smiled.

O'Neil smiled back. "There are angels everywhere," he said.[10]

>> <<

The Cubs, it seems, could even screw up divine intervention in the days when Phil Wrigley sweated details about his ballpark but not his team itself.

The discerning, well-connected O'Neil knew that Brock could be a great player when he saw him playing for Southern. He had speed that reminded O'Neil of legendary Negro Leaguer Cool Papa Bell, but he was a little taller and had big shoulders, making O'Neil believe he had more power than a quick glance at his modest frame (5'11", 170 pounds) suggested. He had both quickness and timing at the plate, centering good pitches and fouling off really good ones.

Brock hit only .140 as a freshman, striking out frequently. But something didn't just click inside him as a sophomore, it exploded. He hit .545 with 13 home runs in 27 games, earning a spot on the U.S. team for the Pan Am Games.

Whenever O'Neil was around Southern visiting with Bob Lee and Emory Hines, who were the baseball coaches, Brock was never far from his mind. He was the kind of kid who hung around his coaches, O'Neil observed, a little shy and in search of affirmation, not unlike a young Ernie Banks.

Banks had been O'Neil's kind of a young player. He had an endless supply of both energy and questions, peppering O'Neil and other older men about the great black ballplayers of the past. He had been willing to work to get better, sometimes demanding that O'Neil hit fifty grounders to the right of him and fifty to the left of him, and then asking for even more. "You got a few more in you, Skip?'" O'Neil remembered Banks asking. "I'm going to wear your hands out."[11]

It was easy for O'Neil to insert Brock for Banks in that mental picture. He had skill but also a certain infectiousness, which was just waiting to get out. But for O'Neil, it was never a slam dunk to get the Cubs to sign one of his players.

He had raved about Brock to the men back in Chicago, but he didn't carry a checkbook himself.

When Brock decided he was ready for pro ball, he hopped on a bus for St. Louis, where he had been promised a tryout with the Cardinals. But that didn't happen, as a communications breakdown left no one expecting him. The St. Louis scouts had dropped the ball. Brock was down to his last $10, which got him a bus ticket for Chicago, where he planned to stay with a friend from Southern.

Brock went right to work in Chicago, washing walls and floors at a YMCA near Noah Pates' apartment and awaited tryouts. The first came with the White Sox at Comiskey Park, but they weren't interested. The Cubs were intrigued, based on O'Neil's recommendation, and a two-day tryout at Wrigley Field went well. The ice was broken for Brock when veteran first baseman Ed Bouchee offered him a pair of spikes to replace his raggedy ones, and he hit the ball so well in one pregame workout that Phillies manager Gene Mauch told one of the coaches that he'd sign Brock if the Cubs took a pass.

Brock signed for $12,000, with the first installment of $5,000 paid to him before he hopped on a Greyhound to go home.[12]

Brock spent his first pro season at St. Cloud, Minnesota, in the Class C Northern League. He hit .361 with 14 homers while establishing himself as a center fielder with great range and a base-stealer with tremendous raw speed.

"He was a great guy, and he could really play," remembered Joe Macko, a longtime equipment manager and club official of the Texas Rangers who was Brock's manager in St. Cloud. "He bunted a lot, but he had good power and was a line-drive hitter. He'd hit it in the hole, and he could fly. He had a lot of doubles, triples, and some [inside-the-park] home runs, too."

Brock was playing in the low minors, three or four rungs away from the National League, depending on how you counted. Yet the reports on Brock were so good, so promising, that General Manager John Holland allowed Vedie Himsl, Charlie Grimm, and others involved in the College of Coaches to bring him to the big leagues for a cup of coffee that September and then take a serious look at him the following spring.

Brock would never play another day in the minor leagues, ending his apprenticeship after only 128 games. Macko almost lost his job arguing that he needed more time for seasoning.

"I told them how stupid they were," Macko said. "They wouldn't listen. They wanted to have the kid, and they didn't want to wait.... That was the way they were running things in those days."

When the Cubs left Mesa, Arizona, in early April 1962, Brock was on the team. Ernie Banks, eight years older and then a veteran of eight full big-league seasons, was his roommate on the road. Brock played center field and batted leadoff on Opening Day, when the Cubs visited no-frills Colt Stadium for the birth of one of baseball's two expansion teams, the Houston Colt 45s. He struck out against Bobby Shantz in his first at-bat and went 0-for-3 as the home team won 11–2, the only real sign of life in the visitor's dugout came when Texan Ernie Banks hit a home run.

That was the beginning of a 0–7 start that showed Brock how difficult life with the Cubs would be. He got a hit the next day and would have three in a 15-inning loss to the Cardinals in the Wrigley Field opener, including a home run and a triple.

Reporters and fans loved Brock based as much on his potential as his actual contributions. One reporter, the *Chicago Tribune*'s Richard Dozer, had speculated in a story at the end of that spring training that the rookie could develop into a .400 hitter—something the major leagues hadn't had since Ted Williams hit .406 in 1941.

Dozer cited a quote from Hall of Famer Rogers Hornsby, who had hit .400 three times in the 1920s. "A .400 hitter nowadays has to be able to bunt," Hornsby said. "He has to be fast; he has to avoid striking out frequently."[13]

Brock told Dozer that he had "beat out about three-quarters of the bunts I laid down last year," and added that 15 of those bunt hits came on two-strike pitches. His only real concern entering that 1962 season was that left-handed pitchers were exploiting their lefty-lefty advantage against him.

"The left-handers have been giving me a little trouble with their breaking pitches," he said. "But as soon as I learn to lay off their outside pitches, I'll be okay."

Brock had long since developed a body that made the concerns he carried to the college tryout seem silly, and it was only going to get more defined as he matured.

Tim McCarver would say Brock looked like he had a body chiseled out of marble. Senator Eugene McCarthy met Brock in 1968 and said that being with

Brock was like being in a room with a superior species of being. "I was ashamed to be in the same locker room with him," McCarthy said.[14]

But baseball is rarely an easy game, no matter your gifts. Brock learned that lesson the hard way when he worked to establish himself on NL diamonds in the early 1960s, regularly facing the likes of Warren Spahn, Lew Burdette, Sandy Koufax, Don Drysdale, Juan Marichal, and a young Bob Gibson. Brock hit .263 in his rookie season, with nine home runs and 16 stolen bases. That latter total could have been higher, but Brock hit in front of Banks, Billy Williams, Ron Santo, and George Altman, and the Cubs were employing a very conservative approach, relying on power and not daring.

Brock remained a regular for the Cubs in '63 and '64, but he was a wildly inconsistent player. He hit some monster home runs, including one into the center-field bleachers at the Polo Grounds that was for a time the talk of the league. Joe Adcock was the only slugger to hit a ball there before Brock. He also used his athleticism to make spectacular running catches, especially in some of the huge parks on the road, but he had trouble battling the sun at Wrigley Field. "Right field in Wrigley Field is the toughest field I've played in any park," Brock said.[15]

Brock's batting average dropped to .258 in 1963 and slipped a little more early in '64, this time to .241 through his first 40 games. He worked with what seemed to him like an endless line of coaches and instructors wearing Cubs uniforms, and not even the regular presence of O'Neil allowed him to solve any of the secrets that were holding him back.

Banks was one of the few consistent voices that Brock heard. He loved how Ernie could describe hitting in simple terms after coaches and so many others made it seem like quantum physics.

Rushed to the big leagues and burdened with high expectations, disappointment weighed heavily on Brock, no matter how hard Banks tried to get his mind off the game with visits to see the Liberty Bell in Philadelphia or the Statue of Liberty in New York. Brock was overprocessing each at-bat before he went to the plate and overanalyzing it afterward. His confusion was evident.

Bob Kennedy, then the Cubs manager (or head coach, according to Phil Wrigley's vernacular), tried an experiment before a game in Cincinnati during the 1963 season. He asked Brock to write his signature on a piece of paper, and Brock complied. Then he told him to write it again, slowly.

"Think about every letter," Kennedy said. "Write each one of them very carefully."

Brock wrote his name again, only this time moving the pen deliberately as he tried to blend the straight lines with the curves perfectly.

The results were startling. The second signature barely resembled the first.

"I bet your couldn't even get your bank to pass that second signature," Kennedy said. "It doesn't look anywhere like your handwriting.... You let your conscious take over from your subconscious on that second try. That's why it looks unlike you. And that's what you do all the time at the plate, my friend. If ever I saw a self-conscious baseball player with his brains tied in a knot, it's you. You are forever thinking about whether your stance is right, whether your shoulders are balanced, whether you're swinging correctly. Tell you one thing— you squeeze the bat so hard, sometimes I think I see sawdust coming out of the handle. You know you didn't do that in St. Cloud."[16]

For most competitors, there's nothing harder than trying less. Brock, deprived of the chance to gain repetitions and confidence in the minor leagues, was living out that nightmare daily at Wrigley Field.

≫ ≪

Two months into the 1964 season, the St. Louis Cardinals were a .500 team stuck in the middle of a large National League pack. They had gone 18 years since last winning a pennant, and their general manager, Bing Devine, was under pressure to keep his job.

For four years Devine and his manager, Johnny Keane, had tried to figure out a way to construct a team without being lucky enough to have one of the game's best players—someone like Mays, Aaron, DiMaggio, Williams, or Mantle. They concluded that there was only one truly reliable trait for a hitter—his speed.[17]

They knew it could be spotted early on, when players were available either to be signed or perhaps acquired cheaply from another team. They knew you couldn't coach a good hitter to be fast, but with patience and hard work you could coach a speedster to be a good hitter.

That philosophy led Keane to follow Brock closely since early in the 1963 season.[18] The Cardinals had glowing reports on him from his time at Southern, and Eddie Stanky, a top man for Devine, had quietly scouted him as a big leaguer, recommending that the Cardinals get him if possible.

"Brock wasn't a really good outfielder," Devine said. "He had trouble playing in Wrigley Field. Occasionally, he'd throw a ball over home plate and into the stands. For a player who could run, he also struck out a lot.... Even given all these factors, we really liked his potential."

Devine approached the Cubs about a deal for Brock after the 1963 season, and then again early in the '64 season. He was politely told no both times. "John Holland always rejected it," Devine said. "He'd say, 'We're not going to deal him.'"[19]

At the time, Banks was slipping past his prime and Holland (who replaced Matthews as the man in charge in 1957) worked to build a winner while Banks was still a cornerstone. Banks had won back-to-back Most Valuable Player awards in 1958 and '59, but his knees hurt him in '63, when he hit only 18 homers in 130 games as the Cubs finished 82–80 in seventh place and 17 games behind the Los Angeles Dodgers. Headlined by Dick Ellsworth and Larry Jackson, the pitching staff led the National League in earned run average, but the Cubs scored only 570 runs, 48 behind the league average.

>> <<

Banks began to get his swerve on again in 1964. He ignored the cold weather to hit .283 in April, followed by another strong month in May.

The roots of his turnaround traced to a house call that winter by his old friend, Buck O'Neil. This was ostensibly a social visit, but Banks had baseball on his mind. After dinner, and while O'Neil smoked a few panatelas, Banks brought out the movie projector. He asked O'Neil if he would look at film of him hitting in 1963 and compare it to earlier years when he had been at the top of his game.

O'Neil initially did more watching than talking. Then he said, "Let's have a few dozen feet of that '63 stuff again."

Shots of Banks striking out and popping up ran over and over on the screen in the darkened living room of Banks' south Chicago home. "Okay," O'Neil said. "Enough of that. Put on the '58–'59 reels again."

O'Neil watched those for about two minutes and walked over to the wall, switching on a light.

"Get me a bat," he said.

It was a night that would stick with Banks for a lifetime, as the simple suggestions O'Neil made helped him remain a respected hitter as he and the Cubs tried to win the title that Banks felt Phil Wrigley deserved.

"You know how Buck is," Banks told the *Chicago American*'s Bill Gleason. "He not only told me, he took that bat and showed me. He demonstrated, right there on the living room rug, how I had hit from a wide stance when I was going good, with my arms away from my body. But in '63 I had brought my feet closer together and brought my arms in."

Somehow, none of the Cubs' many coaches had caught the change as it was happening.

"It's funny, you know," Banks said. "How can I explain it? How can I explain how a batter will hit one way for years then get away from it? I did it—the change, I mean—unconsciously.... This spring in Mesa, I concentrated on my stance and my arms. I had to rediscipline myself."[20]

>> <<

Even with Banks back on form, the Cubs were in seventh place on June 8, hanging around near the Cardinals a week before the trade deadline. Holland started thinking that it might be time to trade Brock for a pitcher. Somewhere in his mind was the thought that the right pitcher would be a white pitcher.

Chicagoans think of themselves as progressive people. They will stereotype the South as the incubator of racism or point to the battle between Irish and blacks in Boston as a shameful chapter in America's development. They aren't always as quick to look in the mirror.

In many ways Chicago has been one of America's true melting pots, with different cultures thriving side by side or mixed together. But all you need to know about the city's institutionalized racism is how the lakefront was developed to the north and south of the museum campus, where the Field Museum, Shedd Aquarium, and Adler Planetarium sit in the shadows of Soldier Field, the monument to sweat and blood that opened in 1924.

The Magnificent Mile's hotels, restaurants, and designer boutiques shine on the edge of bike paths, marinas, and projects like Navy Pier north of the Chicago River. Yet it was the late 1990s before city planners paid more than lip service to development on the south side of the city, where Hall of Famer Kirby Puckett grew up in public housing, throwing a baseball against a wall day after day as a child because there were no Little League teams.

The White Sox played at Comiskey Park on 35th and Shields, and that was where black fans gravitated after the Negro Leagues died. The Cubs' clientele was largely white.

In Banks, Brock, Billy Williams, and Bahamian shortstop Andre Rodgers, the 1964 Cubs had a lineup that was 50 percent composed of players of color. There's little doubt that this ratio—unusually high at almost any time in baseball—made it easier for Holland to pull the trigger on a Brock trade.

In his later years, O'Neil recalled seeking out a meeting with Holland. "I got all these players, but they weren't playing them at the same time," he told George Castle for his book, *The Million-to-One Team*. "I told Mr. Holland we'd have a better ballclub if we played the blacks. Then he showed me a basket of letters from fans saying, 'What are you trying to do, make the Cubs into the Kansas City Monarchs?' We weren't appealing to black fans anyway, playing on the North Side of Chicago."[21]

≫ ≪

The Cardinals were in Los Angeles on June 13, two days before the trading deadline. Bing Devine, fearing for his job, was anxious to make a move. "I was making the rounds by phone from Dodger Stadium, calling the other general managers to see if we could do anything to improve the Cardinals," Devine said.

He noticed a change in the Cubs' position when he called John Holland.

"If you're still interested, we might have to move Brock," Holland said.

"For what?"

"We need a pitcher," Holland said. "You gave me a list of players when we talked before, and we'll take a pitcher off that list. We'll take Broglio."

Ernie Broglio, a six-year veteran from Berkeley, California, won 18 games in 1963 but hadn't pitched the same this season. Devine told Holland he'd have to check with Keane but would get back to him. The two talked on the team flight from Los Angeles to Houston.

"I can remember this so clearly," Devine said years later. "I told Johnny we had a chance to get Brock for Broglio, and he said, 'What are we waiting for?' There were no cell phones then. I told him, 'I'll call as soon as we land and I get to a pay phone.'"

Devine called Holland from Hobby Airport in Houston, telling him the Cardinals were willing to make the deal. Holland wanted to make it a little bigger so that it wouldn't be a one-for-one for the 24-year-old Brock.

"We both put two other players in there—Bobby Shantz and Doug Clemens for the Cards and Jack Spring and Paul Toth from the Cubs—and that was it," Devine said.[22]

June 15 fell on a Monday, and the Cubs were off. Brock was making an appearance at Wieboldt's department store, standing on a small stage with some other players and club officials, when someone said, "Phone call for you, Lou."

Lou Boudreau, then a broadcaster, went for it first, then Coach Lou Klein. But the call was for Lou Brock, from Holland, who got right to the point. He told Brock that the Cubs had called a news conference to announce a trade, which had caused Brock's contract to be transferred.

Brock's initial thought was that he was being replaced by a veteran player and would be returning to the minor leagues. That's how low his confidence was. But Holland kept talking, eventually telling Brock he had been traded to St. Louis.

He returned to the podium and announced the trade himself. "Hey!" he said. "I have just been traded, everybody! I'm going to St. Louis."[23]

Both Holland and Phil Wrigley were thrilled to have added Broglio, who at age 24 had won 21 games in 1960. Wrigley said, "If you want to hit the bull's eye, you have to take a shot at it." Holland went him one better. "We're taking more than a shot at the flag," he declared. "We're cutting loose with both barrels."

Yet there was a sense of shock in the clubhouse. Banks was crushed that the kid he had mentored was sent to a rival so early in his career. Other veteran players knew the risk that was being taken with the trade.

"I can remember sitting and talking with Don Zimmer and Larry Jackson," said Don Elston, a relief pitcher who was in the last year of his career. "Everybody wanted to know what the hell had happened. Why? Nobody could figure it out because we all knew Lou was going to be a star. Nobody could figure out who did the trade or why the trade was made. We just could not understand what had happened and why. We didn't understand it."[24]

Macko, who was on the coaching staff of the Wenatchee (Washington) Chiefs of the Northwest League, was flabbergasted to hear his star pupil had been traded.

"All they had to do was leave the kid alone and he was going to be a great player," Macko said. "I told everyone to just give him some time, that he had so much talent and knew what he was doing. But after they had spent so much time working with him in Chicago, he wanted to come back and play for me."

Conventional wisdom in both Chicago and St. Louis was that the Cubs had pulled off a shrewd move at the Cardinals' expense. Brock still talks about how *Chicago American* sportswriter Brent Musburger referred to the trade as being a Brinks job by the Cubs.

Another Chicago writer, Bob Smith, chirped in his column, "Thank you, thank you, oh, you lovely St. Louis Cardinals," he wrote. "Nice doing business with you. Please call again any time."

In the Cardinals' clubhouse, the deal was panned as badly as on the streets of St. Louis. Veterans Bill White and Dick Groat were among those who felt their front office had been hoodwinked.

In hindsight, the Cardinals were making a move they had explored for a long time—one that was put in motion by solid analysis and shrewd scouting, with Eddie Stanky and others seeing the potential in Brock as it was being wasted in Chicago. From the Cubs' standpoint, it was a spontaneous, knee-jerk move that may have been influenced by the color of Brock's skin.

"When we made that trade, the Cubs were taking a chance and we were taking a chance," Devine said. "You win some, you lose some... sometimes you get lucky.... But you don't get lucky if you don't take the chance."[25]

>> «

Brock had 72 hours to report but wasn't the kind to take his time. He caught an afternoon flight to Houston and went directly to Colt Stadium, where he struck out as a pinch hitter that night. He swung wildly and went down on three pitches against Houston reliever Jim Owens. "I guess our next trade will be Bill White for two broken bats," one Cardinal complained loudly after Brock had returned to the bench.

Catcher Tim McCarver said Brock may have faced some resentment because of Broglio's popularity in the clubhouse. "Everybody loved Ernie," he said, and White later said that there was a feeling Devine had given up too much to get an unproven player like Brock.

The future National League president said Brock "was not a good fielder, struck out too much, and made a lot of mistakes on the bases." Keane realized he had to nip such criticism in the bud, so he called a team meeting to tell his players to zip it.

"Who we trade for is our business, and you guys have no right to criticize what we do," Keane said. "This trade is none of your business."[26]

Brock was in the lineup the next day, playing right field alongside center fielder Curt Flood, and had a triple, single, two walks, and a stolen base—the first of 888 he would have in his 16 seasons with the Cardinals, including a 118-steal season in 1974.

Keane issued strict orders to his coaches—leave the new guy alone. He felt that Brock had been mishandled by an overabundance of coaching (and coaches) in Chicago and wanted to give him a chance to play the game naturally, the way he had when the Cardinals watched him at Southern and again in his one minor league season.

Keane even asked St. Louis reporters to keep their distance. "Don't press him," he said to St. Louis Post-Dispatch's Bob Broeg. "Let him alone. I think he tried too hard in Chicago."

The results were amazing.

Brock, who was hitting .251 at the time of the trade, hit .348 for the Cardinals. He stole 33 bases and scored 81 runs in 103 games, and the team that had been in seventh place when he arrived shot up the standings like an Elvis Presley hit moving up the charts. St. Louis was in seventh place, 6½ games behind Philadelphia when Brock arrived. The team moved into fourth place by late August but watched the gap behind Philadelphia grow to 11 games on August 23. But it would be a magical September at Sportsman's Park and a nauseating one at Connie Mack Stadium in Philadelphia.

While the Cardinals went 22–10 to the wire—with Brock hitting .370 in his last 24 games—the Phillies folded under Gene Mauch, losing 12-of-13 in a late stretch to watch a lead of 6½ games vanish before their stunned eyes. "Brock changed the entire complexion of the team," backup infielder Jerry Buchek said.

Brock had transformed Keane's team into a pennant winner, and he wasn't through yet. He hit .300 and drove in five runs in the World Series, leading the Cardinals to an upset over a Yankees team featuring Mickey Mantle and Whitey Ford.

Keane said the key to the Cardinals' magical run was Brock. "He picked the club up," he said. "The other players suddenly realized how good of a ballplayer he was. Of course, none of us expected to see him come along so fast."

Devine looked like a genius. "At the time we got Brock, we said we didn't want to put too much pressure on him, and we made it clear that we got him for the future as well as for the present," the general manager said. "Lou put everything together quickly. He should continue to get better, and I have to believe he'll hit for more power as time goes on."

Brock himself might have been the least surprised. "I got off to a good start this year, but then I guess I was trying too hard and my batting average went down in a hurry," he said. "You know, Ernie Banks predicted I would hit .320 this year, and I finished at .315."[27]

Brock said Keane and Devine restored his confidence by opening up his game.

"In Chicago, they wouldn't let me run on my own," he said. "Johnny Keane showed tremendous confidence in letting me run on my own. He said the Cardinals got me for my speed. The only sign I have is a don't-steal sign on certain plays."

Brock said the green light on the bases "loosened me up," but he understood why he had not been given such freedom in Chicago, where Bob Kennedy was trying to win around his power hitters. "Of course, I realized that ... where you had Santo, Banks, and Williams, they weren't going to let you steal too many bases," he said. "If I were the manager, I wouldn't let me steal in front of those guys, either."[28]

Pitcher Larry Jackson, a former Cardinal, led the National League with 24 wins for the eighth-place Cubs in 1964. He said Brock was transformed after the trade. "Brock wasn't at all relaxed at first in Chicago," he said. "He'd break out into a big sweat just putting his uniform on. His desire was so intense that he made things tough for himself. He didn't know when to slide and was so fast that, before he realized it, he tore the bag right out of the ground.... Lou seemed to be under too much pressure in Chicago, but he certainly relaxed once he got to St. Louis."[29]

Meanwhile, Broglio went 4–7 with a 4.04 ERA in 100⅓ innings for the Cubs in 1964 and needed surgery on his elbow that winter. He would only pitch in two other seasons, ending his stay in Chicago with a 7–19 record and a distinction as the wrong end of one of the worst trades ever. He was *No, No Nannette* or whatever musical it was that Harry Frazee produced with the money he received from selling Babe Ruth to the Yankees.

"I was the highest paid BP pitcher in baseball," said Broglio, who would come to embrace being a historical footnote. He even kept an autographed photo of Brock in his den. It was inscribed, "You are and were a helluva player."[30]

Banks and the Cubs teammates who had glimpsed Brock's potential weren't nearly as glib about the dubious transaction. Long after his career was over, Banks lamented that he had played on many good teams that were one player short of being great teams.

Brock was the one player.

12

JULY

Fans love to see players from their teams in the All-Star Game, but baseball's annual mid-season showcase does not foretell a team's success. There were eight Cubs at Yankee Stadium for the 2008 game, with Alfonso Soriano, Geovany Soto, and Kosuke Fukudome elected to start, and that collection of firepower would go on to produce zero victories in the postseason, swept by a Dodgers team that had only one All-Star, catcher Russell Martin.

The 1969 All-Star Game was a source of pride for Bleacher Bums and less attention-grabbing Cub fans. The entire infield, including catcher Randy Hundley, went to the game at RFK Stadium in Washington. It gave them a chance to visit with Richard Nixon at the White House.

Someone quizzed Nixon on Banks' age, and it amused Banks greatly that the president said 35. "He gave me three years," Banks said. "Then [commissioner Bowie Kuhn] said, 'No, Mr. President, I think Ernie is 38,' and Mr. Nixon said, 'Well, he looks 35, and don't tell any of those other fellows, but this man deserves a pennant.'"

Nixon confessed to a group that he sometimes wished he had gone into another line of work. "I like the job I have," he said, "but if I had to start over again, I'd like to have been a sportswriter."[1]

A vote by players elected Ron Santo and Don Kessinger as starters. St. Louis manager Red Schoendienst, in charge of the National League team because his team had won the '68 pennant, had named Glenn Beckert, Hundley, and Banks as reserves.

Schoendienst had not named Fergie Jenkins to the team—a point of criticism given Jenkins' 13 wins, 2.69 ERA, and 194 innings at the All-Star break. But in interviews before the game, Schoendienst told reporters he had originally selected Jenkins but not Banks and later rearranged his roster at Kuhn's suggestion.

This was Banks' 14th All-Star Game, but he hadn't gone to the '68 game in the Astrodome. Kuhn felt that with the Cubs in first place it was a good time to throw a lifetime achievement award Banks' way, and while he was batting only .266, he had 15 homers and 79 RBIs at the break—impressive totals in any era.

"There's no question [Jenkins] deserves to be on the team, but when it was suggested to me that Banks should be included, I agreed," Schoendienst said. "Banks has done so much for his club, and I think he's great. People kept saying I didn't pick Jenkins. They think I picked the pitchers. It's not so. The other managers voted on it, and I went by what they said. I'm glad Banks is on the team, but I would have liked having Jenkins, too. You can't have everybody."[2]

Banks momentarily felt terrible, as this would have been only the second All-Star Game for Jenkins. "My goodness, Fergie is my roomie, and there's no other person I'd rather see make the All-Star team," he said. "I feel bad about that. I never dreamed of making the team. Fellows like Willie McCovey and Lee May have been doing fantastically."

But Banks would bask in the attention from reporters, who were forced to look for one news cycle's worth of feature stories when rain postponed the game (a 9–3 victory for the NL) one day. The UPI's Milton Richman wrote that Banks was rightfully rewarded with his spot for being such an outstanding representative of baseball, always signing autographs, smiling, and maintaining a cheerful attitude in the face of losing seasons in Chicago.

"I can't find anything to complain about," Banks said, insisting he was only doing what comes naturally. "It's just part of my nature. I truly enjoy being around people and associating with the ballplayers. You watch me out there before the game today. I think I'll be just like a kid, getting autographs, taking pictures and whatnot."[3]

>> <<

For Banks and his teammates, the trip to Washington was a potentially valuable diversion during a troubling time. The Cubs ended June with a 50–27 record, 7½ games ahead of the Mets, but they went 11–10 before the All-Star break, allowing their lead to shrink to five games.

The first of those losses was in Montreal—an 11–4 shellacking in a day game that followed a contentious, water-logged loss ending after midnight the night before. Leo Durocher had waged war against the Expos' management for allowing the June 30 game to be played in horrible conditions and against umpires for somehow ruling that a ball Banks had driven over the Jarry Park fence had skipped through a hole under the fence.

Durocher childishly wouldn't announce his July 1 lineup until he carried it to the plate,[4] but he was left stewing when the Cubs played one of their worst games behind starter Ken Holtzman, even allowing the recently discarded Adolfo Phillips to steal home on a dash from third while Holtzman appealed that he had missed second. Holtzman's throw was low and dropped by Don Kessinger, giving Phillips time to score a Little League run.

Holtzman, a bachelor, loved going to Montreal, as ballplayers would until the Expos were no more in 2005, becoming the Washington Nationals. He had made arrangements to spend time after a game with a girl he met at the stadium beforehand, one of the usherettes, and Durocher shamelessly asked to be set up with her friend.

"I got a tap on my shoulders from Leo, and he says, 'You know that broad? You talked to her in French? You asking her out after the game?... That blonde right next to her is her good friend, so you ask her if she'll go out with me, okay?'"

Holtzman found the request bizarre, considering his manager had 40 years on him and probably even more on the girls, but Durocher was the boss. So after the ugly loss Holtzman wound up on a double date that ended with the two couples partying until they returned to the Queen Elizabeth Hotel at about 3:30 in the morning.

Disgracefully, Durocher would not make it to Jarry Park the next day. The Cubs said he had an upset stomach, which was no doubt true, but Holtzman knew why Durocher wasn't himself. "Monique said that, according to her girlfriend, Leo woke up at 9:30, threw up, then threw up again at 2:00," Holtzman said. "He called Jake [team doctor Jacob Suker] and she finally went home.... Apparently she was too much for him."[5]

Durocher somehow would play the victim the next day, complaining to Chicago reporters that the *Montreal Star* newspaper had spoiled his rest with a series of phone calls to his room, claiming he had even turned away reporters at his hotel door.

Poor Leo. Poor Cubs.

>> <<

None of their losses in 1969 would be worse than one the Cubs suffered when they traveled to Shea Stadium for a series in the second week of July. This was a key stretch of the schedule, especially for the chasing Mets, who relished the opportunity to host the Cubs in New York and then travel to Chicago for another three-game series.

Banks loved trips to New York. He loved the excitement of the city. He loved the attention he was paid by reporters for America's biggest newspapers. This trip was no different.

Before the series opener on July 8, Banks was standing outside the visiting dugout, humming the Mets' theme song, "Meet the Mets," occasionally throwing in ad-libbed lyrics like "Beat the Mets, beat the Mets."

He had no shortage of time for his usual small talk with reporters.

"What a beautiful day for baseball," Banks said. "New York. The melting pot. The Great White Way. What's going on?"

"The Mets," a reporter said.

"What about *Oh, Calcutta*?" Banks asked. "Twenty-five dollars a ticket and you can't get a hold of them."

"Don't tell us that beneath that sunshine smile beats the heart of a dirty old man," said a reporter.

"No, no," Banks answered, smiling. "You can't say that. What will all these kids think?"

Talk eventually turned to the Mets.

"People used to laugh and laugh at the Mets," Banks said. "But not anymore. Now they have a good team. They have good pitching, and they play together. People laughed a few years ago, but the Mets play together now."[6]

One of the cruel aspects about baseball's 162-game season is that sooner or later it will expose a team's weaknesses, and this was the time that the Cubs would pay for never finding an All-Star center fielder after trading Andy Pafko to Brooklyn in 1951.

Frank Baumholtz had held the job the next two years, but the Cubs changed primary center fielders for 12 consecutive seasons before Phillips arrived in 1966. You can argue that Lou Brock lacked the arm to ever become a top center fielder, but he still would have looked good between Billy Williams and Jim Hickman in '69.

Phillips might have been fine, as well, had Durocher not insisted on making the weak hitter a leadoff man, then burying him in his doghouse when he failed to turn into Maury Wills. The guy that Durocher wound up counting on was the 23-year-old Don Young, and it was clear even to *Sports Illustrated*'s Robert H. Boyle that this was a risky proposition.

In his glowing article on the Cubs, Boyle said the question with Young was whether he'd hit. "The center fielder, Don Young, hit only .242 last year for Lodi in the Class A California League," Boyle wrote. "Defensively he is excellent. Young is long-legged ["split high" is the expression] and he goes after a ball in what seems an effortless glide. [GM John] Holland says, 'He never looks like he's running hard, but he's there to get the ball.'"[7]

Most of the time, anyway.

The Cubs were leading the Mets 3–1 on July 8, with a solo homer by Banks part of the minimal support it appeared Jenkins would need, but much would change in the span of three batters in the bottom of the ninth. Young played like the neophyte he was, and there was no one to catch him when he fell. Instead, Durocher and Santo would make this worse than just a three-run rally by the second-place Mets.

Ken Boswell led off with a high pop into right-center. Young should have gotten to the ball but broke slowly and was only able to play it on a hop, as Boswell hustled into second base with a leadoff double. Jenkins got Tommie Agee to hit a pop foul for the first out, but the newly acquired Donn Clendenon followed with a smash toward the fence in left-center.

Young's long legs got him to the ball, but it went in and out of his glove as he crashed into the wall. It was another double, and Jenkins was unable to escape from the jam. The Mets won on a bloop single by Ed Kranepool after Cleon Jones tied the score with the third double of the inning—the only one Young didn't have a chance to take away.

Gil Hodges called it one of the most important wins of the year, helping to "make believers out of all you unbelievers." Jones and his Mets teammates were ecstatic.

"Somebody said the Cubs aren't taking us seriously," he said. "Maybe they'll take us seriously now."[8]

The Cubs had been swept in St. Louis before arriving in New York, and losing the opener in this fashion not only cut their lead to 4½ games but clearly unsettled Durocher. After the game, with no regard to Young or anyone else within earshot, Durocher ranted like a madman. "It's tough to win when your center fielder can't catch a fucking fly ball!" he bellowed. "Jenkins pitched his heart out. But when a man can't catch a fly ball, it's a disgrace. He stands there watching one, and then gives up on the other. It's a disgrace!"

Durocher, according to reports, moved closer to where Young was sitting, a dazed look on his face, no doubt fighting to hold back tears.

"My son could have caught those balls!" he shouted. "My fucking three-year-old could have caught those balls!"[9]

There was dead silence in the clubhouse for perhaps 15 minutes afterward, and when it ended Young was slipping away, leaving the stadium by himself rather than waiting for the bus. Santo stopped him and said a few words but did not prevent Young from leaving by himself. Then Santo gave an interview to reporters that he would regret for the rest of his life. "I know the Dodgers won pennants with just pitching, but this Mets lineup is ridiculous," he started. "Maybe I'd better not say anything else because my mouth will get me into trouble."[10]

He would have been fine if he stopped there, but he turned his attention to Young. "He was thinking of himself, not the team," he said. 'He had a bad day at the plate, and he's got his head down. Don's a major leaguer because of his glove. When he hits, he's a dividend, but when he fails on defense, he's lost—and today he took us down with him. He put his head between his legs."

Santo had broken the unwritten rule about not criticizing a teammate in the press, and he felt horrible about it almost immediately. He called some reporters to his room early the next afternoon to say he had made a mistake[11]—which only cast more attention on the situation—after apologizing to Young.

Durocher had never mastered the art of the apology, however, and wouldn't have seen the need to make amends anyway. This was a guy who had once been accused of stealing Babe Ruth's watch. He was a hard man who felt his hardness had helped make him successful in a hard game.

If Young couldn't take a little criticism, well, that was on him. Maybe he was a gutless baby who shouldn't be playing the game.

Seaver was waiting on the other side of the ashes. He took advantage of the fraying Cubs to throw an almost historic game the next day. Only a one-out single in the ninth inning by Jimmy Qualls stopped Seaver short of a perfect game.

Qualls, it should be noted, started in center field. Young would start only five of the remaining 21 games in July, and he shared center field with Qualls and the 19-year-old Oscar Gamble the rest of the season.

>> <<

Durocher, the guy who said a three-year-old could have caught the balls that Young missed, again displayed childishly self-indulgent behavior the first weekend after the All-Star break. He snuck out of Wrigley Field during a nationally televised game against the Dodgers on Saturday, July 26. Pete Reiser or another of his coaches told the press box that Durocher had a "stomach disorder."[12]

This was surely believable, as reported illnesses had already played a role in him missing frequent games during spring training and the regular season, including the one in Montreal a few weeks earlier. But this disappearance—the only one that remains memorably notorious—was different because it was preconceived and would never have been excused if it was engineered by a player.

In the early innings of the game, Durocher went into the clubhouse, closed the door on his office, changed clothes, walked outside the stadium, and caught a cab to nearby Meigs Field. There he met his wife of two months and her two daughters, and joined them on a flight to Wisconsin. They were headed to Eagle River in the northern part of the state, which was home to Camp Ojibwa, where 12-year-old Joel Goldblatt was attending camp.

Lynne Walker Goldblatt Durocher later said she wasn't sure her husband was going to join her until she got word as the Cubs were facing the Dodgers' Bill

Singer. "I went to Meigs with my two daughters and had Leo's ticket with me just in case," she said. "And, sure enough, he called me from the dugout during the game and said, 'I think I can make it. We can't lose this one!'"[13]

Durocher apparently made the snap decision at some point after Hundley singled to score Santo in the second inning, giving the Cubs a lead they would later lose before winning 3–2 in the 11th on another Hundley RBI single.

Perhaps Durocher wouldn't have left had Dick Selma not been as sharp as he was, striking out six the first time around the order. Or maybe Durocher would have justified it as the Cubs having no chance to win if they had fallen behind early. With a leader this erratic, who can know?

Durocher had not cleared his absence with Phil Wrigley or John Holland, even though he would miss Jenkins' loss to the Dodgers on Sunday. It was crazy to think he could get away with this disappearing act—especially since he was going to attend parent's weekend; especially since many of the campers were from Chicago and its northern suburbs; and especially since this was 1969, not '66 or one of the franchise's other on a long list of forgettable seasons.

Durocher's team was in first place when he bolted, five games up, and one would have figured the attention of the manager would have been required for the next day's game when Jenkins was scheduled to start on one day of rest after leaving a Friday start when he was hit in the right thumb by a Willie Crawford line drive. Shouldn't the manager have been there to make sure his ace was physically okay, or at least well enough to handle such an unusual schedule?

When Durocher wasn't at the park on Sunday, Dr. Suker announced he was home, recovering from gastritis, and would be back Monday. Reporters took the Cubs at their word until Jim Enright of *Chicago Today* received the inevitable call from a Chicagoan who had been at Camp Ojibwa with Durocher.

One of Enright's next calls was to Wrigley's home in Lake Geneva, and Wrigley was rightfully steamed. He should have fired the manager as soon as he had confirmed Enright's information. Brickhouse and others believed his first reaction had been to sack the unreliable manager. But Wrigley's management style was to seek solutions, not confrontations, and amazingly he would find a way to excuse his manager.

"For about two hours, Leo was fired," Brickhouse said years later. "Wrigley was really upset, but [his wife] Helen calmed him down and warned him to cool off before making a decision. He did cool down, thought it over, and gave Leo a chance to explain ... [Leo] almost got down on his hands and knees to kiss their shoes."[14]

Monday's *Chicago Tribune* landed on lawns and newsstands without a mention of the situation, however; for one news cycle it was *Chicago Today's* exclusive property. And Durocher strode into Wrigley Field for a Monday game against San Francisco as if nothing had happened.

When reporters asked where he'd been, he dismissed their questions contemptuously. "This is a private matter," he said, "and I don't discuss my private life with anyone."[15]

But Wrigley had not yet dismissed the affair. He told reporters he was disappointed in Durocher and had scheduled a meeting for Tuesday.

"My concern is that some of the players, who have been busting their boilers to win the pennant, might wonder if the manager is equally dedicated," Wrigley said. "I'm sure he is, but I don't want anything to happen to upset us at this stage."[16]

The Cubs, who had lost on Sunday with the sore Jenkins allowing five runs on 10 hits in 4⅓ innings before Reiser gave him the hook, beat the Giants in dramatic fashion on Monday. They trailed 3–2 with two outs in the 10th against Juan Marichal, but lightning struck in the form of a walk to Willie Smith and consecutive singles by the top three hitters in the lineup—Don Kessinger, Glenn Beckert, and Billy Williams.

Did this out-of-nowhere rally against an All-Star pitcher en route to his sixth 20-win season convince Wrigley that Durocher still had his players' support? There's no way to know, but it would have been a factor if Wrigley was wavering at all, as it appears he was.

Monte Irvin, it seems, had it right about Durocher's "unbelievably good luck." The coach received only a brief lecture when he stopped by Wrigley's apartment on Tuesday, and the incident was swept under the rug.

Durocher told reporters his meeting with Wrigley lasted five minutes. "We understood each other perfectly—as we always have," he said. "It's as simple as that."

Wrigley, not wanting to be perceived as a complete pushover, differed on one point. "It lasted 10 minutes," he said of the meeting.[17]

Durocher's wife, Lynne, said later that the aftermath of the weekend in Wisconsin "stunned" Durocher.[18] That seems startling if it's true. But there's no question that Durocher was operating like the ruler of a banana republic. Not only was he allowed to do whatever he wanted, but in his mind the people dealing with him were going to like it, by God.

Players did not rebel at their manager's actions and even decades later seemed to consider the Camp Ojibwa affair more a source of amusement than an impediment to their success. They seemed to relax when Durocher wasn't around, which might be why they had gone 5–1 when he wasn't in the dugout for regular season games.

The *Tribune*'s Robert Markus, like Durocher himself, wondered why some people were saying Durocher should have been canned. He compared the latest absence to organized sickouts that were being held around the country, which he said had become "an accepted way of life … now poor Leo does it and everybody climbs all over him."

Markus wrote that the Cubs were in such a commanding position that Durocher's work was done.

"Leo has already accomplished the job that owner Phil Wrigley gave him four years ago," he wrote. "He took a group of dispirited baseball players, participated in a couple of judicious trades, infused them with his own unquenchable will to win, and presto change-o, the miracle Cubs!

"Durocher can set the Cubs on automatic pilot and spend the rest of the season in Wisconsin if he chooses without affecting the course of destiny. The Cubs, thanks to Durocher, are winners now and would win the pennant with Zsa Zsa Gabor at the helm."[19]

≫ ≪

Gil Hodges continued to set an example for Bobby Cox, Tony La Russa, and others in the next generation of managers to follow both by seeking platoon advantages in his running of games and in his ability to demand results from players without dehumanizing them, as Durocher had done to Don Young.

Having climbed within four games of first place on July 18, the Mets began to backslide after the All-Star break. They lost 7-of-10 in one stretch, including a horrific doubleheader sweep by the Astros at Shea Stadium, after which Tom

Seaver proclaimed it "the worst day I've seen as a Met,"[20] saying this must have been what it was like in 1962, the 120-loss season.

The bullpen collapsed after Jerry Koosman threw seven innings in the opener, resulting in a 16–3 loss. Gary Gentry was knocked out in the third inning of the second game, which Houston won 11–5. But the biggest switch came after reliever Nolan Ryan served up a double to Johnny Edwards, the first man he faced.

Cleon Jones jogged toward the ball in the left-field corner. He then lobbed it indifferently back toward the infield as a crowd of almost 30,000 booed.

Out popped Hodges from the first-base dugout. He headed toward Ryan but didn't stop when he got to him. He marched out, furious, toward shortstop Bud Harrelson, who wondered what he'd done wrong. But he kept walking, all the way to Jones. They talked for a moment and then both made the long walk to the dugout, Jones a few steps behind his manager, who would send Ron Swoboda to left field in Jones' place.

Hodges had taken charge, showing that he was serious when he demanded maximum effort. His wife, Joan, told him that night that he shouldn't have embarrassed Jones, and Hodges admitted he acted impulsively. "You want to know something?" he said. "I didn't even realize I was doing it until I was past the pitcher."[21]

But Hodges had not raged when he reached left field. He listened to Jones, hearing him say he had coasted on the ball because the field was wet and he was protecting a sore ankle. And according to Jones, the manager sought him out a few days later to talk.

"He said, 'You know I wouldn't embarrass you like that, but I look at you as a leader on this club,'" Jones said. "'Everybody seemed like they were comfortable getting their tails kicked, and I didn't like that.'"[22]

Jones appreciated the explanation and said, "In a way it proved a point and woke us up."

Durocher would try to prove his points, too.

When the Cubs headed west in early August, he ordered the plane to leave after a refueling stop in Las Vegas while Enright was in the terminal, making phone calls. And on another leg of the trip, when he noticed Enright wasn't on the team flight from San Diego to Tacoma for an exhibition game against the Triple A team, he called Enright's boss to report him missing.

"Fair is fair, and right is right," Durocher said. "If he can call my boss and get me into trouble, I think this is only fair."

Durocher didn't realize that Enright had been assigned to spend the day at Camp Pendleton, interviewing White Sox slugger Carlos May, who was hospitalized after losing his thumb in a mortar accident during a Marines training exercise. How petty can one look? How foolish?[23]

Yet this was the guy the Cubs were counting on to keep them at the top. No wonder Banks was already having trouble sleeping.

13

STEP FOR STEP WITH THE HAMMER
AND THE SAY HEY KID

Jim Brosnan wasn't just another guy in the Cubs' bullpen. The bespectacled intellectual ran against the grain of baseball's scratch-and-spit mentality. He was as much an observer as a player, a George Plimpton in baseball spikes.

Brosnan wouldn't write his first book until after the Cubs had traded him to St. Louis for aging infielder Alvin Dark, who would move from shortstop, his natural position, to play third base alongside Ernie Banks. That's too bad for Chicago fans. Had Brosnan turned the microscope that produced *The Long Season* on the Cubs of the 1950s, it would be a treasured document, if only because it would have allowed readers to ride along with Banks at the zenith of his career.

But Brosnan's insights on that era were preserved in *Wrigleyville*, an oral history of the franchise written by Peter Golenbock that was published in 1996.

Brosnan recounted the bizarre way he received an unexpected raise before the 1958 season. "In 1958 I was designated by [manager] Bob Scheffing as the Cubs' Opening Day pitcher," he wrote. "Bob Rush was hurt, Moe Drabowsky and Dick Drott were serving their army hitches, and I was the fourth pitcher on the staff. So by default I opened.

"I had a very good spring training, and Mr. W. [Wrigley] was there at the ballpark. Art Meyerhoff, who was hired by Mr. Wrigley to do the advertising for Doublemint gum, Catalina Island, and the Biltmore Hotel, invited me over for dinner. I had worked for Art in the off-season while I was in the minors. Art was in charge of advertising for just that one gum, Doublemint, He didn't have Juicy Fruit and the other gums. He worked on the Doublemint twins.

"Art said, 'We'll ride with Gus.' I didn't know who Gus was. Gus was P.K. Wrigley's chauffeur. We got in the car, and P.K. was in the back. Meyerhoff got in the front seat, and I sat in the back with Mr. Wrigley, and he said, 'Congratulations.'

"For what?"

"'That you're starting, that you're our Opening Day pitcher. I think you deserve congratulations.' Then he said, 'What do you think of my new idea about paying starting pitchers $15,000 a year?' His idea was that as long as you started for the Cubs, he would pay you $15,000 a year. If you didn't remain a starter, then you would get paid for whatever you signed for. I had signed for $10,500. Which was what I deserved after three barely competent years.

"I said, 'I think that's an excellent idea, sir. I really do. Thank you, sir.' It was an incentive, a one-time offer, just for that year.

"We took the limo back to Mr. Wrigley's mansion. He had a true mansion up on a butte overlooking the grounds of the Arizona Biltmore, and he pointed out various Frederic Remingtons he had, introduced me to his wife, who was standing at the top of the stairs.

"'This is our starting pitcher for opening day.'

"'Yes, dear.'

"She gave less of a shit about baseball than he did.

"We never had a deep pitching staff because the Cubs always had a budget and never spent enough on pitchers. Once Mr. Wrigley began paying $60,000 for their starting pitchers, that didn't leave much in the pitching budget for the other guys who had had to be under ten grand or less. . . . Talk about a bad businessman. . . . Shit, Phil Wrigley *gave* away the radio, *gave* away the television rights. He should have been charging for those things. . . . His slogan was, 'Come out and have a picnic,' and the other teams usually did."[1]

Brosnan said attitudes weren't great around Wrigley Field in that era.

"A lot of malcontents ended up playing for the Cubs, or it seemed that way because they bitched a lot. That club had more than its share of gripers. They griped about meal money, travel, griped about what time the game started, everything. Some people just griped. It was part of their personality."

Brosnan had pitched 18 games as a reliever for the Cubs in 1954, Banks' rookie season. He spent all of '55 at Triple A Los Angeles, then won a big-league job to stay in '56. He was stunned by the development of Banks and Gene Baker while he was away.

"The year I was in L.A., Banks became a hitting star, and the Cubs fans loved him. A Cubs fan will embrace any kind of human being if that human being can hit the ball, catch the ball, throw the ball, score runs, and help win ballgames. ... In his prime, Ernie Banks was one of the most dangerous batters in the game."[2]

In 1956, the Cubs set a new franchise record with 94 losses and compiled a .390 winning percentage, their worst since 1901 when they were known as the Chicago Orphans. Reaching that nadir would finally prompt Wrigley to make significant changes, ousting general manager Wid Matthews and manager Stan Hack. Wrigley picked John Holland, who had been the GM with the Los Angeles Angels, as his new front man, naming him and former manager Charlie Grimm, who the Associated Press referred to as "an old standby of the club," as vice presidents.

Holland's father had been a minor league GM, and John had worked in baseball his entire life, beginning as head of concessions for his father's Oklahoma City team. He joined the Cubs organization in 1946 after working in an aircraft plant during World War II and arrived with the belief that the team didn't hold enough talent to win.

"Baseball has been built on changes," Holland said. "The farm system, as we know it today, is the lifeblood of the game, but you can't find success on that alone. We're going to have to try and make trades for proven experienced major league talent."[3]

After he'd been on the job a little more than two months, only 13 players remained from the hapless '56 team. Those players were referred to by the *Chicago Sun-Times'* John C. Hoffman as "survivors from the conglomeration of misfits inherited by the [executioner]."[4]

Banks, of course, was included in the group. He had hit .297 with 28 homers and 85 RBIs, but he and outfielder Walt Moryn were the only players to drive in more than 57 runs. Holland's biggest challenge was to find run-producing hitters to put around Banks, and by the start of the 1958 season, Moryn would be the only regular still left in the Cubs' lineup.

Holland had traded for a couple of aging All-Star hitters—Bobby Thomson, who had delivered the "Shot Heard 'Round the World" in 1951, and first baseman Dale Long. The latter came from Pittsburgh in a trade that cost the Cubs Gene Baker but netted them young outfielder Lee Walls, who some pegged as a future star.

Holland had brought with him Los Angeles manager Bob Scheffing, a former Cubs catcher, as manager. He was immediately challenged in his first spring training, as Banks was bothered by a sore shoulder that forced him to miss much of the exhibition schedule.

Because Banks was having trouble with the throw from short, Scheffing considered moving him across the infield to first base. But Banks returned for a barnstorming trip home and was in the lineup as usual, playing shortstop and hitting cleanup, on Opening Day against Milwaukee.

Gene Baker, now playing third base, was the No. 5 hitter. However, demonstrating the need to continue looking for ways to improve the lineup, Holland sacrificed Baker less than three weeks into the season, sending him and Dee Fondy to Pittsburgh for Long and Walls.

Banks had gotten off to the worst start of his career. He was hitting .152 on the day of the Baker trade and went 1-for-12 the next three games, sliding to .138. But after that, if he was feeling sorry for himself about losing a friend, you couldn't tell it. Banks piled up 13 hits in the next seven games and never really looked back, finishing with vintage numbers—.285 batting average, 43 home runs (second in the NL to Henry Aaron's 44) and a league-high 156 games (including two ties that were made up).

"Of course I missed having Gene out there at second base, but that had nothing to do with the slow getaway I had with the stick," Banks said. "Not having Baker there had nothing to do with my hitting. It was just one of those things. All batters have their slumps. I'm just happy mine came early in the season and that I was able to snap out of it later when we won 29 of our last 56 games."[5]

Walls had an interesting take on his new teammate's value. "You can't exactly say that without him we'd be in the cellar," he said, "but without him we'd be a lot deeper in the cellar."[6]

Banks just missed the home run crown in 1957. After he hit three solo home runs against the Pirates in the second game of a September 14 doubleheader at Wrigley, he and Aaron were tied at 40 apiece. They would both homer three days later, making it 41–41, and Banks moved ahead with his 42nd the following day. Banks was on hand to see Aaron tie him off the Cubs' Drott on September 22nd—an opposite-field blast into the surprisingly full right-field bleachers. The crowd was 25,561—more than these same teams had drawn back on Opening Day.

This wasn't Sammy Sosa and Mark McGwire 1998 style, but it was a good contest between good men, and fans were captivated. The Milwaukee Braves had to bring in extra staff when the team returned home the following day, with a crowd of 40,926 going home in ecstasy after Aaron hit a game-winning homer in the 11th off St. Louis reliever Billy Muffett, wrapping up a pennant. The homer gave Aaron a 43–42 lead over Banks, and he extended it with a blast off Toothpick Jones (traded to St. Louis in the flurry of trades the previous December) the following day.

Banks also homered on September 24—off Cincinnati journeyman Bud Podbielan in the second game of a doubleheader. He had four games to play, all on the road, but he wouldn't hit another homer. You can't say he didn't go down without a fight, however, as he was 5-for-5 with three doubles in the season finale. He could have beaten Aaron, or at least tied him, had he got a little more elevation on a couple of balls that day.

» «

Banks couldn't wait to get to Arizona the following spring. The Cubs had gotten ambitious in hiring a new hitting coach, giving the job to Hall of Famer Rogers Hornsby. A .358 career hitter, he had been a player-manager for the Cubs in the early 1930s and had managed once his career ended but without the success he had when he was on the field.

Hornsby, who had been without a job in baseball since being fired from a job as Cincinnati's manager in 1953, had spent a week working with Cubs' hitters in '57. He was a semi-degenerate gambler, who loved to hang out at racetracks, including Chicago's Arlington Park. He was crusty. He was old school. And some had also considered him to be racist.

"He generally didn't care for colored players," El Tappe had told writer Charles C. Alexander in 1992.[7] But if Hornsby was biased against blacks, it didn't show up in Mesa, where his work with Banks was particularly productive.

Hornsby worked more on approach than mechanics, selling a hitter's confidence and willingness to work from behind in the counts as "the big thing." He told the Cubs' hitters that those two factors, confidence and determination, are always keys "with anyone who becomes a success at anything."[8]

Hornsby felt baseball was in a period where it paid too much attention to home run hitters. He felt too many sluggers considered themselves "the whole show," and that the culture of the game empowered that kind of thinking. But when reporters asked him about Banks, who had almost won the National League's homer crown the year before, Hornsby was quick to make an exception. "I hope Ernie gets a lot more homers," he said. "He's a fine ballplayer."[9]

Banks was eager to work with Hornsby. He was just eager to work, period, feeling he could build off the momentum he had created by overcoming his slow start in '57. He was even excited about the schedule, which had the Cubs traveling to Los Angeles and San Francisco in April, when they normally were at Wrigley Field, using hot-water bottles and anything else available to try to stay warm.

"Usually I have my troubles with the cold weather we get around Chicago and in the East," Banks said.[10]

Hornsby told reporters that Banks was the best young hitter in the game, if not just the best hitter. "[He] is a better hitter than Aaron," he said. "Banks has been up here for five years, proving he can do it. He has great wrist action, and he is learning the strike zone."

Banks absolutely killed the ball that spring. He was 41-for-106 with 25 extra-base hits, including 14 home runs.

"Did you ever see home runs go so high and so far?" Scheffing asked one day. "Those outfielders keep moving back like they'll catch 'em for easy outs, and before they know it they're standing against the fence watching the ball go over."[11]

Long after his career was over, Banks would remember that stretch of hitting as the best of his career. He remembers not just the results but the way other players reacted to him.

"Everybody was looking at me saying, 'What is this guy doing?'" Banks said.

With more protection behind him, Banks would go 3-for-9 in the first two games of the season, both wins in St. Louis. It was the start of a season-opening seven-game hitting streak that left him with a head start on his goal to hit .300. He hit home runs in three consecutive games during that streak.

Walls got off to a huge start in 1958, hitting nine home runs in his first 14 games, including a three-homer flurry off Don Drysdale and the Dodgers' bullpen at the Los Angeles Coliseum, where it was forever to the wall in right-center but only 250' to the stands down the left-field line.

With those two providing run support for a staff that used a league-high 20 pitchers and finished sixth in ERA, the Cubs broke to a 13–7 record out of the gate, leading the NL for 16 of the first 24 days. They encountered their familiar losing streak, however, this time a seven-gamer that dropped them to fourth place.

The team never really recovered, although Scheffing and Banks received huge billing when the Cubs climbed back into a tight race in July, trailing Milwaukee and San Francisco (who were in a virtual tie) by 2½ games as late as July 18. The altitude got to the team, however, as they then went through a 6–16 stretch that took them out of the race.

Banks barely noticed. He was on a mission and nothing was going to stop him, including problems at home with Mollye. Except for a two-week period in late May, Banks kept his batting average above .300 all season, finishing at .313. He was consistent in hitting long balls, too, never going more than 10 games without a home run.

Hornsby said Banks improved by making one of the universal adjustments available to a hitter—learning to use the whole field.

"We tried to make him hit the good balls down the middle and to right field," Hornsby said. "Before he was a dead left-field hitter, and they were getting him on outside pitches."

There was talk Banks could become the fifth NL player to hit 50 homers. "I don't know," he said. "I guess you have to be lucky to do that. I'll be swinging; that's all I can do."[12]

Banks was making baseball look easy. "He's a good shortstop; nothing flashy, but a good workman," Scheffing said. "He's such a good athlete that he doesn't even work up a sweat on a hot day, and that's something."

When Banks hit his 39th and 40th home runs in a win over the Pirates on August 21, reporters and fans began to talk about whether he could seriously challenge Babe Ruth's record of 60. The odds were massively against him, of course, as there were only 32 games left, but it was something to talk about.

Banks wouldn't take the bait. "All I ever think about is winning the ballgame," he said.[13]

That wasn't all he thought about, of course.

As always, there was the beauty of the game—"I love to see the ball go over the fence," he said—and the business of the game. In some ways Banks had never stopped being the kid who had to be bribed by his father to play catch.

"The more homers I hit," he said, "the more money I make." Banks' salary was estimated at $40,000, but the talk was that the breakout season could drive that above $50,000, perhaps even to $55,000.[14]

While the Cubs stumbled home at 72–82, their 12th consecutive losing season, they couldn't take Banks down with them. He led the NL with 47 homers, 12 more than runner-up Frank Thomas. Banks had 129 RBIs, 20 more than Thomas.

Despite the Cubs' fifth-place finish, there was little doubt Banks would be named the NL's Most Valuable Player. He would receive 16-of-24 first-place votes from members of the Baseball Writers Association of America, easily outdistancing the second-place finisher, Willie Mays.

≫ ≪

Two months after the MVP vote was revealed, Banks was back in the headlines, and this time they were not flattering. Little had ever been known about Banks' life away from the field—had many people other than Buck O'Neil, Gene Baker, and a few other friends really cared?—but that changed with newspaper stories about Mollye filing for divorce.

The court papers revealed she was charging Banks with cruelty. She said they had been separated only since December 13. But these problems didn't come out of the blue. Monte Irvin said that Banks' marriage had been "on the rocks" when they played together in 1956, and by the '58 season Ernie and Mollye were rarely together.

Banks chose not to contest the action—in fact, he may have wanted it sped up—as he had met another woman of interest. In a hearing before Judge John A.

Sparbaro, the Cubs' star was ordered to pay Mollye a $65,000 settlement in lieu of alimony, as the couple had no children.[15]

This was a huge amount of money for any baseball player in the 1950s, but not for Phil Wrigley. Neither Banks nor the Cubs' owner ever discussed where the settlement money came from, but the belief around the team was that Wrigley had stepped in to help his star player.

Banks, who married Eloyse Johnson as soon as the ink was dry on his divorce, went to work the following spring as if it had been a typical winter. His play in 1959 was a continuation of '58, and for a long time it looked like this might be the year the Cubs compiled a winning record, if not becoming true contenders. They were 8–8 in April, 15–16 in May, and hung around .500 through June and July, sitting in fourth place in the NL with a 50–48 record on July 28. But the game at County Stadium the following day proved to be a turning point.

The pitching matchup—Dave Hillman vs. the Braves' Lew Burdette, who had won 20 games the year before and was on his way to 21 wins this season—favored Milwaukee, but Banks homered off Burdette twice. That wasn't enough, however, as Henry Aaron also homered twice, and the Braves turned back the Cubs 8–5. They won 6–2 behind Spahn the next day, and the Cubs were headed for another seven-game losing streak and renewed irrelevance in another pennant chase. Walls and other players who had created excitement the year before could not back up those seasons, leaving too much in Banks' hands.

Banks finished the season hitting .304 with 45 homers and a league-best 143 RBIs while also setting two fielding records. He was charged with only 12 errors, the fewest ever by a shortstop who played enough to qualify as a regular, and he had a .985 fielding percentage. Banks probably would have traded those for a second home run title, but as in 1957 he was edged by a Brave.

Banks led Mathews by two homers late in the season, 42–40. Mathews homered on September 20 off future Hall of Famer Robin Roberts, cutting that lead to one entering the final week. Banks hit his 43rd in St. Louis on the 21st, off the yet-to-be-known-as-infamous Ernie Broglio, but Mathews hit a pair at Pittsburgh that night, making it 43-all. The Cubs came home to Wrigley Field for series against the Giants and Dodgers, and Banks delivered No. 44 on Wednesday off San Francisco's Johnny Antonelli and No. 45 on Friday off Los Angeles' Danny McDevitt, who was pitching in relief of Don Drysdale.

Mathews wouldn't slow down. He couldn't, really, as the Braves were swapping leads with the Dodgers in a tense race for the pennant. Mathews had matched Banks by hitting his 44th on Wednesday at Pittsburgh and then, after a travel day, he hit his 45th on Friday at County Stadium off the Phillies' Don Cardwell. Banks and Mathews were tied 45–45, and Banks had a problem.

Johnny Podres hit him in the leg with a pitch in the third inning on Saturday. Banks played through the pain to finish the game, but he could barely get around the clubhouse afterward. Scheffing announced that was it—Banks couldn't play on Sunday.

Banks didn't start the Cubs' final game, but he did play, emerging from the dugout in the seventh inning to pinch hit for pitcher Glen Hobbie. Fans went crazy, and Banks popped up to shortstop Maury Wills. The fans stood and cheered as Banks hobbled back to the dugout.

He was so touched by the response of the Wrigley Field fans that a couple of years later he called that moment the favorite in his career. "I wanted to play," Banks told the *Chicago Tribune*'s Dave Condon in 1961. "I felt I should. The Dodgers and Braves were neck-and-neck in the race, and it was the obligation of the other clubs to do their best to whip both. Anyhow, I wasn't able to play the next day, but [Scheffing] had me on the bench to pinch hit. The chance came, and I limped out. The greeting the crowd gave me made all my baseball career worthwhile. Then I went to the plate and popped out. The real thrill came next—an ovation as I limped back.

"Was that my greatest thrill? I'd say it would have to be one of a very few top ones. Probably my most appreciated thrill because they cheered me when I hadn't done a thing."[16]

Mathews, who like Banks didn't homer in either of the last two games, got to keep playing as the Dodgers and Braves ended the year with identical 86–68 records. He hit No. 46 in the second game of a best-of-three playoff series with the Dodgers, and rules called for such tie-breaking games to be considered regular-season games. Thus Banks lost his share of the crown.

Banks got the last laugh when the MVP voting was announced. He received only 10 first-place votes this time around (six fewer than a year earlier) but was elected MVP as the Braves' Aaron and Mathews and the Dodgers' Wally Moon split the other 13 votes. One writer was apparently so perplexed he simply didn't vote, as only 23 of the 24 ballots distributed were cast.

Banks received 232 points in the BBWAA's vote, followed closely by Mathews (189), Aaron (174), and Moon (161). Since MVP voting began in 1931, no NL player had previously won two years in a row. It had happened four times in the American League, with Jimmie Foxx, Hal Newhouser, Yogi Berra, and Mickey Mantle repeating.

Scheffing, through some unexplained formula he had contrived, figured that Banks was "directly responsible" for 27 of the Cubs' 74 wins in 1959, the team's 13th consecutive losing season, and said that the Yankees' Joe DiMaggio was the only player he'd ever seen that he would rate more highly than Banks.

Rob Neyer, a disciple of numbers genius Bill James who serves as an analyst for ESPN, found it a little too overly simplistic to credit any player as "directly responsible" for 36 percent of his team's victories. He and others who use statistics to design metrics that reveal value over replacement player (VORP) and fielding prowess (UZR, ultimate zone rating) have often been critical of baseball writers' subjective votes, believing they lean too heavily on a players' "intangibles," and other non-quantitative factors that favor the conventional choice.

If ever a player could have benefited from popularity, it was Banks. He was not only beloved in Chicago but also became a favorite of some top New York writers, including the *Times'* Arthur Daley and the *Daily News'* Dick Young, who is credited as being a pioneer in working to get to know players and air their viewpoints, not just those of management.

Did Banks really deserve those back-to-back MVP awards? Would they stand up over the performance of Mays, Aaron, and Matthews?

According to Neyer, who weighed that question with the benefit of more than 50 years' historical perspective, the voters got it right both times.

"It's generally not hard to figure out why players won MVP Awards in the 1950s, as the voters typically favored 1) catchers who posted big hitting numbers for pennant-winning teams, or 2) players who drove in huge numbers of runs.

"A great deal is made of Banks winning two straight MVP Awards while playing for a fifth-place team, but just a few years earlier Hank Sauer had won the award while playing for a fifth-place Cubs team. What else did Banks and Sauer have in common? Both led the National League in RBI in their MVP seasons. [Sauer also led the NL in home runs, and Banks did in one of his MVP seasons.]

"And in all three cases, these candidates benefited from the [however slightly] subpar performances of others. We know that the voters preferred big RBI men on pennant-winning teams. But in 1952 when Sauer won, the pennant-winning Dodgers didn't have that big RBI man. Gil Hodges led the Dodgers with 102 RBIs, but that figure paled beside Sauer's 121 and Hodges finished 19th in MVP balloting [well behind five teammates]. Basically, the voters couldn't support Hodges when he so obviously wasn't even close to being the most valuable *Dodger* [and it didn't hurt that Roy Campanella had a poor season, by his standards]. Similarly in 1958 and '59, Banks' MVP competition just sort of fell away.

"In '58 the Braves won the pennant, and many MVP voters would love to have voted for a Brave. But their best player was Henry Aaron, and Aaron didn't drive in 100 runs. Eddie Mathews drove in 77 runs and didn't get a single mention in the MVP balloting. Warren Spahn led the NL with 22 wins...but teammate Lew Burdette won 20 games *and* finished with a lower ERA. If the Braves had a catcher or a middle infielder with big numbers, maybe he would have given Banks a fight...but they didn't."

Aaron, who was on a better team in '59, topped Banks in OPS—the simple metric that became popular after the turn of the millennium. It adds on-base percentage to slugging average to get one simple rating of a player's contributions at the plate, both in reaching base and in generating extra-base power.

Aaron's OPS was 1.037. Banks' was .970 (down from a career best .980 in '58). Yet Neyer said it was Banks who was the most deserving because there's more to baseball than hitting.

"The Braves had two outstanding MVP candidates in Aaron and Mathews... but they split the vote *and* the Braves didn't actually win the pennant, losing a best-of-three playoff series to the Dodgers," Neyer said. "I don't know—perhaps some or most or all of the voters had already sent in their ballots before the playoff series. But the combination of the two Braves splitting the vote and the Dodgers' relatively weak lineup—Wally Moon finished fourth in the MVP balloting with 19 homers and 74 RBIs and Charlie Neal finished eighth—made it relatively easy for Banks.

"Which seems only fair, as Banks probably was the best player in the National League in 1959. Yes, Mathews had a higher slugging percentage, and Aaron topped Banks in both slugging percentage *and* on-base percentage. But neither of those guys were shortstops. Banks was a shortstop, and a good one.

"In fact, from 1955—when Banks switched to a particularly light bat— through 1960, he was probably as good as anybody in the National League. Mickey Mantle might have been better in the American League. And Willie Mays was probably *as good as* Banks.

"Banks wasn't a perfect hitter. He didn't usually hit for a high batting average, and he didn't draw a great number of walks. But his power and his defensive skills made him as valuable as anybody in the league for six years."

Only 28 years old, Banks already had almost everything you could have in baseball—everything except a championship ring.

≫ ≪

When Ernie Banks talks about the Cubs' teams of the 1960s, the ones that teased a generation of fans with a core of players that included Billy Williams and Ron Santo, he speaks of the closeness they had despite such different lives away from Wrigley Field.

"We played together, and we lived apart," he said. "Most of the players lived north. I lived south, me and Billy."

Not by choice.

In Chicago in that era, African Americans were not welcome in many neighborhoods and were legally excluded by housing covenants. Exceptions were made for some athletes and entertainers but not always—and some didn't want to be treated as exceptions.

Segregated neighborhoods weren't just an issue in Chicago, of course. Even cities as progressive as San Francisco could act as if they were being run by Bull Connor.

Willie Mays was the talk of that city after Horace Stoneham announced plans to move the Giants westward in 1957. He had said and done all the right things about the move, working not to alienate his fans and friends in New York while cultivating new ones in San Francisco.

191

Once in '57 a reporter asked if he had thought about playing a "dirty trick" by not making the move to California with his team. "Mister, I like to play ball," he said. "I'd walk barefooted to San Francisco just to get in the lineup."[17]

Mays received tremendous coverage from a January press conference in which he was given a $67,500 contract for the 1958 season, which was the third largest in baseball (behind Ted Williams' $100,000 and Stan Musial's $80,000). But Mays had been in the news a couple months earlier as the result of house hunting with his wife, Marghuerite.

They headed to San Francisco shortly after Mays had completed his annual barnstorming tour and quickly fell in love with a new two-story home at 175 Miraloma Drive. It was just north of Daly City, next to the exclusive community of St. Francis Wood.

In James Hirsch's biography of Mays, it is described as being "set on a steep, winding hill, its most distinctive feature a span of large glass windows that offered a sweeping view of the Pacific Ocean." The house was perfect, except that after Mays had paid a $100 binder as part of his offer ($37,500 in cash) for the house, the developer had begun working to make the deal go away.

Walter A. Gnesdiloff said that after he received Mays' offer on the house, he and his wife began receiving calls from agitated residents in the neighborhood who did not want an African American family to move in. The calls, he said, made him fear for his own livelihood.

Suddenly the house was mysteriously taken off the market. Someone had tipped the *San Francisco Chronicle* to this personal drama, and Edward Howden, director of the city's Council of Civic Unity, created to combat racial inequality, received a call from Mays' real-estate broker.

The situation had turned into a mess and officially became a nasty black eye for the city when the *Chronicle* ran a front-page story on the standoff between Mays and his prospective neighbors. "I'm just a union working man," Gnesdiloff told the newspaper. "I'd never get another job if I sold this house to that baseball player. I feel sorry for him, and if the neighbors said it was okay, I would do it."

Another home builder, Martin Gaehwiler, was among the most vocal opponents of the deal. He was bold enough to state his objections for the record. "I happen to have quite a few pieces of property in that area, and I stand to lose a lot if colored people move in," Gaehwiler told the *Chronicle*. "I certainly wouldn't like to have a colored family near me.... I told [Gnesdiloff] to use his own conscience but that he'd get a bad name if he went through with this."

Howden, on the other hand, referred to the situation as "nothing less than a civic disgrace." For his part, Mays was gracious, saying that if neighbors don't want you, what's the good of buying? But he also spoke a truth when he pointed out the blatant inequality.

"They'll talk about a thing like this all over the world," he said, "and it sure looks bad for our country."

Media pressure quickly collapsed the opposition, and Gnesdiloff agreed to sell the house to Mays. Newsmen and cameras tracked the final steps, which were not without their own drama as Gnesdiloff was under pressure from both sides. The broker representing Gnesdiloff elected to forego his $1,125 commission rather than do business with a black man.

Mays again took the high road.

"I'm glad this is over," he said. "I didn't want any trouble in the first place. All I wanted was a nice house in this town where I'll be playing ball. And I don't think the neighbors will make any trouble, either. They'll calm down now that it's over."

His wife wasn't as forgiving. "Sure they'll calm down," Marghuerite said. "We're not planning to have tea and crumpets with them."

Hirsch reported that Mays moved from his home in New York that winter, bringing with him "five televisions, his raft of trophies, his pool table, and his white Cadillac convertible," and that by February, Gray Line buses were swinging through the neighborhood and stopping in front of 175 Miraloma Drive so that tourists could get a look at where Willie Mays lived.[18]

≫ ≪

His divorce from Mollye in the works, Banks wouldn't be single for long. He met Eloyse Johnson in a random encounter at an office in Chicago's Loop after the 1958 season, and they had a whirlwind courtship.

The recently crowned MVP acted fast when he and Johnson were both in Los Angeles that winter. Eloyse was visiting her parents, and Ernie was there to be honored at a sports banquet. The new couple went to dinner together, and afterward he asked her to marry him.

"When?" Eloyse asked.

"Right now," Banks answered.

As easily as that, as if marriage was a hanging curveball, he swung for the fences with his future. He and Eloyse caught a taxi for Los Angeles International Airport, where they bought tickets for the first plane headed to Las Vegas. Later that night, in a 24-hour chapel, they exchanged vows.[19]

They had twin sons, Joel and Jerry, the following fall, with Ernie celebrating his second MVP Award. That put Banks in need of a home that was suited to a growing family.

Banks was earning enough money to live wherever he wanted. He could have afforded a condo with a view in one of the nicest high-rises downtown or along Lake Shore Drive on the Gold Coast. He could have joined teammates in moving to a quiet suburb like Park Ridge or even an affluent one like Winnetka or Glencoe.

But Chicago's housing market was controlled by covenants that prohibited sales to differing ethnic groups—usually non-whites, but some neighborhoods even limited development to certain areas or origin, such as families of Irish and Italian backgrounds.

Banks knew what Mays had gone through to purchase his home in San Francisco. That was the kind of discussion that would often be held privately, including time together on the barnstorming tours. And he knew that Chicago was not ahead of San Francisco on issues like segregation and racial tolerance. Just because he was Mr. Cub didn't mean he could expect to be welcomed next door to Mr. and Mrs. Bob Smith, unless the Smiths were also black.

So Ernie and Eloyse were forced to look south of the city's ghettos. They found a large brownstone on a corner lot at 8159 S. Rhodes Avenue, on the corner of Rhodes and 82nd.

He had been closer to Wrigley Field when he stayed at the Pershing Hotel with Buck O'Neil and the Kansas City Monarchs. According to Mapquest, his new house was 11.6 miles away from Wrigley Field, but because Chicago's highway system was still being designed—the Dan Ryan Expressway running south from downtown wouldn't open until the winter of 1961–62—he might as well have been twice that far away.

Banks, as was his pattern, had chosen the path of least resistance. His decision to do so was reinforced once when he accepted an invitation from a white sportswriter to visit his house for an interview over dinner.

The writer lived in a whites-only neighborhood, and Banks must have attracted attention as he drove slowly down the street in his Cadillac, checking out street addresses.

"When he went out to go home, all the tires were flat," remembered John Kuenster, who covered the Cubs for the *Chicago Daily News*. "Somebody had cut the tires. Can you believe that? I don't remember if we had to get a new set of tires or just found somebody to fix them, but we got Ernie's car up and going again and he went home, almost like nothing had happened. He never said anything about it."

Billy Williams, who had joined the Cubs earlier that season, and his wife, Shirley, moved near Banks after he established himself as a fixture in left field. He and Banks would sometimes car pool to the ballpark in the late 1960s, when Chicago was on fire with change, much of it relating to the cultural bias against African Americans.

Williams has said they would talk about the times and their own experiences with discrimination on the ride but that the topic always changed to baseball when they were in sight of the ballpark.[20] There was life and there was baseball, and it was the latter that Banks knew he could count on because he didn't need anybody's help.

"What I learned [through the years] is I played in the game with nobody there but me," Banks said. "I didn't think about the fans because we didn't have [many]. I didn't hear them, didn't see them. I just played the game, me and the ball. I don't care who's throwing it, I'm going to hit it. I'm going to catch it. I'm going to throw it. I'm going to do the things as if I'm playing by myself. … This is just me doing this, and that's just it. Sometimes I'd walk out of the ballpark, walk right past my kids like they weren't even there. Everybody thought I was crazy, the way I've been."

14

AUGUST

There are times that you can't ignore feelings of mortality. Ernie Banks came face to face with real doubt toward the end of the 1968 season.

Although the Cubs were in the process of finishing strong, going 53–37 to grab third place behind St. Louis and San Francisco after a slow start, a finish that would build the optimism they carried forward, Banks felt all of his 37 years. To feel his age was a new experience, and he couldn't shake the feeling that he was approaching his last stand.

"I try not to think about it, but it's always there," Banks said. "It's got to come. Maybe this year. I wouldn't say it at the start of the year, like Roger Maris did. That'd be like playing with half your heart, knowing it was over. I wouldn't want to be just (playing) 100, 115 games like Willie Mays does now. I couldn't sit on the bench. If I'm playing, I got to play."

Banks still ran into his share of home runs but batted only .211 the last couple months of the '68 season. He didn't know how much longer he could continue hitting old rivals like Don Drysdale and Bob Gibson and newcomers like Tom Seaver and Jerry Koosman, especially if he didn't start feeling better.

"I wore down last year," Banks said. "The last month or two, I was just dragging. I didn't admit it to anyone. I didn't ask out of any games. But I had no bounce. It was a struggle.… The end's coming. I feel it. It scares me. It saddens me."[1]

There were no small slumps for Banks as 1969 wound down. He had gone 1-for-12 in a stretch of five games that included Leo Durocher's camping adventure, starting only three of them, but he homered off San Francisco's Bobby

Bolin on July 31, his 16th homer of the season. The Cubs were in first place, and Banks was fully focused on delivering when it mattered most.

Yet he couldn't get the words of Roberto Clemente out of his head. And it wasn't just Clemente who questioned whether the Cubs had what it took to hold on.

Unlike the belief expressed by the *Chicago Tribune*'s Robert Markus and so many others who had followed the '69 Cubs since the dramatic first act, many people wearing baseball spikes were skeptical about the Cubs' chances. They knew success was never preordained.

"Leo Durocher is an excellent manager, but the Cubs have got to put a little faith in their gloves and bats and not so much in Durocher," Cincinnati's Pete Rose said. "He can't swing their bats for them."[2]

As he had with Clemente, Banks went to opposing players he considered to be friends seeking thoughts about the Cubs' chances of hanging on. The answers were unsettling.

"I'm saying this now in love," Banks told a crowd of Cubs' fans at the Highland Park library in 2010. "I would talk to Clemente, Hank Aaron, [Willie] Stargell, when we were leading.... I'd ask them, 'Hey, what are our chances of winning the pennant?' They'd look at me and just start laughing.

"'Come on, tell me the truth, what are our chances of winning the pennant?' Ha, ha, ha, ha, ha. They would say, 'Ernie, let me tell you this, you guys have no chance of winning the pennant.'

"'Why not? We're leading the division now.' Well, when you all get closer and closer to winning, you're gonna have five players—I'm not going to [repeat] who they are, but they told me—who are not going to be able to catch the ball, they're not going to be able to hit the ball, not going to be able to do anything.'

"From that I learned winning a world championship when you get close to the end, is tough, really, really tough. You have to have the heart. What they were saying is there are going to be many players dropping balls, making errors, throwing fastballs for home runs, all kinds of stuff. What is that? It means that when you are going for the World Series, it is tough. If we had played seven-inning games, we'd have won about 15 different World Series."

>> «

From July 31 through August 19, the Cubs went 13–4, extending their lead over the Mets from 5½ games to as many as 10 games at one point. Jenkins won four of his five starts in this stretch, including back-to-back shutouts at San Diego and San Francisco, both times starting on only three days of rest, as he would in 28-of-42 starts that season. But the crowning moment, the one Chicagoans haven't stopped talking about, came when Ken Holtzman faced Atlanta on August 19, a Tuesday afternoon when the park was packed.

It was a typical late-summer day—76 degrees but the strong wind blowing in off Lake Michigan making it chilly in the shadows. Phil Niekro, the knuckleballer who would win 23 games that season, opposed Holtzman. He was annoyed with the Cubs, who had traded his younger brother, Joe, to San Diego after Durocher told him to stop screwing around with a knuckleball, but he always enjoyed pitching in Wrigley Field.

"You go out and take BP, shag fly balls, you can talk to the people," Niekro said. "They're right there. I'd go out there to just smell the place. You'd smell beer, popcorn, catsup, mustard. You'd see the ivy.… Sometimes when I wasn't pitching, I'd go down and sit in the bullpen just to enjoy the park, the people. I'd stick my hand behind my back and somebody would give me a little popcorn, maybe even a hot dog. What a great place."

Niekro also got a kick out of Banks, who was Wrigley's unofficial greeter.

"He always had that smile," Niekro said. "It was always a beautiful day. I don't care if it was cold, snowing, 105 degrees with humidity. He always had that smile. It was a good day for baseball. He just brightened your day.… He always talked to you. You'd be taking BP, and he'd walk by and say, 'Hey, Niekro, how's that knuckleball?'"

On this day, the knuckler took a little while to get going but then became devilish. He allowed a three-run homer to Ron Santo after singles by Don Kessinger and Glenn Beckert in the first inning, but he gave up nothing else. It didn't matter as everything the Braves hit off Holtzman was right at somebody.

"He didn't have a strikeout against us," Niekro said. "I remember hitting a line drive to right field that I thought was going to be a hit. In came the right fielder and caught it at his knees."

Holtzman walked shortstop Gil Garrido in the third inning, catcher Bob Didier in the fifth, and left fielder Rico Carty in the seventh, but the Braves couldn't manage a hit. Leading off the seventh inning, Aaron lifted a blast that seemed headed for Waveland Avenue.

"Everybody said, 'There it is, a home run,'" Niekro remembered. "[Billy] Williams went all the way back to the wall and was looking up, like he knew he couldn't get it, and all of a sudden he's coming back [toward the infield] and he caught it."

Holtzman knew he'd been lucky. "Should have been a home run," he said. "I'll never forget the look Hammer gave me. Let's face it. When Hammer hits it, you know it's gone. ... He was almost to second base when he saw Billy catch the ball. He made a U-turn around second base and ran about 4' from me as he came past the mound. He just looked at me, puzzled, quizzical, and I just looked back at him. Nothing was said. Nothing needed to be said."[3]

Holtzman faced Aaron again in the ninth, this time retiring him on a screaming groundout to Beckert. Durocher was ecstatic afterward, praising the 23-year-old lefty as being "this far short of Sandy Koufax," with his hands about 6" apart.

There were 40 games left to play, and it was still the Cubs' world.

≫ ≪

Holtzman's no-hitter came in his 29th start of the season. He had opened the season as the Cubs' No. 3 starter. His Mets counterpart, rookie Gary Gentry, also started on August 19. It was his 25th start. The difference was typical for the two staffs, with Durocher choosing the then-standard four-man starting rotation while Gil Hodges spread out the workload across five primary starters.

Fergie Jenkins, Bill Hands, Holtzman, and Dick Selma (who had taken over the spot that had belonged to Joe Niekro at the start of the season) were not visibly fatigued. Hands was en route to the only 20-win season of his career, and Holtzman had just thrown the Cubs' first no-hitter since 1960. But as a staff they were beginning to hit the invisible wall between peak performance and diminished results despite stubborn effort, and Banks and their teammates couldn't help but notice.

Few people talked about the workload that the starting pitchers were carrying because these guys inspired confidence. The concern was more for the durability of the players in Durocher's set lineup. With the exception of center field and right field, the Cubs almost always played Randy Hundley, Banks, Beckert (except when he was injured), Kessinger, Ron Santo, and Williams.

Hundley was one of baseball's all-time iron men. He played more than any National League catcher that season, and the group of catchers included Johnny Bench, Tim McCarver, Manny Sanguillen, Tom Haller, and the Astros' Johnny Edwards. Those five and the other six regulars averaged 134 games caught, with the Mets' Jerry Grote (who platooned with J.C. Martin) catching only 113 games. Hundley caught 151, including the 145 times that he started.

The year before, Hundley had set a record that will never be broken. He caught 160 of the Cubs' 162 games and probably would have matched that mark in '69 had he not gotten beat up. Hot summers were always a problem for Hundley—as the lack of lights at Wrigley meant nothing but day games when the Cubs were home—but Durocher was such a believer in toughness that he never saw the benefit of resting a player to keep him fresh for the end of the season.

Hundley said fatigue became an issue by August every season. "I lost so much weight I couldn't reach the warning track," he said. "But Leo wanted me out there every day handling the pitchers."

Other players were showing the wear and tear, too. Kessinger lost so much weight that season—perhaps as much as 15–20 pounds—that one account said his uniform hung off him like drapes.[4] But pitching is always the area where fatigue takes the biggest toll on a team.

The Cubs played 13 games in the last 12 days of August, going 6–7 with the starting pitchers compiling a 4.42 ERA. Meanwhile, the Mets had quietly found a sixth gear.

They had enough pitching to handle a schedule that would have crushed a team relying on only star players and pitchers, playing 12 doubleheaders in the second half of the season (compared to only three for the Cubs). They swept doubleheaders against the last-place Padres on August 16, 17, and 26, allowing Preston Gomez's expansion team to score only nine runs in those six games.

The Mets were putting heat on the Cubs, and it started with Tom Seaver, Jerry Koosman, Don Cardwell, Jim McAndrew, and Gentry. The Mets went 14–3 in the last 16 days of August, with the starting rotation compiling a 1.83 ERA.

Tired? These guys were just getting started.

>> <<

Some good things were still happening for the Cubs. They produced a wild victory at Wrigley Field in the opener of a doubleheader against Houston on August 24.

Down 8–2 after the Astros jumped on Jenkins and lefty Rich Nye, the Cubs fought back to win 10–9. Banks homered twice in the game, including an eighth-inning shot off Fred Gladding that put the Cubs ahead, as the Bleacher Bums and everyone else in a sellout crowd went delirious.

Chicago Today's Rick Talley described the scene. "While Banks was trotting around the bases, I watched the fans," he wrote. "They didn't have horns or they would have blown their heads off. No balloons either. No confetti. No tubs to thump. So they just jumped in place and screamed and screamed, fists clenched and thrust toward P.K. Wrigley's sun. Cushions, programs, and beer cups flew through the air, and those people with enough strength picked up their chairs and held them triumphantly over their heads. It was enough to bring tears, and there were probably some of those, too."

Who cared if you had to pay $3 to park your car near Wrigley and another $1.50 for a standing-room-only ticket?

But that win was followed with a 3–2 loss in the second game when Banks could summon no more magic no matter how badly he tried. He was 1-for-3 against Don Wilson, who he hated to face, and the hit was a leadoff single that led nowhere.

In New York, Seaver and Koosman were pushing each other like few teammates ever have, both before and since. Every time he sent out his young aces, Hodges expected they would pitch very well, if not win, and after the middle of August they never disappointed him.

Seaver, a workout fiend, set the tone. He saw baseball as a game about little advantages, and he felt he gained one by driving himself hard.

"It's why you run wind sprints in 104-degree heat in the middle of the afternoon in St. Louis in the summer," he said. "In the ninth inning with the game on the line, you draw strength from that."5

Seaver could see the mental toughness of the Mets building.

"The difference between the physical abilities of the players in the major leagues is not that great, and something going hand in hand with that, the difference between the teams is not that great," Seaver said. "So what it comes down to is that the dividing factor between the one that wins and the one that loses is the mental attitude, the effort they give, the mental alertness that keeps them from making mental mistakes. The concentration and the dedication— the intangibles—are the deciding factors, I think, between who [wins] and who [loses]. I firmly believe that. I really do."6

Reinforcements matter, too. And while the Mets were given a jolt when Donn Clendenon was added via trade, the Cubs mostly had to do with the players they had. John Holland had made two early moves that were important—trading for Dick Selma and utility man Paul Popovich—but he knew his pitching staff was still thin. The trading deadline long since past, he could make only a minor addition and purchased 36-year-old right hander Ken Johnson from the New York Yankees on August 11.

Johnson started the second game of that August 24 doubleheader but was no match for Wilson. He was a Band-Aid, and the Cubs' problems were hardly superficial. They had essentially wasted a roster spot on No. 3 catcher Ken Rudolph all season, but now it was all hands on deck. Holland summoned the 19-year-old center fielder Oscar Gamble from Double-A San Antonio, where he had hit .298, and Durocher threw him into the lineup.

When the Mets left for a 10-game West Coast trip in late August, the Cubs discovered a new way to become fatigued. Many of the players, Banks included, would stay up late to get the Mets' scores before going to bed.

On the night of August 27, after Holtzman had lost to Cincinnati, Banks waited through the evening news in hopes of hearing that the Padres had beaten the Mets. But the game was still going when the Chicago newscasts went off the air, so Banks took matters into his own hands. He tracked down a telephone number for the San Diego press box and placed a call to San Diego Stadium.7

Koosman had done it again—a two-hitter to win 4–1, cutting the Cubs' lead down to 2½ games.

Oh brother. Banks' worst fears were coming true. He knew it had been a mistake to let himself think ahead to the World Series. But how could he stop himself?

Almost three weeks earlier, the Chicago Bears had announced an agreement to play their October 12 game against the Minnesota Vikings at Northwestern University's Dyche Stadium in the event that Wrigley Field, their normal home, was needed by the pennant-winning Cubs.[8] Surely it would be needed, wouldn't it?

15

JOHN BOCCABELLA,
JOHN HERRNSTEIN, AND
OTHER TRESPASSERS

Players can only control so much in team sports. Few knew that lesson better than Ernie Banks, but he never complained about the mediocrity and silliness that often swirled around him at Wrigley Field. It's a wonder he could talk at the end of his career given how often he must have bit his tongue.

Year in and year out, he arrived in spring training carrying the highest expectations for the Cubs only to see them dashed, often before they had blossomed into real hope.

This was the case in 1960—a season that would be a line of demarcation for Banks' career. It was the last season that he was in his peak form both at the plate and at shortstop, and it was the last time that the Cubs' management would simply leave him alone and let him play.

If there was a blessing, it was that he had to know right away that it wasn't going to be his year. Phil Wrigley and his top baseball man, John Holland, had fired Bob Scheffing, arguably the easiest manager that Banks ever had a chance to play for, and replaced him with "Jolly Cholly."

Charlie Grimm was the company man who, when managing the Milwaukee Braves, would regularly refer to Hank Aaron as "Stepin Fetchit," the comic character played in movies by Lincoln Perry that perpetuated the stereotype of blacks as lazy and unintelligent. But Wrigley didn't bother to consider whether the 61-year-old was right for the changing times, instead seizing on the fact that the Cubs had won three pennants in Grimm's two previous stints as manager, most recently in 1945.

"Every time he manages, we win a pennant," Wrigley reasoned.[1]

Unlike Phil Cavarretta in 1954, Grimm at least made it out of spring training. But he was hardly around long enough to win one more pennant, sacked by Wrigley after the Cubs got off to a 6–11 start.

Grimm hadn't trusted the organization's young players, including 20-year-old third baseman Ron Santo and 22-year-old outfielder Billy Williams, in spring training. He went with veterans to start the season and they let him down, prompting Wrigley to make one of his most unusual moves—he ordered that Grimm swap roles with Lou Boudreau, who was Jack Quinlan's color man on radio broadcasts.

Boudreau managed the last 137 games of the season, ushering in both Santo and Williams along the way. The one thing he had going for him on a team that finished 60–94 was the hitting of his shortstop.

Banks was very much the same player who had won MVP awards the previous two seasons. He finished with a .271 average, 41 home runs, and 117 RBIs—20 homers and 53 RBIs more than any of his teammates. He won his second home-run crown, edging Aaron by one and Eddie Mathews by two even though he failed to hit a homer in his last 56 at-bats after hitting one off Sandy Koufax on September 17.

Banks finished fourth in MVP voting behind Dick Groat, Don Hoak, and Willie Mays.

The election of Groat, a shortstop who won a batting title for the pennant-winning Pirates, ended a streak of seven years when the MVP had been won by an African American—a stunning feat considering that this was only the 14th season blacks had been allowed to play.

Lonnie Wheeler, author of the Aaron biography *If I Had a Hammer*, calculated that less than 8 percent of major leaguers were black in their first decade of participation, yet they had managed to dominate the National League.

Ten MVP awards were handed out in the 1950s, and eight went to blacks— Roy Campanella three times, Banks twice, and Don Newcombe, Mays, and Aaron once. Black players had combined to hit .280, compared to .261 for whites, and for every 20 home runs that black players hit, white players hit 13 in the same number of at-bats. For every 10 bases that a black player stole, a white player stole four.

Across the board, the 1960s would be an even better decade for black players in the National League. Banks witnessed it all in Chicago, but he would regularly be betrayed by his body (especially his knees) and his franchise.

>> <<

As the start of the 1960 season approached, Banks told a reporter that he sometimes couldn't believe the life he was leading. "This whole thing is so great," Banks said. "It scares me sometimes."[2]

In many ways, the 1960s would remain great for Banks. He maintained his stature as Mr. Cub and was presented with business opportunities he couldn't have imagined when the 1950s began with him riding buses alongside Buck O'Neil and his Monarchs teammates. These included involvement in a bowling alley and, in partnership with former Tuskegee Airman Robert Nelson, a Ford dealership on S. Stony Island Avenue, near his home on the South Side.

But Chicago was on fire with racial unrest and social change throughout the decade, and Banks was constantly being tugged toward a responsibility that always seemed an odd fit for a man happiest when traveling America with a baseball team.

Banks ran unsuccessfully for alderman in Chicago's 8th Ward at the start of the decade, failing to unseat a Democrat; traveled to Europe with Eloyse; took courses at the University of Chicago in sociology and the problems of juvenile delinquents; and at the end of the decade he toured Vietnam on a goodwill mission with some other players and baseball executives.

He added a daughter (Jan) to the family that included twin sons. He also played for nine different managers, surviving Wrigley's confusing concept of the College of Coaches and then waging a cold war with Leo Durocher, who never got over managing a player who had more leverage with management than he did. He experienced near-trades, position changes, and even questions about his eyesight, which once had been judged as 20/13.

Much of the time, Banks seemed on top of the world. He not only toured Europe for three weeks with Eloyse after the 1966 season but was given an audience with the Pope. He visited London, Vienna, Budapest, Rome, Florence, and Paris.

"Florence. What a city!" he told the *Chicago Sun Times'* Jerome Holtzman. "It's a paradise for women—but purgatory for men. All those shops.... Just imagine—15 years ago I'm a kid playing on a high school field in Dallas and there I was in Vienna—eating goose liver with violin and Gypsy music in the background."[3]

Banks was understandably moved after the 16-day tour of Vietnam. He had done little more than play baseball and organize basketball teams during his two-year hitch in the army, but the troops he met after the 1968 season were confronting death daily, which prompted them to unwind by abusing drugs and alcohol when they had a chance.

"If they're not fighting Charley—that's what they call the Viet Cong— then they're working, piling up sandbags, or with guns and all that," Banks told Holtzman upon returning. "They're always busy. They never have any free time. Every day is Monday and every night is New Year's Eve. That's the way they refer to it."

Banks brought back a sign he'd seen on a bulletin board in a hospital waiting room. It read: "Who cares about the pension? The work here kills you before you're 65, anyway."

Banks' trip to Vietnam came after the summer in which Chicago police had waged combat with war protesters at Lincoln Park and elsewhere in the city. He sounded very much like the establishment talking to Holtzman.

"Over here you see a lot of young people complaining, people who hang out in the streets and who don't want to work," Banks said. "But over there, young men 19 and 20 years old are flying helicopters that cost $400,000. And you see lieutenants, maybe 21 years old, leading men into battle. It really proved to me that young people, when they're called upon, can do the job. It was a pleasure meeting them."[4]

Banks himself was not a complainer. He hadn't been one growing up in Dallas, and he hadn't been one when he was in the Negro Leagues and the army. He certainly wasn't going to start as a baseball player, even if he was on a team that lost habitually and, as Jim Brosnan had noted, had its share of "malcontents."

"Baseball can be fun, even when you're not on a championship club," Banks said. "Being with the Cubs has been fun for me. Do you know of a better way to earn a living than playing baseball? Baseball isn't work to me, it's a game. If I was with the Yankees, I couldn't play any more innings than I do for the Cubs."[5]

Banks had controlled the game on the field in his first seven seasons in Chicago. However, he would begin an 11-year pattern of adjustment in 1961.

Banks took a hard grounder off his left knee during spring training that year and would have trouble with it all season, repeatedly having fluid drained to relieve pressure and pain. As a result, he wasn't moving as well as normal.

Jerry Kindall meanwhile awaited a chance to play his natural position. The Cubs had invested $35,000 in Kindall in 1956 after he had led the University of Minnesota to an NCAA title.

A two-sport star who also played basketball for the Gophers, Kindall attracted attention from most of the teams in the majors and eventually received offers from about 10. The Cubs made the biggest offer, he said, and it came at a time that he needed cash as his father was working two jobs, trying to keep up with medical bills that resulted from his mother's battle against multiple sclerosis.

Given the Cubs' usual lack of aggressiveness in the Wrigley years and their confidence in Banks, it was surprising that they would win a bidding war for another young shortstop, who scout Ray Heyward labeled as the "nearest to Banks I have seen."

As a bonus baby, Kindall came directly to the big leagues in '56. He was on hand that August to replace Banks when a badly infected finger forced him from the lineup after playing 424 consecutive games, a record for a big leaguer starting his career. Banks would miss two weeks but returned to begin another marathon streak of consecutive games.

The young Banks wasn't about to give somebody else a shot at his job. He was driven by an awareness of how quickly his success could end.

"I tried to sign every kid's autograph," Banks said, "because in my mind I thought that one day I might have to ask this kid for a job."

The rules involving so-called "bonus babies" kept Kindall in Chicago through the end of the '57 season mostly being used as a backup second and third baseman. He then spent two years in the minors, working, he said, to "learn how to hit that slider they throw up here."

Kindall was back in '61, and many in the organization wanted to see him play some shortstop. Vedie Himsl, among those managing the team in the College of Coaches, was among those.

Banks had only played shortstop and third base for the Cubs, but Himsl approached him about a possible move to left field. Banks was surprised, but it wasn't his style to say no.

"Fine," Banks said. "If you think it will help the team."[6]

On May 23 at Wrigley Field, with Philadelphia in town, Himsl filled out a lineup card that had Banks in left field. Banks felt like the proverbial fish out of water as an outfielder but kept his complaints to himself.

Richie Ashburn, the Cubs' center fielder, sensed Banks' awkwardness and loudly shouted out directions for Banks to move on fly balls. "Back, back, back," or "in, in, in." Fans in the bleachers could hear Ashburn guide Banks on every ball hit his way, but Banks never did feel comfortable playing behind Kindall in left field. He played 23 games in left field and says he still doesn't know how he escaped making only one error, as every ball seemed like an adventure.[7]

At the time, Williams, a fine outfielder who had ended his minor league apprenticeship, was serving as a fourth outfielder behind Ashburn, George Altman, and Banks. First baseman Ed Bouchee, acquired the year before from Philadelphia with pitcher Don Cardwell for Cuban infielder Tony Taylor, was struggling to keep his batting average above .200.

Elvin Tappe, who had taken over for Himsl in the position Wrigley called "head coach," summoned Banks to discuss a move to first base. Banks smiled even bigger than normal. "Had he asked me to catch I would have done it," Banks said. "Anything to get out of left field."[8]

Banks worked out there one time—before the June 16 game at Candlestick Park—and then played there in the game. He says he had both feet on the bag the first time he had to cover first and would have been run over had Joey Amalfitano not swerved to miss him.

Banks started seven games at first base—long enough to bang his left knee off the brick wall at Candlestick Park chasing a foul ball from Orlando Cepeda—but was moved back to short on July 1.

With the Cubs in Cincinnati on July 15, Banks was removed late in a game. It appeared his knee was bothering him but there was also talk about his vision. He hadn't been himself, hitting just one home run in 19 games and going 2-for-13 in the last three games. The team was going from Cincinnati to St. Louis, Pittsburgh, and Philadelphia on a 12-game trip, but Banks wouldn't be making it.

He had been ordered home by Wrigley after a conversation with Tappe, deciding that Banks should be thoroughly examined and rested before being allowed to play again. A streak of 717 consecutive games played was over.

So with the Cubs in St. Louis, Banks sat in his back yard with sportswriter John Kuenster, discussing his predicament. He admitted the knee was requiring attention but said it was not limiting him. "I am not conscious of it," said Banks, who was then hitting .286 with 13 home runs. "I make up my mind to think about other things."

He said he hadn't been bothered by the position changes but admitted he'd felt wasted in left field. "Not much action there," he said.

He hoped to play shortstop when he returned, and he hoped it would happen soon. "I'm anxious to get back," he said. "This is a game you've got to play every day."9

Banks was in uniform on July 25, the Cubs' first game back at Wrigley, but Tappe started Kindall at short. He turned to Banks as a pinch hitter in the eighth inning, and he flew out. The next day, pinch-hitting again in the eighth, Banks delivered a home run over the left-field bleachers off Cuban reliever Ed Bauta.

He was back to stay and finished the season hitting .278 with 29 home runs. But it would be his last as a shortstop as Tappe and his colleagues in the College of Coaches decided Banks should move permanently to first base for 1962.

An expansion year that brought with it a 162-game schedule, 1962 would be the first (and still only) 100-loss season in the franchise's history.

With Andre Rodgers at shortstop, Banks hit 37 home runs and drove in 104 runs. He was selected to the All-Star Game for the eighth consecutive season. But the production he provided was no longer quite as valuable in the big picture, as almost every team had a first baseman who could hit for power and drive in runs. He wasn't as special of a player as he had been at shortstop, and John Holland often thought of a trade he almost made when Banks' value was at his highest.

Before the 1961 season, Holland had quietly let it be known that he might be willing to trade his best player if he could get enough talent back to help the team become competitive. He was motivated by economic fear, as the Cubs had played one game in September 1960 with only 1,013 fans at Wrigley.

The Milwaukee Braves had won pennants in 1957 and '58, but when they finished second the following two seasons, their attendance fell by almost a million fans. John McHale, the Braves' GM, was intrigued by adding Banks' bat as a compliment to Aaron and Mathews, giving Milwaukee one of the all-time collections of sluggers. And the Braves had done well stocking their farm system, creating a potential match with their neighbor.

Reports said the Braves offered a 6-for-1 package of talent for Banks: young pitchers Joey Jay, Don Nottebart and Carl Willey, center fielder Billy Bruton, shortstop Johnny Logan, and first baseman Frank Torre.[10]

Jay was one of the game's top young pitchers (he would win 21 games in both 1961 and '62 after being traded to Cincinnati), and Nottebart was a top prospect. Holland was more than intrigued. He wanted to make the deal, but Wrigley wouldn't let him. He couldn't imagine a team without his favorite player.

When the *Sun-Times* reported on the trade talks, Holland essentially confirmed them by saying that no player was "untouchable." But if the Cubs were ever going to trade Banks, that would have been the time. His value would plummet when he was moved across the infield and continue downward throughout the decade, binding him even more tightly to the franchise.

There would be other trade rumors, of course. The most reliable of those was a potential swap of first basemen with the Giants. Leo Durocher, just hired to manage the Cubs, was so skeptical about Banks' ability to remain a contributor that he was willing to deal him to San Francisco for Orlando Cepeda, who seemed back on form in spring training 1966 after a bad knee sidelined him much of the previous year. The Giants weren't interested in another first baseman, however, as they had decided to make Willie McCovey's move from left field to first base permanent.

Durocher still wanted Cepeda, feeling that Holland would have to find someone to take Banks if he had acquired Cepeda to replace him. Appeasing the new manager, Holland offered San Francisco left-hander Dick Ellsworth (14–15 in '65) for Cepeda, but the Giants felt they were getting a better deal from St. Louis, so they sent him to the Cardinals for lefty Ray Sadecki.[11]

Durocher had long liked the potential of left-handed-hitting first baseman John Herrnstein, a former University of Michigan football captain who had lost his chance to replace Dick "Dr. Strangeglove" Stuart as a Phillies' regular when Bill White was acquired from St. Louis. Durocher offered pitcher Bob Buhl for Herrnstein but would turn that starting point into a far better deal when the Phillies suggested expanding the trade.

The Cubs wound up with Herrnstein, center fielder Adolfo Phillips, and 23-year-old Canadian pitcher Ferguson Jenkins for Buhl and Jackson.

Herrnstein talked his way out of Philadelphia, expressing exasperation at his own situation after the Phillies added White. "I've got to know where I stand," said Herrnstein, who told Phillies GM John Quinn that he wouldn't go back to Triple A. "I can't go on forever as a borderline player.... I know my trade value is zero, as little as I've played, but I sense some sort of deal is going to be made here."[12]

He was right, of course, but being sent to Chicago as a possible replacement for Ernie Banks is a dubious gift. It was almost as if Quinn was laughing so hard about screwing Herrnstein that he didn't bother to ask his coaches about Jenkins.

Herrnstein, acquired on April 21, would get 17 at-bats for Durocher before the Cubs traded him on May 29, this time to Atlanta. That deal came one day after Holland had made another deal with the Braves, acquiring another potential Banks replacement, 30-year-old Lee Thomas, for pitcher Ted Abernathy.

Durocher's arrival signaled a new era for the Cubs, one in which they more often looked outside the organization to attain the credibility they had been lacking since 1945 when they last went to the World Series.

When Phil Wrigley hired Durocher, he was making a statement to his fans about becoming more serious about producing results on the field. Durocher would not be a miracle cure, suffering though a 10th-place season in 1966, but he developed a core of players who would finally give the team a chance to compete with Banks in uniform.

The two players upon whom Durocher perhaps most put his stamp were catcher Randy Hundley and second baseman Glenn Beckert.

Hundley was only 23 when he was acquired from San Francisco along with Bill Hands in a trade for Lindy McDaniel and Don Landrum. Beckert came up through the Cubs' system after playing baseball and studying political science at Allegheny College. Along with shortstop Don Kessinger, who made up in desire what he lacked in tools, they were badly needed supporting actors in a cast that had a variety of star players in eventual Hall of Famers Banks, Billy Williams, and Fergie Jenkins, as well as Ron Santo, the perennial Hall of Fame argument.

When Banks was in his prime, the six-year run from 1955–60, he hit .294 with an average of 41 home runs and 116 RBIs while playing shortstop. But between 1961–68, he averaged .263–26–88 while transitioning to first base and losing much of his speed. The presence of Williams and Santo made it impossible to pitch around him, as teams once had.

Jerome Holtzman noticed the difference as early as 1963. In his report on a game that season, he noted that Houston manager Harry Craft had decided to pitch to Banks with runners on second and third—something that hadn't happened since early in his career.

Banks' base-running was always a source of irritation for Durocher, who would continue to try to upgrade on a player he felt was getting a free pass from fans and reporters. He was always shouting from the dugout for Banks to get bigger leads at first base, and often the players and some of the coaches felt Durocher was doing it just to call attention to Banks' biggest weakness.

Durocher was always trying to make Banks feel his mortality as a player. The coach gave playing time at first base to a variety of players, including Thomas, Altman, Clarence Jones, Willie Smith, Gene Oliver, and Dick Nen. Banks bristled when he wasn't in the lineup but never took on his manager verbally. It just wasn't his style.

In a *Sporting News* feature in 1966, Banks said he could understand why Durocher would explore other options. "There comes a time in every player's life when he must face up to this sort of thing," said Banks, who was then 35 and would play six more seasons. "As we get older, we have to make way for the younger players.... I won't say it doesn't hurt because it definitely does. However, I simply have to adjust to it, just as every player does when he gets older. Personally, I don't feel like my playing career is over."[13]

The greatest of Durocher's first-base hopes was John Boccabella, a Californian the Cubs signed in 1963. He flashed serious power in the minor leagues but never put it together with an ability to hit for average. Yet Durocher gave him chances to take away Banks' job every spring—a cat-and-mouse game that never ended with Leo getting the cheese.

"Leo was always giving Ernie Banks' job away," Jenkins said. "Every spring he'd give it to John Boccabella or George Altman or Smith or Lee Thomas, and Ernie would win it back again.... Leo felt pressure in the respect that Ernie was more popular than he was. Leo had his charisma and his position, but you couldn't take away the fact that Ernie was the Cubs organization. He had been there, done so much, and he was still there. When Leo came on the scene, two spots Leo wanted to improve [were] center field and first base. When he got me, he got Adolfo to play center and John Herrnstein to play first.

"[Herrnstein] was a left-handed first baseman, and he hit well in Wrigley Field. Ernie won the job back again from him. Ernie just kept playing and winning the job back. Ernie would get in there and get some hits and get back in the lineup, and you couldn't take him out. He was a hitter."[14]

Jenkins and Banks spent time as road roommates.

"Ernie knew that Leo didn't like him," Jenkins said. "[But] you play hard for yourself, not the manager. So Ernie was always going to spring training, and someone always had his job, and Ernie would always win it back.... Ernie would say to me, 'Oh, Boccabella's got my job,' or, 'Lee Thomas has got my job.' Shoot, Ernie would hit 25 home runs, and Lee Thomas would be on the bench. Boccabella got traded to Montreal. Because Leo knew Ernie's ability but didn't have confidence in him. One year Ernie had a bad leg, and another year he had a bad hip, but he could still hit. He could flat-out hit."[15]

Even when he couldn't hit like he once did.

16

SEPTEMBER

The Cubs led the Mets by 4½ games when September arrived. This would have been considered a fairly comfortable lead under some circumstances, but given that the margin was only half as large as it had been on August 16, as well as the reality that this was a season Chicago fans had awaited since at least 1945—the franchise hadn't won a World Series since 1908—the comfort level for everyone involved was zero on the good days and somewhat less the rest of the time.

Leo Durocher, who should have lost his job five weeks earlier, was like a lion who had just been introduced to a cage. He, like Pat Pieper, the 83-year-old public address man at Wrigley, knew that it was wrong to assume anything.

"I've seen too many things happen in this game," said Pieper, who had attended almost every Cubs home game since 1906. "You wouldn't believe it, but in the 1918 World Series between the Cubs and the Red Sox, I saw Babe Ruth [bunt]. You never know what can happen in baseball."[1]

Durocher knew that firsthand.

He managed the 1942 Brooklyn Dodgers, which led the Cardinals by 10 games on August 5 only to get passed while playing well (30–20 down the stretch to finish with 104 wins), and more recently had been on the right side of a dramatic finish. Durocher's 1951 New York Giants trailed the Dodgers by 13 games on August 11 but then ran off 16 wins in a row en route to a 37–7 finish that put Bobby Thomson into position to hit his game-winning homer in a playoff.

Managerial strategy—that is, running a game from the dugout—is often overvalued.

Bill James developed a formula that looks at team statistics to determine how many games a team *should* win, and it shows the greatest managers in history might help their teams by an average of two or three wins a year. Durocher had been good for a +5 rating in '51 and in '42 had produced a +2 rating, while the Cardinals were meant to win 107 games, not the 106 that manager Billy Southworth (who was inducted into the Hall of Fame as a manager posthumously in 2008) produced.

Durocher had averaged a +1 rating in his first 13 years as a manager but would slide to a -1.5 average over the final 11 seasons, including his seven with the Cubs. He was en route to a -1 rating in 1969—compared to a +8 for Gil Hodges—although that only partly shows the poor job Durocher was doing.

The limitation in James' formula for rating managers—the so-called Pythagorean standings—is that it does not reflect how a manager aids and detracts from the performance of his players. Durocher had left his players physically and mentally exhausted entering a stretch when they would need every ounce of strength they could find.

Few players trusted him. Many feared him. And down the stretch, when Durocher had to make a decision, it was almost always the wrong decision.

"He wasn't the same guy he was in the late '40s," one observer said.

Durocher said in his autobiography that Ernie Banks was a great player in his time. "Unfortunately, his time wasn't my time."[2] But as the biggest month of Banks' career began, the exact opposite case was building.

Durocher may have been a great manager in his time, but his time wasn't the 1969 Cubs' time.

≫≪

Banks and his teammates had looked at the September schedule so often in July and August that they knew it by heart. They had split the first 14 of their 18 games against the Mets, and they were set to play at Shea Stadium on September 8–9 and at Wrigley on October 1–2, the final games of the season.

Before they could get to New York, however, they had to play three at home against the Pirates, and that was never a series that could be overlooked. Those watching would include scouts Jim Russo of the Orioles and Cal Ermer of the Twins, who had been sent to gather intelligence about the Cubs with the World

Series in mind; the Cubs' John Holland had likewise sent scouts Buck O'Neil and Rube Walker to watch the Orioles and Twins.[3]

Banks thought about baseball so much when he was at home or in a hotel that he wanted to talk to friends scattered around the major leagues, and he was a serial phone caller. He would often seek out the men he felt closest to, mostly those like Willie Mays and Hank Aaron, who he had bonded with on barnstorming trips and in All-Star clubhouses.

The Pirates came to Chicago in the middle of a 10-day road trip and were off on September 4. Willie Stargell, who had hit a long home run at Wrigley off Dick Selma in June and hit three homers in a day there in '68, was on Banks' mind. He knew Stargell would be at the Pirates' hotel, so he called him there.

"What would they charge me for you not to hit a home run at Wrigley Field?" Banks asked Stargell. "I don't want the Pittsburgh Pirates taking batting practice at Wrigley Field on us."

Stargell just laughed. "Come on, Ernie," he said. "I love to hit at Wrigley Field."

Ken Holtzman and the bullpen held Stargell hitless in the series opener, but the Pirates still rolled to a 9–2 win behind Steve Blass. Manager Larry Shepard rested Stargell against Fergie Jenkins the next day, but the Pirates had enough firepower to crush the Cubs 13–4.

Center field remained a problem that Durocher couldn't answer. Jenkins had unraveled after Don Young allowed a soft pop from the diminutive Freddie "The Flea" Patek to fall between him and Jim Hickman. The play was bad enough that the next day's *Chicago Tribune* carried a picture that had been doctored to show a large arrow pointing to the ball as it fell to the grass with the caption, "It's the White Thing, Boys!"

Jenkins' shoulders slumped when the play wasn't made, and he allowed eight hits and six runs in 2⅓ innings before getting the hook. "With all his physical talent, Fergie is just one of those fellows who gets upset by things like that," pitching coach Joe Becker said.[4]

Durocher was steaming when he left Wrigley Field and hadn't calmed down the next day. He called a team meeting in which he blasted the Cubs' efforts in the previous two games, saying one thing he could never stand was having "a quitter" on the mound.[5]

Never mind that Jenkins had already won 19 games and made 37 starts en route to 42, the most in the National League since 1917. Never mind that he had come back to start two days after taking a screaming line drive off his thumb in July (with Durocher missing that game because he bolted for his stepson's camp in Wisconsin). And never mind that if the Cubs were going to stay ahead of the Mets they needed Jenkins to offset the brilliance of Tom Seaver.

Durocher was mad, and the emperor would have his pound of flesh. Jenkins admitted a day later that the manager "got all over me" but did not lash back. "He's got a right to handle the club in his own way," Jenkins said. "I know what my job is, and I'm not going to say anything. I want my five more starts."[6]

The Cubs still had one game left against the Pirates before heading to New York, and Stargell would make it an unforgettable one for Banks and the large crowd at Wrigley. The Cubs had rallied from a 4–2 deficit to go ahead 5–4 on Hickman's homer off Chuck Hartenstein in the bottom of the eighth (one batter after Durocher lifted Banks for a pinch runner) and were within one out of a victory they badly needed. But up came "Pops" Stargell.

Durocher had lefty Hank Aguirre available in the bullpen, and Aguirre had neutralized the left-handed-hitting Stargell throughout the season (1-for-5 with an infield single and three strikeouts). But Durocher stuck with Phil Regan, and Stargell lifted a home run into the right-field bleachers.

Banks, stuck in the dugout, was probably the least surprised person in the park. This was a microcosm of his career with the Cubs, which once was summed up as being "like doing 10-to-20 at Folsom; a fine season…was one in which they flirted with mediocrity."[7] So was Banks surprised at what happened next? How could he be?

Since he had been lifted for a pinch runner by Durocher, a move that resulted in no gain, Banks was left sitting on the bench, unable to do anything. Naturally, his spot in the batting order came up with men on first and second and no one out in the 10th inning. It was hero time, and Banks had been relegated to being a cheerleader.

Willie Smith drove a liner right at third baseman Richie Hebner, who fired to first base to double off Ron Santo. Bad luck and bad base running, for sure. But Banks was certain he could have ended the game had he gotten his chance against rookie lefty Lou Marone.

That's what he was thinking when Hickman was intentionally walked, bringing Randy Hundley to the plate. The catcher grounded out, killing the rally, and Banks and his teammates told reliever Ken Johnson to hold 'em another inning. But just like that, a Don Kessinger error opened the door for two Pittsburgh runs, and Bruce Dal Canton escaped another Cubs rally in the bottom of the 11th, sealing the win when Glenn Beckert, like Smith before him, lined into a double play. The Cubs were off to O'Hare for the flight to New York, their lead down to 2½ games.

>> <<

New York can be a good trip for players and their families, and the city was alive in the late summer of 1969. It had not suffered like Chicago, Los Angeles, and so many other cities during the turbulent decade.

There had been a five-day clash in Harlem between police and angry African Americans after an off-duty police officer shot a 15-year-old boy whose crime had been spraying water from a hose onto his building superintendent, but New York somehow contained the national outcry that followed Martin Luther King's assassination. The only significant incidents of civil unrest in New York in '69 were the so-called Stonewall riots, a series of spontaneous, violent demonstrations after a police raid on a gay bar in Greenwich Village back in late June. Talk in Manhattan had long since moved to the Mets and the Jets, who had a transcendent celebrity star in Broadway Joe, the flashy quarterback Joe Namath.

But neither the schedule nor the circumstances suggested sight-seeing trips to the Statue of Liberty (one of Banks' favorite activities) or evenings in the theater. The Cubs were to be in New York for only about 48 hours, and there was no energy to waste.

At the start of a new series, teams hold meetings with the manager, pitching coach, pitchers, and catchers, discussing how to pitch the opponents' hitters. It was in one of those sessions in the Shea Stadium clubhouse on September 8 when Bill Hands declared war against the Mets, who had long since stopped being a nuisance.

Hands, who was pitching better than any of the other Cubs starters, was set to start the opener of the two-game series. He remembered Tommie Agee, the

Mets' leadoff hitter, taking him deep the last time he had pitched in New York—but even more he remembered how Tom Seaver had knocked down Santo when the Mets swept the Cubs in a May 4 doubleheader at Wrigley Field. Hands had responded by hitting Seaver in the wrist, and Seaver closed that series of events by drilling Hands in the leg.

So Hands decreed that Agee was due a bow tie, if not worse. "Agee is going on his ass the first pitch," Hands said, and none of his teammates were especially surprised.[8]

"When Hands said that, we *knew* Agee was going on his ass the first pitch," the late Gene Oliver told Peter Golenbock for *Wrigleyville*, his oral history of the Cubs.

In the bottom of the first inning that night, every Cubs player was up on the top step of the dugout when Agee settled into the batter's box. Guys were standing even out in the bullpen because everyone knew what was coming.

Sure enough, Hands' first pitch was a fastball, high and tight to Agee, who went sprawling as Durocher shouted, "Stick it in his ear!"

Don Drysdale couldn't have done more to send a message. "I have never seen a better knockdown pitch," said Oliver, the backup catcher who had recently been appointed as an extra coach. "It was just right under the chin. Asshole, helmet, bat—that's all you could see of Agee."

Agee popped to his feet and stepped back into the batter's box, not in the least flustered. "He did not even make a face at Hands," Oliver said.[9]

In memory, it's easy to think Agee exacted instant revenge. But what he did was hit a grounder to Santo for the first out. Hands worked a 1-2-3 first, which brought Santo to the plate to start the second. This must have made the Mets very happy.

Santo, you see, was the perfect target. Not only was he Durocher's captain, but he had made dismissive comments about the Mets throughout the season. When Hands beat Seaver in July at Wrigley Field, he had clicked his heels while headed to the clubhouse. No one on the Mets' side had forgotten that.

Koosman knew what he was going to do. "They threw at Tommie, and I had to do it to end it right there," he said. "If Tommie doesn't think I'm working for him, he won't work for me—and I want Tommie Agee working for me."[10]

Santo, like everyone in the Cubs' dugout, knew what was coming next.

"Retaliation was inevitable," Oliver said. "We *knew* Santo was going on his ass, and Koosman hit him right on the elbow."[11]

"Koosman," Santo said, "could throw the ball right through you."[12] He was hurt but he wasn't leaving the game. He no doubt would have loved to barrel into Mets shortstop Bud Harrelson, but Koosman didn't give him a chance, striking out Banks, Hickman, and Hundley after the beanball.

Hands and Koosman went at each other on the mound, determined to give up nothing. But Agee—who else?—gave the Mets a 2–0 lead with a homer in the bottom of the third.

"Everybody went, 'Huh?'" Oliver said in the 1995 interview. "He let the air out of us. We were going to let the air out of him. He let the air out of us. He took an offensive situation we were trying to create, and he turned it into a negative for us. We thought we were going to intimidate them, and they were not about to be intimidated."[13]

The Mets scored a contested run in the sixth inning—Agee, who had led off the inning with a double, scored on a Wayne Garrett single, although Hundley and others with the Cubs still believe umpire Satch Davidson blew the call at home plate—and won 3–2. Koosman piled up 13 strikeouts.

Two of those came against Banks, who found himself in a 2-for-38 slump. Ernie had faced Koosman in the eighth inning with Glenn Beckert on third base as the tying run after Santo grounded into a double play, taking much of the steam out of a situation that could have turned around the game.

Banks would have given almost anything to blast a home run, which would have been the 496th of his career. He would have been thrilled to drop a soft single into the outfield or even to have hit a grounder that Harrelson couldn't handle. But Koosman got him to two strikes and then did what pitchers had been doing the last few years, firing a fastball just above the belt on the inside part of the plate. He had crushed those pitches when he was younger, when he had the most of the bat speed he felt he gained picking cotton, but as he got older he couldn't catch up to them. He had a hard time laying off them, too, which was the tendency Koosman took advantage of to strike out Banks and escape the eighth-inning jam.

But in a funereal clubhouse that found Santo sitting with his head in his hands for 20 minutes, Durocher saying he had "nothing to say" and Billy

Williams saying he couldn't "add anything to what already has been said," Banks at least tried to act like the sun would come up tomorrow.

"Well, you know, the guys have a reason for not saying anything," Banks said. "We're always this way when we lose. But we're still in front."[14]

The lead down to 1½ games, the most level-headed Cub had reason for despair the next day. Banks was not in Durocher's lineup for the second game, replaced by the left-handed-hitting Willie Smith, as Durocher searched for kryptonite to use against Seaver, who had picked up win No. 20 in his last start.

A decade earlier, Banks would have been the guy most likely to get the big hit that was desperately needed. But at 38, the odds of him doing damage against baseball's top young gun were not good. He had gone 1-for-12 off Seaver in 1969 and 4-for-29 lifetime, with two home runs. A sentimental manager might have understood what this time meant for Banks and given him a chance, but Durocher was putting together a lineup, not handing out lifetime achievement awards. Sitting Ernie seemed like a no-brainer.

There was one major surprise on Tuesday. Durocher had decided to start Jenkins instead of Ken Holtzman, the scheduled starter. He did this even though Jenkins had only two days of rest and, most curiously, Durocher had just labeled him a "quitter" in front of the entire team. Go figure.

Durocher explained that moving Jenkins in front of Holtzman would delay Holtzman's scheduled weekend start, avoiding a conflict with Rosh Hashanah. But the Jewish calendar had been set for centuries. It seems unlikely that the situation wouldn't have been considered before Tuesday. The more plausible idea is that Durocher simply wanted his top starter to face the Mets' top starter, ready or not. It turned out to be another bad mistake.

After a black cat strolled past the Cubs' dugout in the top of the first inning, Jenkins allowed two runs on a Ken Boswell double in the bottom of the first and two more on a Donn Clendenon homer in the third, and the Mets were rolling toward a 7–1 victory that literally shook the foundation of Shea Stadium and what was left of the National League East race.

Holtzman lost in Philadelphia on Wednesday, the big hit coming from backup catcher Dave Watkins, who batted .176 that season and never got back to the big leagues. And afterward, in a scene that maddened the Cubs' pitchers,

Coach Joe Becker acted as a Durocher stand-in by criticizing Holtzman's pitch selection against Watkins.

Becker had once been an outstanding coach, working to help the teenaged Sandy Koufax iron out control problems that threatened to derail his career before it launched. But as the Cubs unraveled, Becker turned into a finger-pointer.

Watkins' home run had come on a change-up, which Holtzman said he threw because Watkins had been called a "fastball hitter" during the pregame meeting. But Becker wasn't happy. "You go with your best pitch all the way," he said. "With this guy, you are doing [him] a favor when you throw a change-up."[15]

Had Jenkins stayed on schedule and worked with his normal rest, could he have shut down the fifth-place Phillies? Probably. He was 4–0 against them with two shutouts. But Durocher gambled and failed, and now the Cubs had lost their seventh straight. This defeat dropped them out of first place after a season-long run of 155 days.

No team had ever led for so long without winning a pennant. But for Banks and his teammates, the long ride had not led them to the destination they had sought, and there was no getting there now.

>> <<

The final 22 days of the season were like the last days of the Nixon administration. The comedy of errors would have been funny if it wasn't so sad.

The Cubs lost eight in a row and 11-of-12 in the stretch that knocked them out, ultimately ending with an 8–18 record after September 2, which was worse than any other team in the majors except a Cleveland squad led by Ken Harrelson.

When the Cubs lost again in Philadelphia on September 11, Dick Selma called for a trick play that Ron Santo missed, resulting in a throw that sailed over an unoccupied third base with the Phillies' runners on first and second. After the game, Selma was so worried about Durocher's reaction that he hid from him and was detected by Coach Joey Amalfitano only because his shoes stuck out from behind clothes hanging in a trainer's room locker.

John Holland, clinging to hope, brought in yet another center fielder. Jimmie Hall arrived from the Yankees on September 11, becoming the seventh player to start in center (and the ninth to play there). Durocher called another clubhouse meeting on September 21, this time apparently because someone with clout had complained that Oscar Gamble was spending too much time in the company of white women.

"Here we are in September, trying to save our asses in a pennant race, and he's screaming at Oscar, 'If you ever do that again, I'm going to send you so far out of town … I'm going to send you to outer Mongolia!'" Holtzman said. "Those were the exact words."[16]

Jenkins finished 21–15 and led the National League with 273 strikeouts, but he was never himself after getting dressed down on September 7. His spirit was damaged, and like other key members of Durocher's pitching staff, he was exhausted.

This wasn't the case with the Mets, who sprinted to the finish line. They won 38 of their last 49 games, with Seaver and Koosman going 13–1 with a 1.68 ERA in their final 16 starts including eight consecutive complete-game wins for Seaver. From August 20 until the end of the season, the Mets' depth, and Gil Hodges' careful handling of his staff, paid off.

The Cubs' top three starters had been great through 122 games (46–26 with a 2.75 ERA) but were average, at best, down the stretch (12–16 with a 3.99 ERA in the last 40 games). The Mets' top five starters weren't as good as the Cubs' starters for the bulk of the season (46–39 with a 3.00 ERA through 122 games) but put on one of the great displays of pitching at the end (22–5 with a 1.97 ERA in the last 40 games). During the decisive stretch, the Mets' bullpen had a 2.87 ERA compared to the Cubs' 4.18.

But the Cubs' freefall wasn't just about pitching. They had averaged 4.7 runs through August but produced only 3.3 per game in the final month, scoring two runs or less in 12-of-27 games.

Banks hit only .208 in September but matched the team's strongest finisher, Billy Williams, with 14 RBIs. He ended the season with 106, the fifth best total in the league. Hickman (.222–4–8), Beckert (.211–0–6), Kessinger (.186–1–2), and Hundley (.151–2–4) also had little gas in their tanks at the end.

On September 23, Banks denied published reports he was going to retire. He pointed out he was already signed through 1970, and Holland said he wouldn't be surprised to see Banks last even longer. "He told me not long ago that he felt like a young man physically," Holland said. "The way he stays in shape, he could go on for a long time."[17]

A day later, the Cubs were mathematically eliminated. There were 2,217 at Wrigley Field to see them beat Montreal, but the last thread of hope was cut when Gary Gentry's shutout of the Cardinals was completed in New York.

"I admit we played horseshit in the last few weeks," Durocher said on the last day of the season when a hollow victory over the playoff-bound Mets gave the Cubs a 92–70 record. "We've played some of the worst baseball I've seen in years. But that doesn't discount the fact that the Mets played like hell. If they had played like the Pirates or the Cardinals, we would have been all right. But they got in a streak and couldn't lose."

As players packed to head to their winter homes, it was Beckert, not Banks, who broke into song.

"We shall overcome," he sang. "We shall overcome. We shall overcome… someday."[18]

17

EVERYTHING BUT THE RING

"I hate to say it, but in a few years people are going to forget Ernie Banks." —unnamed Tribune Company executive, 1983[1]

"I always looked at everybody as if they had an invisible sign on their back saying, 'Please Handle With Care.'"
—Ernie Banks, 1971[2]

On his last day with the Cubs in Chicago, Ernie Banks bounced around Wrigley Field with just as much boyish verve as he'd had when he arrived at age 22. He hadn't officially retired, declining to call it quits just in case Phil Wrigley hadn't noticed his favorite player had degenerated into a .193 hitter, but everyone in Chicago knew that September, 26, 1971, was going to be his farewell appearance—including Banks.

The Cubs were 82–76, in third place in the National League East, and finally ready to jettison manager Leo Durocher. The Philadelphia Phillies were 65–94, bringing up the rear.

As the teams crossed paths on the field during batting practice, many players wearing jackets to protect them from the chilly wind blowing off Lake Michigan, Banks worked the room the way no ballplayer ever had before him, nor ever would after him.

Banks chatted up Tim McCarver, a catcher who had the annoying habit of trying to catch Banks napping whenever he took a lead off first base. McCarver had been doing it since 1963 and kept doing it, even though Banks rarely wandered more than a step or two from the bag in his final few seasons.

"Hey," Banks yelled at McCarver. "Are you inspired?"

"Now I *know* you're crazy, Banks."

"*Inspired*," Banks continued. "You must be *inspired*."

"It's too damn cold to be inspired."

"Ah, but you must remember those who have to work for a living," Banks said. "You must put it in the proper perspective."

McCarver turned away, heading into the cage to get in his swings. Banks wandered off, speaking, as he so often did, to no one in particular.

"Isn't it a beautiful day," he yelled, and then he broke into song.

"*On a clear day, you can see forever...* "

Then he went into his broadcaster's voice, doing his best imitation of Jack Brickhouse. "The Cubs of Chicago versus the Phillies of Philadelphia in beautiful, historic Wrigley Field," he said. "Let's go, let's go. It's Sunday in America."[3]

Left-hander Ken Reynolds was pitching for the Phillies. Banks batted cleanup between Carmen Fanzone and Ron Santo as a crowd of 18,505 watched at Wrigley Field.

Jack Brickhouse had the call on WGN, and 85-year-old Pat Pieper manned the public address microphone as he had throughout Banks' career.

In the bottom of the first, Banks hit a grounder that was misplayed by third baseman Deron Johnson. Banks reached first before the ball was retrieved and thrown across the infield to rookie Greg Luzinski, and after a moment's deliberation to reach the obvious conclusion—benefit of the doubt goes to the 40-year-old legend playing his last home game—the call was made and the hit sign was illuminated on the ancient center-field scoreboard.

Banks finished that game 1-for-3 with a walk and did not play in the final three games of the season in Montreal. He ended his career with 512 home runs, which ranked eighth on the all-time list, and 2,583 hits.

Banks played 2,528 games without getting into the World Series. That was the most ever when he retired, and through 2010 it still stood as the fourth most all-time behind Andre Dawson, Ken Griffey Jr., and Rafael Palmeiro, the new holder of the dubious record at 2,831 games and no trips to the World Series.

"Many athletes didn't get into the playoffs, but they always mention my name," Banks says. "I'm the poster boy. As you move on in your life, you come to think you really don't have to win to win. I'd see a woman surviving with five children and no husband and wonder, how in the world could I do that? Another time, a woman in a shop or something asked me, 'What is it like to do something you love and get paid for it?' I was stunned by the thought."

The Hall of Fame didn't hold the Cubs' lack of success against Banks. He was elected at the earliest possible opportunity, receiving 321 of 383 votes from 10-year members of the Baseball Writers Association of America in 1977, his first year on the ballot. But he was denied something else he had once dreamed about—the chance to be baseball's first African American manager.

There was speculation about Banks possibly replacing Durocher as manager. He had been named a player-coach late in 1967 and had been all but adopted by Phil Wrigley since their first meeting in 1953. Yet before promoting Whitey Lockman from his job as Triple A manager, Wrigley made it clear that Banks was not a candidate. He did it in the kindest manner possible.

"Ernie has such a beautiful reputation in baseball, it would be a shame to ruin it by making him a manager," Wrigley said. "I'm too fond of Ernie to make him manager of anything. Managing is a dirty job. It doesn't last long, and it certainly isn't anything I would wish on [Ernie]."[4]

Banks did serve as a first-base coach under Lockman, but his mind wandered during games. There were times when Lockman couldn't catch his attention because he was chatting with umpires and even sometimes standing next to the wall, visiting with fans. Yet because of a run of injuries and ejections, Banks wound up managing when Lockman was booted from a game on May 8, 1973, in San Diego, becoming the first African American to even temporarily call the shots for a big-league team. The Cubs won that game on a double by pinch hitter Joe Pepitone, inserted into the game by Banks, but it would be the only time Banks managed.

He was again mentioned as a candidate to manage when Lockman was sacked during the 1974 season, but Wrigley had not warmed to the idea of putting the legend in charge.

"Why would Ernie want to be a manager?" Wrigley asked. "It's the next thing to becoming a kamikaze pilot."[5]

Banks would draw a check from the Cubs almost his entire life, but he would never be given a job with authority or even real influence. The low point in his relationship with the team came in June 1983, shortly after the Tribune Company had purchased the team from the Wrigley estate.

With Wrigley and many of his longtime staffers gone, Banks was suddenly viewed as something of a crazy uncle who hung around the house for no apparent reason. He was paid to be a team ambassador, but nobody knew what to do with him. The Tribune suits decided to sever ties and did it in a manner that was as ugly as Wrigley's handling of Banks' managerial ambition was graceful.

Team officials fed anonymous quotes to reporters explaining that Banks had to be fired because he was unreliable, saying they had spent too much time apologizing for his tardiness or no-shows. *Sun-Times* reporter Joe Goddard credited one anonymous member of the Cubs' front office with one of the dumbest statements ever uttered, saying that Banks would soon be forgotten.

Instead, someone brokered a truce, and Banks was again making appearances for the team in a variety of capacities. He loved the attention, for sure, and the money helped. Banks never made more than $85,000 as a player, retiring before the twin engines of salary arbitration and free agency drove baseball earnings into the celebrity stratosphere, but he never seemed short of money.

He has never forgotten Phil Wrigley. How could he? Every time he pulled into the driveway of his home in Marina del Rey, a stone's throw from the Pacific Ocean west of Los Angeles, or got behind the wheel of his Lexus, he was benefiting from one of the wisest investments anyone ever made.

Wrigley once accompanied one of his top financial advisors to a meeting with Cubs players. There was no pension for players, and he had grown tired of dealing with the financial ruin that so often followed the end of playing careers, so Wrigley offered to help manage his players' money.

Legend has Banks as the only player who trusted Wrigley enough to buy into the idea of building a retirement fund. Other players either didn't feel they made enough to set aside significant savings or didn't trust the owner of their team to handle their affairs, yet Banks authorized Wrigley to withhold 50 percent of every check. He did this for roughly half his career, funneling an estimated $750,000 to this fund, with the understanding he could not touch the money until he turned 55.

Shortly after January 31, 1986, a check arrived in the mail. It was for about $4.5 million.[6]

Banks had the financial freedom to do as he wished in his later years—loving the people in his life and chasing outlandish dreams in the name of world peace and harmony. On that summer night in 2010, 20,806 days after he first walked into Wrigley Field in 1953, he considered himself one of the luckiest men in the world.

A championship or two would have completed his career. But there's no tragedy in being the greatest player to never win a baseball championship.

As Chicagoans who had loved him 50 years or more hung on every word, Banks told how 1969 and his other 18 seasons playing for the Cubs had helped prepare him for all the battles that life can present.

"What I learned as a player was how to overcome losses in my life," he said. "I learned you lose, you come back the next day. You win, you come back the next day. You can learn a very, very strong lesson. You just deal with it."

Always moving on, always going forward, never back. Satch was right about that.

"Somebody said what about the Cubs?" said Banks, who then answers his rhetorical question. "Loyalty."

And one more thing.

"Patience."

After Banks finishes, he is mobbed by a crowd of people wanting to take a picture or sign something they've kept for years, sometimes decades, awaiting the chance to present it to him. It does not appear many have forgotten him.

NOTES

Chapter 1: Killing With Kindness

1. David Halberstam, *October, 1964.* (New York: Random House, 1994), p. 353.

2. David Haugh, *Chicago Tribune,* July 24, 2005.

3. Malcolm Moran, *New York Times,* October 4, 1984.

4. David Haugh, *Chicago Tribune,* July 24, 2005.

5. John Roseboro with Bill Libby, *Glory Days with the Dodgers* (New York: Atheneum, 1978).

6. Rick Talley, *The Cubs of '69* (Chicago: Contemporary Books Inc., 1989), p. 155.

7. Mark Kram, "A Tale of Two Men and One City," *Sports Illustrated,* September 29, 1969.

8. Henry Aaron with Lonnie Wheeler, *I Had A Hammer* (New York: HarperCollins, 1991), p. 138.

9. *The Tim McCarver Show,* August 2, 2010.

10. Ernie Banks and Jim Enright, *Mr. Cub* (New York: Rutledge Books Inc., 1971), p. 36.

Chapter 2: February

1. Peter Golenbock, *Wrigleyville* (New York: St. Martin's Press, 1996), p. 396.

2. Steven Travers, *The 1969 Miracle Mets* (Guilford, Conn.: The Globe Pequot Press, 2009), p. 24.

3. Doug Feldmann, *Miracle Collapse* (Lincoln, Neb.: University of Nebraska Press, 2006), p. 63.

4. Ibid., p. 57.

5. Ibid., p. 56.

6. John Heylar, *Lords of the Real* (New York: Villard Books, 1994), p. 91.

7. Ibid., p. 84.

8. Ibid., p. 92.

9. George Langford, *Chicago Tribune,* February 25, 1969.

10. Bill Libby, "Why They Call Ernie Banks Baseball's Beautiful Man," *Sport,* June 1969.

11. John Heylar, *Lords of the Realm* (New York: Villard Books, 1994), p. 92.

12. George Langford, *Chicago Tribune,* February 23, 1969.

13. Ibid.

14. John Heylar, *Lords of the Realm* (New York: Villard Books, 1994), p. 92.

15. Ibid., p. 95.

16. Doug Feldmann, *Miracle Collapse* (Lincoln, Neb.: University of Nebraska Press, 2006), p. 47.

17. George Langford, *Chicago Tribune,* February 26, 1969.

Chapter 3: Two Different Americas

1. Ernie Banks and Jim Enright, *Mr. Cub* (New York: Rutledge Books Inc., 1971), p. 27.
2. Ibid., p. 26.
3. Ibid., p. 28.
4. Ibid., p. 29.
5. James Enright, *The Sporting News*, February 17, 1960.
6. Ibid.
7. Dave Condon, "The Cubs' $500,000 Shortstop," *Sport*, July 1956.
8. James Enright, *The Sporting News*, February 17, 1960.
9. Ernie Banks and Jim Enright, *Mr. Cub* (New York: Rutledge Books Inc., 1971), p. 31.
10. Ernie Banks, *Chicago Tribune*, June 23, 1969.
11. Ernie Banks and Jim Enright, *Mr. Cub* (New York: Rutledge Books Inc., 1971), p. 32.
12. Ibid., p. 32.
13. Barry Horn, *Dallas Morning News*, September 19, 1997.
14. Ibid.
15. Ernie Banks and Jim Enright, *Mr. Cub* (New York: Rutledge Books Inc., 1971), p. 33.
16. Jim Fisher, King Features Syndicate, April 29, 1977.
17. William B. Furlong, "P.K. Wrigley: Baseball Magnate," *Saturday Evening Post*, Summer 1972.
18. Ibid.
19. Jerome Holtzman, *Chicago Sun-Times*, April 13, 1977.
20. Bill Gleason, *Chicago Sun-Times*, April 13, 1977.
21. William B. Furlong, "P.K. Wrigley: Baseball Magnate," *Saturday Evening Post*, Summer 1972.
22. Ibid.
23. Ibid.
24. Ibid.
25. Jerome Holtzman, *Chicago Sun-Times*, April 13, 1977.
26. Ibid.
27. William B. Furlong, "P.K. Wrigley: Baseball Magnate," *Saturday Evening Post*, Summer 1972.
28. Bill Veeck with Ed Lynn, *Veeck: As In Wreck* (Chicago: University of Chicago Press, 2001), p. 39.
29. Peter Golenbock, *Wrigleyville* (New York: St. Martin's Press, 1996), p. 268.
30. Ibid., p. 28.
31. William B. Furlong, "P.K. Wrigley: Baseball Magnate," *Saturday Evening Post*, Summer 1972.
32. Ibid.
33. Ibid.
34. Jerome Holtzman, *Chicago Sun-Times*, April 13, 1977.
35. William B. Furlong, "P.K. Wrigley: Baseball Magnate," *Saturday Evening Post*, Summer 1972.
36. Bill Veeck with Ed Lynn, *Veeck: As In Wreck* (Chicago: University of Chicago Press, 2001).
37. William B. Furlong, "P.K. Wrigley: Baseball Magnate," *Saturday Evening Post*, Summer 1972.
38. Ibid.
39. Ibid.
40. Jim Enright, *The Sporting News*, July 4, 1981.
41. Ibid.
42. Joe Goddard, *The Sporting News*, July 4, 1981.
43. Jerome Holtzman, *Chicago Sun-Times*, April 13, 1977.

Chapter 4: March

1. Steven Travers, *The 1969 Miracle Mets* (Guilford, Conn.: The Globe Pequot Press, 2009), p. 40.
2. Ibid., p. 33.
3. Ibid., p. 13.
4. Ibid., p. 13.

5. Ibid., p. 27.
6. Ibid., p. 17.
7. Doug Feldmann, *Miracle Collapse* (Lincoln, Neb.: University of Nebraska Press, 2006), p. 42.
8. George Langford, *Chicago Tribune*, March 6, 1969.
9. Doug Feldmann, *Miracle Collapse* (Lincoln, Neb.: University of Nebraska Press, 2006), p. 31.
10. Ibid., p. 32.
11. Ibid., p. 30-31.
12. Doug Feldmann, *Miracle Collapse* (Lincoln, Neb.: University of Nebraska Press, 2006), p. 53.
13. George Langford, *Chicago Tribune*, March 15, 1969.
14. Doug Feldmann, *Miracle Collapse* (Lincoln, Neb.: University of Nebraska Press, 2006), p. 32.
15. Ibid., p. 51.
16. Steven Travers, *The 1969 Miracle Mets* (Guilford, Conn.: The Globe Pequot Press, 2009), p. 39.
17. John Heylar, *Lords of the Realm* (New York: Villard Books, 1994), p. 99-101.
18. Jerome Holtzman, *Chicago Sun-Times*, March 20, 1969.
19. United Press, March 26, 1969.
20. *The Sporting News*, August 2, 1969.
21. Ibid.

Chapter 5: A Friend for Life

1. Ernie Banks and Jim Enright, *Mr. Cub* (New York: Rutledge Books Inc., 1971), p. 36.
2. Ibid., p. 38.
3. Ibid., p. 38.
4. Ibid., p. 39.
5. Bob Broeg, *St. Louis Post-Dispatch*, August 7, 1977.
6. Ibid.
7. Ernie Banks and Jim Enright, *Mr. Cub* (New York: Rutledge Books Inc., 1971), p. 42.

8. Ibid., p. 50.
9. Ibid., p. 51.
10. Ibid., p. 52.
11. Ibid., p. 56-57.
12. Ibid., p. 57.
13. Ibid., p. 61.
14. Barry Horn, *Dallas Morning News*, September 19, 1997.
15. Ibid.
16. Posnanski, Joe, *Soul of Baseball* (New York: HarperCollins, 2007), p. 4-7.
17. Jack Etkin, *Kansas City Star*, July 21, 1985.
18. Steve Wulf, "The Guiding Light," *Sports Illustrated*, September 19, 1994.
19. Ibid.
20. Ibid.
21. Posnanski, Joe, *Soul of Baseball* (New York: HarperCollins, 2007), p. 107-114.
22. *Chicago Daily News*, May 29, 1962.
23. Steve Wulf, "The Guiding Light," *Sports Illustrated*, September 19, 1994.
24. George Castle, *The Million-To-One Team* (South Bend, Ind.: Diamond Communications Inc., 2000), p. 120-121.
25. Posnanski, Joe, *Soul of Baseball* (New York: HarperCollins, 2007), p. 84-86.
26. Dominic A. Pacyga, *Chicago: A Biography* (Chicago: University of Chicago Press, 2009), p. 352.
27. Ibid., p. 329.
28. Ibid., p. 330.
29. Ibid., p. 207.
30. Ibid., p. 333.
31. Ibid., p. 334.

Chapter 6: April

1. George Langford, *Chicago Tribune*, April 9, 1969.
2. Rick Talley, *The Cubs of '69* (Chicago: Contemporary Books Inc., 1989), p. 5.

3. Edward Prell, *Chicago Tribune*, April 9, 1969.

4. George Langford, *Chicago Tribune*, April 10, 1969.

5. George Langford, *Chicago Tribune*, April 11, 1969.

6. Art Shamsky with Barry Zeman, *The Magnificent Seasons* (New York: St. Martin's Press, 2004), p. 25.

7. Rick Talley, *The Cubs of '69* (Chicago: Contemporary Books Inc., 1989), p. 238.

8. George Vecsey, *New York Times*, August 20, 2009.

9. Rick Talley, *The Cubs of '69* (Chicago: Contemporary Books Inc., 1989), p. 8.

Chapter 7: Open Doors into a White World

1. Glenn Stout and Richard A. Johnson, *The Cubs: The Complete Story of Chicago Cubs Baseball* (Chicago: Houghton Mifflin, 2007), p. 199.

2. Ernie Banks and Jim Enright, *Mr. Cub* (New York: Rutledge Books Inc., 1971), p. 70.

3. Henry Aaron with Lonnie Wheeler, *I Had A Hammer* (New York: HarperCollins, 1991), p. 61-62.

4. Ibid., p. 75.

5. Ibid., p. 94.

6. Ernie Banks and Jim Enright, *Mr. Cub* (New York: Rutledge Books Inc., 1971), p. 71.

7. Ibid., p. 72.

8. Dave Condon, "The Cubs' $500,000 Shortstop," *Sport*, July 1956.

9. Ernie Banks and Jim Enright, *Mr. Cub* (New York: Rutledge Books Inc., 1971), p. 72.

10. James Enright, *Chicago Tribune*, September 8, 1953.

11. Dave Condon, "The Cubs' $500,000 Shortstop," *Sport*, July 1956.

12. Mark Kram, "A Tale of Two Men and One City," *Sports Illustrated*, September 29, 1969.

13. Bob Broeg, *St. Louis Post-Dispatch*, August 7, 1977.

14. Ernie Banks and Jim Enright, *Mr. Cub* (New York: Rutledge Books Inc., 1971), p. 73.

15. Dave Condon, "The Cubs' $500,000 Shortstop," *Sport*, July 1956.

16. Charles Walton, "Bronzeville Conversation," Jazz Institute of Chicago.

17. Ernie Banks and Jim Enright, *Mr. Cub* (New York: Rutledge Books Inc., 1971), p. 65.

18. Ibid., p. 67.

19. James Enright, *Chicago American*, September 8, 1953.

20. Ernie Banks and Jim Enright, *Mr. Cub* (New York: Rutledge Books Inc., 1971), p. 68-69.

21. Ibid., p. 73.

22. Scott A. Newman, "Urban Leisure from 1893 to 1945," Jazz Age Chicago Online, June 22, 2005.

23. Ernie Banks and Jim Enright, *Mr. Cub* (New York: Rutledge Books Inc., 1971), p. 74.

24. Ibid., p. 74.

25. Ibid., p. 76.

26. Ibid., p. 77.

27. Ibid., p. 78-79.

28. Ibid., p. 81.

29. Ibid., p. 89.

30. Dave Condon, "The Cubs' $500,000 Shortstop," *Sport*, July 1956.

31. Glenn Stout and Richard A. Johnson, *The Cubs: The Complete Story of Chicago Cubs Baseball* (Chicago: Houghton Mifflin, 2007), p. 212.

32. George Castle, *The Million-To-One Team* (South Bend, Ind.: Diamond Communications Inc., 2000).

33. Glenn Stout and Richard A. Johnson, *The Cubs: The Complete Story*

of Chicago Cubs Baseball (Chicago: Houghton Mifflin, 2007), p. 215.

34. George Castle, *The Million-To-One Team* (South Bend, Ind.: Diamond Communications Inc., 2000), p. 115.

35. Ibid., p. 115.

36. James Enright, *Chicago American*, August 25, 1953.

37. Wendell Smith, *Chicago American*, August 25, 1953.

38. Ibid.

39. Peter Golenbock, *Wrigleyville* (New York: St. Martin's Press, 1996), p. 347.

40. Ibid., p. 347.

41. James Enright, *Chicago American*, September 14, 1953.

42. Howard Roberts, *Chicago Daily News*, March 8, 1956.

43. Peter Golenbock, *Wrigleyville* (New York: St. Martin's Press, 1996), p. 321.

44. Ibid., p. 347.

45. Howard Roberts, *Chicago Daily News*, March 8, 1956.

46. Ibid.

47. Peter Golenbock, *Wrigleyville* (New York: St. Martin's Press, 1996), p. 348.

48. Si Burick, *Dayton Daily News*, June 14, 1963.

49. Dave Condon, "The Cubs' $500,000 Shortstop," *Sport*, July 1956.

50. Ernie Banks and Jim Enright, *Mr. Cub* (New York: Rutledge Books Inc., 1971), p. 89.

51. Glenn Stout and Richard A. Johnson, *The Cubs: The Complete Story of Chicago Cubs Baseball* (Chicago: Houghton Mifflin, 2007), p. 224.

52. Steve Jacobson, *Carrying Jackie's Torch* (Chicago: Lawrence Hill Books, 2007), p. 70.

53. Ernie Banks and Jim Enright, *Mr. Cub* (New York: Rutledge Books Inc., 1971), p. 91.

54. Arthur Daley, *New York Times*, August 24, 1955.

55. Ibid.

56. Ibid.

57. James Enright, *Chicago News American*, September 20, 1955.

58. Ibid.

59. Dave Condon, "The Cubs' $500,000 Shortstop," *Sport*, July 1956.

60. Ibid.

61. Bob Broeg, *St. Louis Post-Dispatch*, August 7, 1977.

Chapter 8: May

1. Nolan Ryan and Mickey Herskowitz, *Kings of the Hill* (New York: HarperCollins, 1992), p. 76-77.

2. Ibid., p. 76-77.

3. Steven Travers, *The 1969 Miracle Mets* (Guilford, Conn.: The Globe Pequot Press, 2009), p. 38.

4. Nolan Ryan and Mickey Herskowitz, *Kings of the Hill* (New York: HarperCollins, 1992), p. 69.

5. Ibid., p. 69-70.

6. Steven Travers, *The 1969 Miracle Mets* (Guilford, Conn.: The Globe Pequot Press, 2009), p. 50-51.

7. Peter Carry, "Baseball's Week," *Sports Illustrated*, September 23, 1968.

8. Doug Feldmann, *Miracle Collapse* (Lincoln, Neb.: University of Nebraska Press, 2006), p. 23.

9. George Langford, *Chicago Tribune*, May 14, 1969.

10. Robert H. Boyle, "Leo's Bums Rap for the Cubs," *Sports Illustrated*, June 30, 1969.

Chapter 9: A Hitter and a Bullshitter

1. Ted Williams and John Underwood, *Science of Hitting* (Fireside, 1986), p. 7.

2. Bill Surface, "The Last Days of Rogers Hornsby," *Saturday Evening Post,* June 15, 1963.

3. Lou Brock with Fran Schulze, *Stealing is My Game* (Upper Saddle River, N.J.: Prentice-Hall, 1976).

4. Dave Condon, "The Cubs' $500,000 Shortstop," *Sport,* July 1956.

5. United Press, January 19, 1958.

6. Dave Condon, "The Cubs' $500,000 Shortstop," *Sport,* July 1956.

7. United Press, January 19, 1958.

8. Henry Aaron with Lonnie Wheeler, *I Had A Hammer* (New York: HarperCollins, 1991), p. 108.

9. Bob Wolf, *Milwaukee Journal-Sentinel,* May 30, 1962.

10. Peter Golenbock, *Wrigleyville* (New York: St. Martin's Press, 1996), p. 385.

11. Leo Durocher with Ed Linn, *Nice Guys Finish Last* (New York: Simon and Schuster, 1975), p. 299-300.

12. Ibid., p. 300.

13. Ibid., p. 348-349.

14. Ibid., p. 352.

15. Glenn Stout and Richard A. Johnson, *The Cubs: The Complete Story of Chicago Cubs Baseball* (Chicago: Houghton Mifflin, 2007), p. 250.

16. Ibid., p. 252-54.

17. Peter Golenbock, *Wrigleyville* (New York: St. Martin's Press, 1996), p. 389.

18. Ibid., p. 387.

19. Ibid., p. 390.

20. Ibid., p. 391-92.

21. Ibid., p. 392.

22. Leo Durocher with Ed Linn, *Nice Guys Finish Last* (New York: Simon and Schuster, 1975), p. 363.

23. Ibid., p. 364.

24. Ibid., p. 365.

25. Ibid., p. 366-67.

26. Ibid., p. 367.

27. Ibid., p. 366.

Chapter 10: June

1. Robert H. Boyle, "Leo's Bums Rap for the Cubs," *Sports Illustrated,* June 30, 1969.

2. Doug Feldmann, *Miracle Collapse* (Lincoln, Neb.: University of Nebraska Press, 2006), p. 143-145.

3. Rick Talley, *The Cubs of '69* (Chicago: Contemporary Books Inc., 1989), p. 10.

4. Art Shamsky with Barry Zeman, *The Magnificent Seasons* (New York: St. Martin's Press, 2004), p. 114.

5. Rick Talley, *The Cubs of '69* (Chicago: Contemporary Books Inc., 1989), p. 162.

6. Robert H. Boyle, "Leo's Bums Rap for the Cubs," *Sports Illustrated,* June 30, 1969.

7. Doug Feldmann, *Miracle Collapse* (Lincoln, Neb.: University of Nebraska Press, 2006), p. 138.

8. Ibid., p. 135.

9. Rick Talley, *The Cubs of '69* (Chicago: Contemporary Books Inc., 1989), p. 10.

10. Steven Travers, *The 1969 Miracle Mets* (Guilford, Conn.: The Globe Pequot Press, 2009), p. xiii.

11. Ibid., p. xiii.

12. David Maraniss, *Clemente* (New York: Simon & Schuster, 2006), p. 195.

13. Ernie Banks, *Chicago Tribune,* June 10, 1969.

14. Rick Talley, *The Cubs of '69* (Chicago: Contemporary Books Inc., 1989), p. 56.

Chapter 11: It's Okay to be Black If You're Willie Mays

1. Henry Aaron with Lonnie Wheeler, *I Had A Hammer* (New York: HarperCollins, 1991), p. 106-107.

2. James S. Hirsch, *Willie Mays: The Life, the Legend* (New York: Scribner, 2010), p. 303.

3. Ibid., p. 302.
4. Henry Aaron with Lonnie Wheeler, *I Had A Hammer* (New York: HarperCollins, 1991), p. 107.
5. James S. Hirsch, *Willie Mays: The Life, the Legend* (New York: Scribner, 2010), p. 303.
6. Ibid., p. 304.
7. Ibid., p. 306.
8. Henry Aaron with Lonnie Wheeler, *I Had A Hammer* (New York: HarperCollins, 1991), p. 138.
9. Lou Brock with Fran Schulze, *Stealing is My Game* (Upper Saddle River, N.J.: Prentice-Hall, 1976).
10. Joe Posnanski, *Soul of Baseball* (New York: HarperCollins, 2007).
11. David Halberstam, *October, 1964* (New York: Random House, 1994), p. 153.
12. Ibid., p. 154.
13. Richard Dozer, *Chicago Tribune,* April 1, 1962.
14. David Halberstam, *October, 1964* (New York: Random House, 1994), p. 135.
15. Robert Markus, *Chicago Tribune,* July 26, 1967.
16. Lou Brock with Fran Schulze, *Stealing is My Game* (Upper Saddle River, N.J.: Prentice-Hall, 1976).
17. David Halberstam, *October, 1964* (New York: Random House, 1994), p. 133.
18. Ibid., p. 134-35.
19. Bing Devine, *The Memoirs of Bing Devine* (Champaign, Ill.; Sports Publishing LLC, 2004).
20. Bill Gleason, *Chicago American.*
21. George Castle, *The Million-To-One Team* (South Bend, Ind.: Diamond Communications Inc., 2000), p. 120.
22. Bing Devine, *The Memoirs of Bing Devine* (Champaign, Ill.; Sports Publishing LLC, 2004).

23. Lou Brock with Fran Schulze, *Stealing is My Game* (Upper Saddle River, N.J.: Prentice-Hall, 1976).
24. Peter Golenbock, *Wrigleyville* (New York: St. Martin's Press, 1996), p. 374.
25. Bing Devine, *The Memoirs of Bing Devine* (Champaign, Ill.; Sports Publishing LLC, 2004).
26. David Halberstam, *October, 1964* (New York: Random House, 1994), p. 136.
27. Neal Russo, *The Sporting News,* October 17, 1964.
28. Robert Markus, *Chicago Tribune,* July 26, 1967.
29. Neal Russo, *The Sporting News,* September 7, 1968.
30. Pete McEntegart, "Ernie Broglio, Big Deal Pitcher," *Sports Illustrated,* August 21, 2000.

Chapter 12: July

1. Ernie Banks and Jim Enright, *Mr. Cub* (New York: Rutledge Books Inc., 1971), p. 199-200.
2. *Los Angeles Herald-Examiner,* July 22, 1969.
3. Milton Richman, United Press International, July 22, 1969.
4. George Langford, *Chicago Tribune,* July 2, 1969.
5. Rick Talley, *The Cubs of '69* (Chicago: Contemporary Books Inc., 1989), p. 57-58.
6. Paul D. Zimmerman and Dick Schaap, *The Year the Mets Lost Last Place* (New York: World Publishing, 1969), p. 14.
7. Robert H. Boyle, "Leo's Bums Rap for the Cubs," *Sports Illustrated,* June 30, 1969.
8. Doug Feldmann, *Miracle Collapse* (Lincoln, Neb.: University of Nebraska Press, 2006), p. 163-164.

9. Rick Talley, *The Cubs of '69* (Chicago: Contemporary Books Inc., 1989), p. 69.

10. Doug Feldmann, *Miracle Collapse* (Lincoln, Neb.: University of Nebraska Press, 2006), p. 164.

11. Rick Talley, *The Cubs of '69* (Chicago: Contemporary Books Inc., 1989), p. 71.

12. Ibid., p. 79.

13. Ibid., p. 80.

14. Ibid., p. 79.

15. *Chicago Tribune*, July 29, 1969.

16. Ibid.

17. Richard Dozer, *Chicago Tribune*, July 30, 1969.

18. Rick Talley, *The Cubs of '69* (Chicago: Contemporary Books Inc., 1989), p. 80.

19. Robert Markus, *Chicago Tribune*, July 30, 1969.

20. Steven Travers, *The 1969 Miracle Mets* (Guilford, Conn.: The Globe Pequot Press, 2009), p. 86.

21. Ibid., p. 86.

22. Art Shamsky with Barry Zeman, *The Magnificent Seasons* (New York: St. Martin's Press, 2004), p. 116.

23. Rick Talley, *The Cubs of '69* (Chicago: Contemporary Books Inc., 1989), p. 81-82.

Chapter 13: Step for Step with the Hammer and the Say Hey Kid

1. Peter Golenbock, *Wrigleyville* (New York: St. Martin's Press, 1996), p. 356-357.

2. Ibid., p. 348.

3. Gil Sloan, *Chicago Daily News*, October 12, 1956.

4. John C. Hoffman, *Chicago Sun-Times*, December 26, 1956.

5. United Press International, January 19, 1958.

6. Bill Furlong, *Chicago Daily News*, August 29, 1958.

7. Charles C. Alexander, *Rogers Hornsby: A Biography* (New York, Henry Holt and Company, 1995), p. 291.

8. *The Sporting News*, March 12, 1958.

9. *The Sporting News*, September 3, 1958.

10. Associated Press, April 12, 1958.

11. United Press International, April 6, 1957.

12. Associated Press, August 8, 1958.

13. United Press International, August 22, 1958.

14. Ibid.

15. *Chicago Daily News*, January 7, 1959.

16. Dave Condon, "The Cubs' $500,000 Shortstop," *Sport*, July 1956.

17. James S. Hirsch, *Willie Mays: The Life, the Legend* (New York: Scribner, 2010), p. 272.

18. Ibid., p. 274-281.

19. Ernie Banks and Jim Enright, *Mr. Cub* (New York: Rutledge Books Inc., 1971), p. 132-33.

20. Billy Williams and Fred Mitchell, *My Sweet-Swinging Lifetime with the Cubs* (Chicago: Triumph Books, 2008), p. 75-76.

Chapter 14: August

1. Bill Libby, "Why They Call Ernie Banks Baseball's Beautiful Man," *Sport*, June 1969.

2. Doug Feldmann, *Miracle Collapse* (Lincoln, Neb.: University of Nebraska Press, 2006), p. 143-145.

3. Rick Talley, *The Cubs of '69* (Chicago: Contemporary Books Inc., 1989), p. 61-62.

4. Doug Feldmann, *Miracle Collapse* (Lincoln, Neb.: University of Nebraska Press, 2006), p. 221-222.

5. Steven Travers, *The 1969 Miracle Mets* (Guilford, Conn.: The Globe Pequot Press, 2009), p. 89-90.

6. Ibid., p. 89.

7. Peter Carry, "Mad Scramble East and West," *Sports Illustrated*, September 8, 1969.

8. Doug Feldmann, *Miracle Collapse* (Lincoln, Neb.: University of Nebraska Press, 2006), p. 189-190.

Chapter 15: John Boccabella, John Herrnstein, and Other Trespassers

1. Glenn Stout and Richard A. Johnson, *The Cubs: The Complete Story of Chicago Cubs Baseball* (Chicago: Houghton Mifflin, 2007), p. 232.

2. Milton Gross, *New York Times*, April 1, 1960.

3. Jerome Holtzman, *Chicago Sun-Times*, November 19, 1966.

4. Jerome Holtzman, *Chicago Sun-Times*, December 7, 1968.

5. David Condon, "Baseball's Hardest Loser," *Chicago Tribune Magazine*, April 2, 1961.

6. Richard Dozer, May 24, 1961.

7. Ernie Banks and Jim Enright, *Mr. Cub* (New York: Rutledge Books Inc., 1971), p. 129.

8. Ibid., p. 129.

9. John Kuenster, *Chicago Daily News*, July 19, 1961.

10. Glenn Stout and Richard A. Johnson, *The Cubs: The Complete Story of Chicago Cubs Baseball* (Chicago: Houghton Mifflin, 2007), p. 235.

11. Peter Golenbock, *Wrigleyville* (New York: St. Martin's Press, 1996), p. 393.

12. Sandy Grady, *Philadelphia Bulletin*, March 22, 1966.

13. Edgar Munzel, *The Sporting News*, July 16, 1966.

14. Peter Golenbock, *Wrigleyville* (New York: St. Martin's Press, 1996), p. 399.

15. Ibid.

Chapter 16: September

1. Doug Feldmann, *Miracle Collapse* (Lincoln, Neb.: University of Nebraska Press, 2006), p. 206.

2. Leo Durocher with Ed Linn, *Nice Guys Finish Last* (New York: Simon and Schuster, 1975), p. 366.

3. Rick Talley, *The Cubs of '69* (Chicago: Contemporary Books Inc., 1989), p. 268.

4. Richard Dozer, *Chicago Tribune*, September 7, 1969.

5. Doug Feldmann, *Miracle Collapse* (Lincoln, Neb.: University of Nebraska Press, 2006), p. 210.

6. Richard Dozer, *Chicago Tribune*, September 9, 1969.

7. Mark Kram, "A Tale of Two Men and One City," *Sports Illustrated*, September 29, 1969.

8. Peter Golenbock, *Wrigleyville* (New York: St. Martin's Press, 1996), p. 416.

9. Ibid.

10. Steven Travers, *The 1969 Miracle Mets* (Guilford, Conn.: The Globe Pequot Press, 2009), p. 92.

11. Peter Golenbock, *Wrigleyville* (New York: St. Martin's Press, 1996), p. 416.

12. Steven Travers, *The 1969 Miracle Mets* (Guilford, Conn.: The Globe Pequot Press, 2009), p. 92.

13. Peter Golenbock, *Wrigleyville* (New York: St. Martin's Press, 1996), p. 416.

14. David Condon, *Chicago Tribune*, September 9, 1969.

15. Richard Dozer, *Chicago Tribune*, September 11, 1969.

16. Rick Talley, *The Cubs of '69* (Chicago: Contemporary Books Inc., 1989), p. 58-59.

17. *Chicago Tribune*, September 24, 1969.

18. George Langford, *Chicago Tribune*, September 25, 1969.

Chapter 17: Everything But the Ring

1. Joe Goddard, *Chicago Sun-Times*, June 12, 1983.

2. Paul Hemphill, "The Last Days of Ernie Banks," *Sport*, December 1971.

3. Ibid.

4. Associated Press, November 11, 1971.

5. James C. Mullen, *Chicago Sun-Times*, August 1, 1974.

6. David Haugh, *Chicago Tribune*, July 24, 2005.

BIBLIOGRAPHY

Nobody does more to help us get to know baseball players than the reporters who cover them daily, from game to game, city to city, spring training through the last game of the year. I was fortunate in having access to the work of many good reporters who covered Ernie Banks, but no one did it better than the late Jim Enright, who was there waiting at the Pershing Hotel after Banks signed his first Cubs contract in 1953, and who co-authored the one Banks biography before this one, Mr. Cub, written in 1971, when Banks was still playing. Rick Talley and Jerome Holtzman, both also deceased, and Jack Kuenster also did fabulous work, which made my job on this project so much easier.

While this is the first Ernie Banks book since the 1971 autobiography he worked on with Enright, a wealth of information on Banks can be found in books written on baseball in the 1950s and '60s as well as on the Cubs' franchise. The Cubs-Mets race in '69 is the subject of many books preserving pieces of that history, and none are better than Talley's The Cubs of '69, which would be worth reading even if he had only interviewed Ken Holtzman.

One of the ways I've tried to explain Banks is through a look at the people who were closest to him, and fortunately many of those people have been the subjects of wonderful works, most notably Joe Posnanski's Soul of Baseball on Buck O'Neil and the Henry Aaron–Lonnie Wheeler collaboration I Had a Hammer. I've also tried to paint a picture of Banks in the confusing, turbulent times he played his career in, and it helped to have books on Chicago's history of African American exclusion—a world I probably can't even imagine.

There likely wasn't a day that went by when I was writing that I didn't check a fact—or dozens of facts—on the Internet. The Baseball Almanac (baseball-almanac.com) is a treasure in quickly providing access to box scores, player logs, and other sources of invaluable data. This wasn't available when many of the '69 books were written, and it's fascinating to sort out fact (Tommie Agee homered in the next at-bat after Bill Hands knocked him down) from fiction (Agee homered on the next pitch from Hands) on lasting moments.

Books

Aaron, Henry, with Lonnie Wheeler. *I Had A Hammer.* New York: HarperCollins, 1991.

Alexander, Charles C. *Rogers Hornsby: A Biography.* New York: Henry Holt and Company, 1995.

Banks, Ernie, and Jim Enright. *Mr. Cub.* New York: Rutledge Books Inc., 1971.

Brock, Lou, with Franz Schulze. *Stealing is My Game.* Upper Saddle River, N.J.: Prentice-Hall, 1976.

Castle, George. *The Million-To-One Team.* South Bend, Ind.: Diamond Communications Inc., 2000.

Devine, Bing. *The Memoirs of Bing Devine.* Champaign, Ill.; Sports Publishing LLC, 2004.

Durocher, Leo, with Ed Linn. *Nice Guys Finish Last.* New York: Simon and Schuster, 1975.

Feldmann, Doug. *Miracle Collapse.* Lincoln, Neb.: University of Nebraska Press, 2006.

Fuerst, J.S. *When Public Housing was Paradise.* Champaign, Ill.: University of Illinois Press, 2005.

Golenbock, Peter. *Wrigleyville.* New York: St. Martins Press, 1996.

Haas, Jeffrey. *The Assassination of Fred Hampton.* Chicago: Lawrence Hill Books, 2010.

Halberstam, David. *October, 1964.* New York: Random House, 1994.

Helyar, John. *Lords of the Realm.* New York: Villard Books, 1994.

Hirsch, James S. *Willie Mays: The Life, the Legend.* New York: Scribner, 2010.

Jacobson, Steve. *Carrying Jackie's Torch.* Chicago: Lawrence Hill Books, 2007.

James, Bill. *The Bill James Guide to Baseball Managers.* New York: Scribner, 1997.

James, Bill. *The New Bill James Historical Baseball Abstract.* New York: The Free Press, 2001.

Jenkins, Fergie, with Lew Freedman. *Fergie.* Chicago: Triumph Books, 2009.

Leavy, Jane. *Sandy Koufax.* New York: HarperCollins, 2002.

Maraniss, David. *Clemente.* New York: Simon & Schuster, 2006.

Pacyga, Dominic A. *Chicago: A Biography.* Chicago: University of Chicago Press, 2009.

Posnanski, Joe. *Soul of Baseball.* New York: HarperCollins, 2007.

Roseboro, John, with Bill Libby. *Glory Days with the Dodgers.* New York: Atheneum, 1978.

Ryan, Nolan, with Mickey Herskowitz. *Kings of the Hill.* New York: HarperCollins, 1992.

Shamsky, Art, with Barry Zeman. *The Magnificent Seasons.* New York: St. Martin's Press, 2004.

Stout, Glenn. *The Cubs: The Complete Story of Chicago Cubs Baseball.* Chicago: Houghton Mifflin Harcourt, 2007.

Talley, Rick. *The Cubs of '69.* Chicago: Contemporary Books Inc., 1989.

Travers, Steven. *The 1969 Miracle Mets.* Guilford, Conn.: The Globe Pequot Press, 2009.

Trouppe, Quincy. *Twenty Years Too Soon.* Los Angeles: S and S Enterprises, 1977.

Veeck, Bill, with Ed Lynn. *Veeck As in Wreck.* Chicago: University of Chicago Press, 2001.

Williams, Billy, and Fred Mitchell. *My Sweet-Swinging Lifetime with the Cubs.* Chicago: Triumph Books, 2008.

Zimmerman, Paul D., and Dick Schaap. *The Year the Mets Lost Last Place.* New York: World Publishing, 1969.

Magazine Articles

Boyle, Robert H. "Leo's Bums Rap for the Cubs." *Sports Illustrated,* June 30, 1969.

Carry, Peter. "Mad Scramble East and West." *Sports Illustrated,* September 8, 1969.

Condon, Dave. "The Cubs' $500,000 Shortstop." *Sport,* July 1956.

Condon, David. "Baseball's Hardest Loser." *Chicago Tribune Magazine,* April 2, 1961.

Furlong, William B. "P.K. Wrigley: Baseball Magnate." *Saturday Evening Post,* Summer 1972.

Hemphill, Paul. "The Last Days of Ernie Banks." *Sport,* December 1971.

Kram, Mark. "A Tale of Two Men and One City." *Sports Illustrated,* September 29, 1969.

Libby, Bill. "Why They Call Ernie Banks Baseball's Beautiful Man." *Sport,* June 1969.

McEntegart, Pete. "Ernie Broglio, Big Deal Pitcher." *Sports Illustrated,* August 21, 2000.

Surface, Bill. "The Last Days of Rogers Hornsby." *Saturday Evening Post,* June 15, 1963.

Wulf, Steve. "The Guiding Light." *Sports Illustrated,* September 19, 1994.

INDEX